D1174942

Lion's Share

How three small-town grocers
created America's fastest-growing
supermarket chain
and made millionaires of scores
of their North Carolina
friends and neighbors

Mark Wineka
and
Jason Lesley

Copyright 1991 by Mark Wineka and Jason Lesley
First Printing, October 1991
Printed in the United States of America

All rights reserved. No part of this book may be reproduced
by any means without permission of the publisher,
except for brief passages in reviews and articles.

Publisher's Cataloging-in-Publication Data
(Prepared by Quality Books Inc.)

Wineka, Mark William, 1956-
  Lion's share: how three small-town grocers created
America's fastest-growing supermarket chain and made
millionaires of scores of their North Carolina friends and
neighbors / Mark Wineka and Jason Lesley. –
  p. cm.
  ISBN 1-878086-07-3
    1. Supermarkets. 2. Business enterprises. I. Lesley,
Jason Ranier, 1949- II. Title.
HF5469   658.878
                                                    MARC

Cover design by Harry Blair
Book design by Elizabeth House

Down Home Press
P.O. Box 4126
Asheboro, N.C. 27204

Contents

DAVIE CO. PUBLIC LIBRARY.
MOCKSVILLE, NC

For Jim Hurley,
our inspiration

Acknowledgements

Jim Hurley
Dwayne Walls
Evelyn Stallings
Ralph Ketner
Bonnie Shaffer
Tom Smith
Wilson Smith
Glenn Ketner Sr.
Addie Ketner
Jim Berrier
Brown Ketner
Ronald Marsh
Donald Marsh
Paul Ritchie
Jerry Bledsoe
Harold "Hap" Roberts
The Salisbury Post
Ronnie Smith
Frank Hinds
Ned Cline
Fred S. Roseman Jr.
Zula Martin
G.K. Brown
William Alsobrooks
Gordon Hurley
Haden Hurley

Nancy Fisher
Joe Junod
Mary Jane Fowler
Sue Wilkinson
The Food Marketing Institute
Charles Wineka
Linda Ketner
Charles Allmon
Helen Goodnight
Rena Hood
Harold Melton
Helen Black
Shirley Palmer
Progressive Grocer
Jeff Ketner
Dennis Davidson
Clyde Kizziah
Rose Post
Doris Jones
Lucille Lesley
Marvin Edens
Todd Swicegood
Elizabeth Cook
Don Stiller
Steve Bouser
Mike Mozingo

Our fellow employees at *The Salisbury Post* who did our jobs while we were on leave to write.

Our wives, Lindsay Wineka and Debbie Lesley, for patience and forbearance.

For permission to reprint from previously published material: Carolina Publishing Group, *The Rise and Decline of the Great Atlantic and Pacific Tea Company*, by William I. Walsh, copyright 1986, a Lyle Stuart Book; and Penguin Books, Penguin USA Inc., *Sam Walton: The Inside Story of America's Richest Man*, by Vance H. Trimble, copyright 1990.

1. 'I'll take it'

Postal clerk Paul Ritchie caught the resolve in Ralph Ketner's eyes as the businessman approached his service window that late summer morning in 1957. And he immediately spotted Ketner's memo pad, its list of names familiar to any mailman in town. Ritchie realized, however, that Ketner wasn't there to buy stamps or mail a package.

"We're going to start a new grocery store," Ketner told him. "We've just about got all the stock subscribed, but I've got 10 shares if you want it. Ten shares for a hundred dollars."

Salisbury was a close-knit, North Carolina community in which word routinely spread fast. Ritchie knew, of course, that Ketner, his brother C. Brown Ketner and their friend Wilson Smith were calling on acquaintances to raise a grubstake for their venture. Someone had told Ritchie they were going to open in the new shopping center being built on the west end of this city of almost 21,000 people.

Though he had known the Ketners since childhood, Ritchie doubted he would hear from them. A postal worker surely didn't have the kind of money they needed, yet here was Ketner, and a hundred dollars seemed affordable. Ritchie trusted the men. He liked the Ketner family and considered Ralph an exceptionally smart fellow. It couldn't be a bad investment, he thought.

"I'll take it," Ritchie blurted out.

Ketner took out a pen and signed him up.

A day or two later, Paul Ritchie saw Ketner again downtown. "How about a couple of hundred dollars more of that stuff?" the

1

postal clerk asked. But Ketner answered that the three men had closed their books.

Ritchie shrugged it off as bad timing, not knowing that his $100 had already bought into a high-stakes lottery. So had many of the other people on Ketner's memo pad.

Not everyone was as eager to invest in this one-store company called Food Town. Economic times could have been better, and Salisbury – the county seat of Rowan County – was typical of the late 1950s. It had one foot deeply planted in the past with the other foot kicking at the dirt, waiting for the explosion of economic development that supposedly was heading south. Layoffs were common at Rowan County's largest employer, the Spencer Shops railroad repair facility. Food Town also faced strong competition from established supermarkets and independent grocers.

Some people who initially said yes to the Food Town organizers backed out. Dorothy Chamblee and Frances Thigpen asked for their money back. Each had bought 10 shares. Thomas A. Clark canceled his request for 50 shares. James L. Moore and his wife put back 25 shares each. S. Holmes Plexico thought better of his $1,000 investment and asked the Food Town men to cancel his 100 shares. Several others joined them.

But the people who stuck with the Ketners and Wilson Smith did it on faith, from reputation and out of friendships that evolve during people's lifetimes in a small town. They believed in the men's character. They respected their work ethic. They had no doubts that the founders knew the grocery business.

Teachers, railroaders, bankers, doctors, salesmen, housewives, lawyers, druggists, mill workers, merchants, mailmen – all walks of life – paid as little as $50 for five shares or as much as $1,000 for 100 shares of Food Town stock in 1957.

The money the new entrepreneurs could raise among themselves had amounted to only half of the $125,000 they needed. Brown and Ralph Ketner assembled $25,000 apiece. Smith mortgaged his house three times, drew cash on his life insurance and borrowed money to put up $12,500. They dreaded it when

2

they realized they would have to put the pinch on friends to raise the other $62,500.

The men paged through the telephone book, A to Z, writing down names of people they knew. The number came to a couple hundred and it so happened that each man felt comfortable calling on a third of the people on their list.

• • •

It's the Southern way to exchange pleasantries, talk of the weather and ask about a friend's relatives or his health before getting around to business. That's especially the case when one is asking for money. But the Food Town principals didn't have time for small talk. Since the summer days in 1957 when they quit their jobs at Winn-Dixie, they had been going without pay while borrowing thousands of dollars. They wanted to open their store as soon as possible. Vice president Brown Ketner and secretary Wilson Smith uncharacteristically found themselves rushing to get to the point of their calls or visits.

The president and treasurer of the new company seldom beat around the bush about anything.

Ralph Wright Ketner always attacked a job as if he were the best man for it. Many times he was, especially when the task involved numbers. His skill in arithmetic bordered on genius and would always work toward confusing salesmen, saving money and, most importantly, selling groceries.

Earlier in his career, when Ketner had been working as a buyer for his oldest brother Glenn's Excel Grocery warehouse, an adding machine salesman paid a visit. After the salesman made his pitch, Glenn Ketner told him he had a brother who could add faster than the new electric machine.

"If he can, I'll give you the machine," the visitor promised. They called Ralph in and the salesman made up a list of 20 to 25 five-figure numbers. He began punching away at his machine as Ralph calmly ran his finger down the list of numbers and wrote his answer on a separate piece of paper.

3

"Give up?" the salesman asked, not halfway finished. "No," answered Ralph. He turned his paper over so the salesman couldn't see it. The salesman finally announced his total. Ralph flipped over his answer and matched him.

Glenn Ketner wouldn't accept the man's machine. He had known his brother would win.

Ralph loved a chance to upstage man or machine. It followed that by the time he was 37 and soliciting money for Food Town, he had already quit countless jobs because they didn't challenge him. Other jobs wound up pitting his sometimes overbearing stubbornness against people who considered him simply forward and obnoxious. Friction usually followed. Ketner had little patience with colleagues who didn't share his obsession with work or paid little attention to details. But the traits that sometimes alienated people also would bring him success. His confidence had a way of persuading others that any task at hand was one of the most important in their lifetimes. In the years ahead, he would find men who adopted his philosophy as their own. They didn't last long otherwise.

The man was a gambler, and this new grocery store was his latest risk. He longed to be different, and that trait would lead to his most important decision as company president a decade later when things looked bleak. He relished a fight, as his competitors would learn to regret. He bucked the system, and sometimes the system gave in.

Ketner was the ultimate salesman, who could present an argument as if it were the only sensible approach to take. He also was served by his knack for twisting words and conversations to his advantage.

The Food Town founders didn't know their method of raising money was against the law – no one told them. During the underwriting process before Food Town stock went public 13 years later, Ralph Ketner learned that any company with more than 10 investors must register with the "SEC." The initials stand for Securities and Exchange Commission, but Ketner delivered a typical rebuttal to the lawyerly reprimand: "I explained we weren't in the Southeastern Conference."

Ralph Ketner was a proud man, but no prouder than his older brother Brown, who carried a similar confidence, stubbornness and flamboyant style that had served him for better or worse in the grocery business. If Ralph was the expert in numbers, Brown was the authority on meats. He knew how to select, cut, package and prepare meat as well as any grocer in the state. Brown Ketner also never met a joke he didn't like or a crowd he couldn't entertain.

The years had proved and would prove again that the Ketner brothers were their own men.

Wilson Smith served as the leavening in this volatile mix – the man who worked behind the scenes and could never shake the notion that customers and employees come first. He was part promoter, part merchandiser, part manager and part workhorse. But he was all company.

The trio sincerely believed they were put on earth to save people money. If they and other people prospered from that mission, so much the better. None of the men envisioned in 1957 what lie ahead for Food Town. They faced simpler concerns.

"We had one problem," Ketner acknowledged many years later, "and the problem was we had no money."

• • •

The Ketners and Smith called relatives, church friends, folks they had grown up with and had done business with in the past. Many were the kind of people whom they knew just well enough to say hello to as they passed on the street.

Smith, whom friends called Bill, drew the assignment of calling Julian Robertson, a local textile executive. When he identified himself as "Bill Smith," Robertson assumed it was his banker friend by the same name.

"How much are you going to put in it?" Robertson asked.

"All I can get," Smith said.

"Well, if it's good enough for you, it's good enough for me. I'll take your word for it." Julian Robertson invested $1,000 in a case of mistaken identity.

Wilson Smith also talked to fellow church member Bill Alsobrooks, a Rowan County native who was working as a Southern Railway machinist at Spencer Shops. Alsobrooks knew the three founders and had gone to school with a couple of the men. "If anybody could do it, they could," he said years later. Despite the troubling times at Spencer Shops, he invested $1,000 – the first time he had invested in any kind of stock.

In the 1950s, employees at *The Salisbury Evening Post* invested $10 a month in a little stock club they had formed called the Old Hickory Investment Club. It rocked along for three or four years before Charlie Barger, a Linotype operator, became suspicious and discovered that the club's last two stock purchases had not been made.

Faced with embezzlement, plus frustration with the bookkeeping and taxes, the club members disbanded and paid out all the money – about $700 to each member. Within a month, Wilson Smith happened to approach Charlie Barger about investing in Food Town.

"I'd bet my house that the Old Hickory's disbandment is where he got the money to invest," said James F. Hurley III, who later became the newspaper's publisher.

Hurley belonged to the Old Hickory Club himself, but he came to own Food Town stock through his father, Jim Hurley Jr., who was publisher of the newspaper at the time.

The senior Hurley bought 100 shares for each of his three sons, Jim, Haden and Gordon, mostly for business reasons. The Post needed the advertising account. The newspaper had lost a good account a year earlier when Winn-Dixie bought out the Ketner supermarkets run by Glenn Ketner. The senior Hurley gave the stock to his sons because he thought it unethical to own stock in a firm competing with other advertisers. The Hurley boys stuck their certificates in safe deposit boxes and all but forgot them.

Fred Roseman worked at the post office across the street from

6

the newspaper with Paul Ritchie and Wilson Smith's brother, Julian. Roseman put up $100. That night he told his children that he would give the stock to them someday but, in the back of his mind, he doubted that Food Town would amount to more than a couple of stores. He had just paid for his house, and his daughter was attending the University of Richmond. With a gambler's spirit, Roseman figured he had nothing to lose.

"I gave him the last $100 in my pocket," he said.

A lot of people were in the same boat. Helen Goodnight's husband, Cress, bought five shares in her name from Ralph Ketner, who had called on their clothing business. That's all the couple could afford at the time because they were sinking everything into their own store. They attended church with Ralph and respected his flair for business.

Wilson Smith approached G.K. Brown, who was doing his best to keep Salisbury Engravers running. In the days before offset printing, Salisbury Engravers made the metal plates for the newspaper's pictures. The three-man company also did other commercial work, things handled routinely now by desktop publishing. Brown bought 10 shares for $100. "I didn't hesitate at all," he said. "I sure did have a lot of faith in the Ketners."

Richard and Zula Marlin were buying a house in Salisbury. They agreed to give their brother-in-law Wilson Smith $100. It was about all they could afford on Richard's salary at Nurick's clothing store on South Main Street. "We had a lot of confidence in them," Mrs. Marlin said years later. "If we would have lost that $100, it wouldn't have broke us. But money was scarce back then. That was about all we thought we could put in it."

Harold Melton spoke often with Brown Ketner, but he knew all of the founders. "I felt like they had experience and know-how, and I was glad to invest," he said. "If it didn't go and I lost it, I wouldn't worry about it." Melton owned Salisbury Cut-Rate Furniture Co. He bought 20 shares.

George Hood was chaplain at Salisbury's 900-bed Veterans Administration Hospital in 1957. Ralph Ketner lived across

Emerald Street from Hood and his wife, Rena. In July of that year, Hood had invested $100 in Lyerly's Funeral Home of Salisbury. By October, one of the Ketners approached Hood after a Lion's Club meeting. Would he be interested in making another investment – this one in a new grocery firm? Hood went home and told his wife of the offer, and Mrs. Hood gave him $100 of her money for 10 shares. Hood put the shares in his wife's name.

Dr. Glenn Kiser had been pediatrician for Linda Ketner, Ralph and Ruth Ketner's daughter, and the two boys of Evelyeen and Wilson Smith. Kiser enjoyed a vigorous practice in the 1950s until retiring at age 37 to take care of his wife, who suffered from a progressive illness. To make a living while tending to her special physical needs, Kiser had decided to dive into various business investments, including stocks and bonds.

Ralph Ketner called Kiser on a Sunday night not long after the pediatrician had taken his early retirement. Kiser had just finished building a small office and store and was preparing to set up a drugstore in the building. Simply put, he was strapped for cash. A plumber friend had even loaned him $8,000, interest free. Still, Kiser jumped at the chance to buy stock in Food Town, telling Ketner he thought he could handle $1,000. To be on the safe side, however, he finally lowered the figure to $300 and told Ketner he would let him know about an additional $700 in a few days.

True to his word, Kiser soon wrote Ketner a note requesting that he be counted in for the additional $700. Like Paul Ritchie, he was too late. In years to come, Kiser's confidence in the Ketners and Wilson Smith remained so strong that he would continually strive to purchase more Food Town stock, in very small amounts, whenever he heard of a willing seller. Many other original investors would not show the same faith or patience.

While Brown Ketner was being examined by his doctor, Kyle Black, he asked him whether he wanted to invest in Food Town. Black bought 100 shares, giving 50 to his wife, Helen. It was her first investment and, for the housewife, sparked a hidden interest in the business world.

J.J. Barger, a druggist in the tiny Rowan County town of Faith, bought 50 shares for himself and wife Zeda, who didn't understand stocks and assumed they were giving Ralph Ketner a loan.

Over a couple of weeks, 139 people said yes. Later, 14 of the 139 backed out, giving Food Town 125 initial investors. There were 12,500 shares outstanding at $10 a share.

Employees of the first Food Town also risked their savings on the new company. A pair of key men, Tommy Eller and Clifford Ray, walked into Food Town's small office one Saturday morning and plopped down a paper bag. In it was the money they each had raised to invest: Ray, $10,000 for 1,000 shares; Eller, $5,000 for 500 shares.

"I borrowed all I could borrow," Eller recalled. "I probably could have borrowed more if I knew more people, but, you know, it was a lot of money."

Ralph Ketner ironically raised much of his $25,000 seed money by selling his former employer's stock. When he joined Winn-Dixie as an executive a year earlier, he was allowed to purchase stock on credit. Over the year, the rapidly expanding Winn-Dixie had seen its stock value rise considerably. At first, the company balked at giving the departing Ketner his stock, while Ketner said he would sign a promissory note to pay Winn-Dixie the money owed for his shares – as long as he received them. It took Ketner's threat of a lawsuit for him to receive his stock, which he promptly sold.

Wilson Smith switched off the television set one night and gathered his sons, Ronnie and Tim, and wife Evelyeen together for a family meeting. He explained that he and the Ketner brothers were going to start a new company. Ronnie Smith thought the news exciting at first until his father began explaining that he would be without a paying job for awhile. The family would have to make sacrifices. Both money and time to spend with the family would be in short supply, Smith explained.

"Tim, there won't be any extra money for candy," Smith told his youngest.

Lion's Share

The boy began to cry. The father scrambled to reassure his son that Food Town might lead to a great opportunity, and the boys would each start with five shares of stock.

• • •

Paul Ritchie would never forget the morning Ralph Ketner walked up to his window. He sensed something about Food Town's future and decided early that he was in for the long haul.

Ritchie had started his career as a postal clerk sorting mail on a train, before entering the service in World War II. After the war, he returned to the mail job on an express run between Charlotte and Atlanta. Motion sickness finally did him in, leading to his more solid position at the Salisbury post office.

Near this dignified post office of white marble, a grass median provided room for a Confederate memorial. The bronze grouping of a muse and her wounded soldier had turned iron black from years of fighting pigeons, car exhaust and the elements. It was a constant, nonetheless – something that had a way of slowing time for residents in a small town. The angel stood watch when Ralph Ketner was a kid hawking newspapers downtown, and it continued its vigilance, uninterrupted, the day Ketner bounded up the post office steps to see Ritchie.

Thirty-four years later, when a revived chapter of the United Daughters of the Confederacy restored the bronze to its original luster, change had come to Food Town and Paul Ritchie, too.

One store on the edge of town had expanded to more than 800 stores in 12 states. A handful of employees had grown to 50,000. The small band of local investors had increased to 40,000 shareholders around the world. Some Salisburians had become very rich.

"I didn't expect anything spectacular," Ritchie recalled. "My investment turned out a lot better than I thought."

His $100 had made him a millionaire.

2. Live and let live

Salisbury had witnessed its share of economic disappointments and tales of the big companies that got away. But Food Town investors in 1957 hardly viewed the new company as a corporate giant in the making.

"I think, realistically, about the most we ever hoped for was 15 to 20 stores," Ralph Ketner acknowledged many years later.

Those conservative goals for Food Town were in line with the way Salisbury residents had always viewed their city. History showed that Salisbury was an economic enigma. Poised before the Civil War to become one of the state's largest cities, the town saw its growth stifled by conservative leadership, ill-timed business decisions, missed opportunities and fate. While nearby Charlotte has grown to a metropolis with close to 400,000 population, Salisbury has never exceeded 25,000. It's hard to imagine that a century earlier Salisbury and Charlotte had an intense rivalry for growth, sparking this 1873 comment from editor J.J. Bruner in Salisbury's *Carolina Watchman:* "There are but two things Charlotte is ahead of Salisbury in, and they are wind and gas."

When it was created in 1753, Rowan County covered a huge area: 26 North Carolina counties have been formed from its original lands. But there was no county seat. James Carter, a member of the Colonial Assembly, selected his own land as the site for a new courthouse. The 350-acre tract sat on a long ridge seven miles south of the Yadkin River. It included a traders' campground with which Scotch-Irish, German and English settlers traveling on the old Trading Path were well familiar.

11

Lion's Share

A courthouse went up and the small village was called Rowan County Courthouse until 1755 when the name was changed to Salisbury, for a sister city in England. The town prospered – Daniel Boone bought his supplies here before his excursions into the Tennessee and Kentucky wilderness – and Salisbury became known as the state's "Queen of the West." It grew to 1,000 people by 1850, then doubled in population over the next 10 years as two railroad links were completed. Salisbury seemed destined to become the state's largest city and "could have had this distinction for the asking," Rowan County historian James Brawley wrote.

But a handful of Salisbury's leaders had big investments in the North Carolina Railroad. Out of fear of competition, they snubbed the other railroads being constructed. Prominent families on the east side of town also opposed fighting the drifting ashes from more trains chugging through Salisbury. Meanwhile, Charlotte determined that its economic future would be linked closely to the railroad. By 1900, it was three times bigger than Salisbury.

The editor of *The Salisbury Herald* in 1885 summed up his town's approach toward commerce: "The businessmen have the reputation of being the safest dealers in the state."

Thanks to its tobacco factories, distilleries and beginning textile mills, Salisbury could still be called prosperous in the 1880s. Fate methodically ate away at these advantages, too. Washington Duke began monopolizing the tobacco industry. The small industrialists in Salisbury failed to keep pace because they were making chewing tobacco and cigars while the trend was toward cigarettes. Local history, with some hint of exaggeration, says Salisbury's conservative leadership originally discouraged Duke from locating here, so he went to Durham. The same was said of R.J. Reynolds who headed for Winston-Salem. By 1900, the town's tobacco industry was dead.

In 1908, North Carolina voted in prohibition, effectively killing Salisbury's major industry: distilleries. Salisbury had a reputation until then as the "wettest and wickedest town in North Carolina."

12

The lack of competing railroads serving Salisbury meant that the town was paying more than Charlotte for bales of cotton. While Winston-Salem and Durham had surpassed Salisbury in tobacco, Concord, Charlotte, Gastonia, Greensboro and Kannapolis passed it in textiles.

The entrenched leadership even spurned efforts by Southern Railway to put its repair shops in Salisbury and asked the company to locate just outside the city boundaries, so as not to upset the sleepy community. Southern president Samuel B. Spencer could not overlook the importance of his two main lines intersecting in Salisbury, so he decided to build Southern's huge steam repair facility just north of Salisbury in 1896. The town around the shops became known as Spencer, but Salisbury and all of Rowan County benefited from the huge new industry.

So Salisbury grew in spite of itself. Between 1910 and 1920, the population increased from 7,153 to 13,844. A 1915 annexation tripled the size of Salisbury to 5 square miles.

By 1923, George Robert "Bob" Ketner had moved his family to Salisbury so he could open a meat market. He saw opportunity in Salisbury that didn't seem at odds with his own conservative philosophy – in fact, his cost-conscious ways prompted the move.

• • •

Standing on a crate so he could reach the butcher block, a young Brown Ketner was cutting meat one day when a representative from A&P came in and had a talk with his father, Bob. The man wanted Ketner to become part of the world's largest retailer, A&P, but that would mean some changes. He chastised Ketner for selling his meat at too low a price.

"No, I'm making all I want to make," Ketner replied.

"Now look, Bob," the man continued. "We'll take over this store, put the A&P name on it. You'll have a straight salary coming in. You'll run it just like you're running it now, only we'll tell you what prices to sell it at."

Ketner told the A&P representative goodbye. Young Brown had taken it all in.

"Later on, the fella who tried to hire Daddy went to work for us," Brown says. "Now that sounds crazy because he was boosting one of the biggies, A&P. But I think he liked our philosophy better."

Born November 27, 1888, George Robert Ketner was the oldest of seven children of Luther Jeremiah and Mary Clementine Phillips Ketner. Their German ancestors, Lutherans, came from Pennsylvania in the late 18th century and settled in southeastern Rowan County. George Robert Ketner – friends called him Bob – grew up on the family's large farm and eventually married Effie Yost in 1911. They started their own family on a farm in the Rimertown community exactly 10 months and two days after their marriage. The first born was Glenn, followed by Robert Ray in 1913, Clifford Brown in 1915, Harry Luther in 1919, Ralph Wright in 1920, Mary Virginia in 1923 and Dorothy Elaine in 1924. Harry lived only six days.

Bob Ketner farmed and butchered, taking beef, veal and pork to Salisbury and Concord markets. One day, he came home with eight pounds of round steak in his hand and said, "Effie, by God, I'm going to open a store in Salisbury. This steak I brought home cost me more than I got for the whole beef."

In August 1923, Ketner bought Taylor's Meat Market at 501 North Main Street in Salisbury and moved his family into a bungalow behind it. Operating initially as G.R. Ketner's Meat Market, he doubled his space within eighteen months by expanding into an adjoining building. He cut through a wall and put in groceries for the first time. He also sold fish when he could get them from the coast on weekends.

Ketner never lost sight of the reason he got into the business: fair pricing.

"His theory," Brown Ketner says, "and I heard him say it many times in talking to us kids: 'When you charge a customer a nickel more than you need to make a profit, you're as crooked as if you

14

shortchanged them a nickel in their change. Now if you wouldn't shortchange somebody, don't shortchange in the price.' And it made sense to us."

Ketner operated primarily on credit and delivery, and it didn't take him long to realize that collecting overdue accounts was sometimes difficult. At the same time, he concluded that a cash-only approach could save his customers money. The savings were enough so that customers began recognizing the advantages for themselves. Thus, Ketner changed the name of his business to Ketner's Cash and Carry. By 1925, he opened a second store in the Dixonville community. A third store followed at the corner of South Main and East Fisher streets in January 1928; a fourth store on South Main Street later in 1928; a fifth store on East Innes Street in 1929; and a sixth store in Kannapolis, 16 miles south of Salisbury, near the ballpark in 1931. Ketner's business was booming.

Brown Ketner recalls that the corner store at South Main and Fisher streets had an automatic door opener. The cashier pushed a pedal on the floor so people could come in or go out.

"Mostly, it was to help them get out," he says. "And it was so crowded on weekends, they would hire two policemen to mix with the crowd to keep them from walking out with the meat – that was only meat there. It was just terrific. It was thrilling. Right past the register was the first meat case, and then it just went right on back. On weekends, there would be a person at every slot waiting on you. In other words, you didn't follow the customer. The customer would go on down and you got what they wanted that was in front of you. You weighed it up, wrapped it up, marked the price, then collected it. It worked pretty good."

Ketner tried to price his groceries fairly, too. During Ketner's Cash and Carry Market's eighth anniversary sale on August 21, 1931, tender round steak sold for 17.5 cents a pound, pork chops for 18 cents, three cans of Vienna sausage for 20 cents, potatoes for 5 cents a pound, corn for 15 cents a dozen and canned pineapple, two for 25 cents.

15

Lion's Share

Bob Ketner tried to sum up his business philosophy in the same ad:

"It is a fact that a man does do business with an eye to serving his community as well as making a living for himself. Any man with a growing business should consider his obligation to the good people of the community who support him. Most men like to know that they are conducting their business on a live and let live basis; in recognition of the other man with whom he deals. This live at home policy means just what it says. Live at home and make your life count at home and for home folks. A grocery can help people live at home better and longer. The Ketner policy has been these eight years to provide a satisfactory market for the products of Rowan County and North Carolina and to bring these products to the consumer at the lowest possible price."

To help his steady trade, Ketner came up with promotional ideas to spark public interest. In 1928 he brought what was considered the biggest slab of cheese ever to be displayed in town and placed it in a front window. The Swiss cheese was 35 inches in diameter and six inches in thickness, and Ketner promised a prize for the person guessing nearest the exact weight.

In what must have been a slow week for entertainment even by Salisbury standards, 2,500 entries came in with eleven guessing within a pound of the cheese's weight of 155.5 pounds by Friday night, July 27. Ketner saw another opportunity to prolong public interest by having a drawing from among the eleven finalists on Monday. J.E. Shepherd won first prize: a $2.50 gold piece. Second and third prizes, one-pound blocks of cheese, went to Doc Massey and Willie Sue Aldridge. The local newspaper followed the story of the cheese contest closely.

Before Ketner's Cash and Carry entered the Kannapolis market, pork chops sold for 35 cents a pound. Bob Ketner sold his for 10 cents a pound. Reflecting on his father's stores years later, Ralph Ketner said the philosophy of "live and let live" prices stayed with the sons. Even the father's approach to advertising would find rebirth, especially with Ralph. "It's unbelievable,"

Ralph said, "but in one place he said, 'Make our price challenge comparison.' Well, I've run ads that say, 'Make the pantry test.' We've got ads where we list our prices and we dare you to go into your pantry and see how you're paying too much for groceries."

Bob Ketner also owned a 15-acre farm in the Franklin community of Rowan County that was used almost exclusively to raise and butcher hogs. He raised some vegetables and cattle, but his operation became so large that he was buying most of his beef and considerable amounts of pork from farmers and wholesale meat markets.

Although working on a low margin of profit, Ketner kept his large family fed and the bills paid. He was always able to get credit to open a new store. And he expected his sons to work. Effie, his wife, also pulled duty at the store besides taking care of the household. Life, it seemed, couldn't be better for the Ketners. But the family story was soon to take a tragic turn.

Effie died of pneumonia March 10, 1926, during a flu epidemic in Salisbury. She was 33 years old. Prospects didn't look good for five-year-old Ralph either. Doctors put a tube in his side to drain fluid from his lungs. "I remember to this day that they didn't even put me to sleep," he recalled 65 years later. "I was too weak, and they held my hands and operated on me." Meanwhile, good-hearted aunts and uncles approached Bob Ketner and said they would be willing to raise a particular son or daughter. Glenn Ketner would always remember his father's answer: "Absolutely not."

Glenn received his early education in a one-room country schoolhouse where a single teacher taught all seven grades. After his family moved to Salisbury, Glenn worked long hours in his father's stores, delivering groceries before and after school, learning from his father and gradually developing a keen business sense. Glenn met Addie Glover at Boyden High School about the time his mother died and soon began courting her. He carried her books home from school. Occasionally they saw a movie together. After graduation, Addie became a cashier at Ketner's Cash and

17

Carry at South Main and East Fisher streets. That same year, 1928, Bob Ketner married Addie's older sister, Allene Glover Lyerly. Glenn's girlfriend's sister became his stepmother.

In January 1929, Addie traveled to Dayton, Ohio, with her sister Hazel's family and while there landed a good office job with McCall's, the magazine publisher, then a maker of sewing patterns. She corresponded with Glenn until he decided to follow her to Dayton in the summer of 1929.

He was 17 and he soon became a grocery store manager in Dayton, later a door-to-door salesman for the Cook Coffee Co., where he became the firm's top salesman. It took Bob Ketner until November of 1931 to persuade Glenn to bring Addie – by then they were married – back home to manage the new Ketner's store in Kannapolis. Glenn was only 20.

Like their older brother, Ray and Brown grew up fast. Ray had the reputation of being a free spirit and quite the athlete. Brown also was happy-go-lucky, but he paid close attention to what his father could teach him about selecting and cutting meat. He often assisted his Uncle Charlie Ketner in the butchering on the Franklin community farm.

Looking for the best kind of meat, Brown learned that the biggest factor was its shape and a marbeling that most people wrote off as fat. But in those times, when a customer bought a steak that was only dark and lean, he ended up with tough beef. Brown looked for little flakes of fat grained all through the lean – then the customer would have steak he could cut with a fork.

Ray became amateur boxing champion for his weight class in North Carolina. He turned professional one night for $50, and didn't know it. Ray, Brown and some of their friends visited a nighttime carnival on Innes Street, and they passed a man offering $50 to any person who could stay in the ring for three rounds against his boxer.

"Hell, Ray, you're good," Brown told his brother. "You can beat him."

"Well, I know," Ray said in a halting tone.

18

The next thing his friends knew Ray was in the ring with a pair of boxing trunks on. "I think it lasted about seven seconds," Brown later recalled. "Ray knocked him out. Then the fella didn't want to pay because he didn't stay three rounds."

Ralph Ketner learned to kill and dress chickens in the back yard of his house in Salisbury. A neighbor, Bobby Harrison, would help, and the boys received a penny for each chicken they plucked. Ralph's grandfather would chop the chickens' heads off, and the birds would flap wildly around the yard. Ralph and Bobby would grab a bushel basket and slap it over the kicking bird until it quit moving. If they broke the skin while plucking a chicken, it cost them a nickel, meaning they would have to dress five free of charge just to get back even. The secret in plucking chickens was not to allow the water to get too hot. And if he left them in the water too long, Ralph learned, he paid the price.

The Ketner sons grew to be stubborn, independent thinkers, like their father. As adults, this trait showed itself in the religious denominations they chose. Glenn stuck with the Lutheran faith of his ancestors. Brown favored the Baptists, the religion on which his mother had been raised. Ralph became a Presbyterian, the discipline adhered to by his stepmother, who played a large role in raising him and his two younger sisters.

With his sons' help, Bob Ketner had built a solid business, scraping out a decent living during the early days of the Depression. By 1932, he had sold one of his stores but still had four in Salisbury, plus the store Glenn was running in Kannapolis. He had run unsuccessfully as a Republican candidate for the county board of commissioners in 1930 and was rumored to be a possible Republican candidate for Rowan County sheriff in 1932.

But one night late in February 1932 Bob was rushed to the hospital. Shock swept friends and family when he died in early March. He was 43.

While his doctor was out of town, a substitute misdiagnosed Ketner's appendicitis. He treated him for constipation. The appendix burst; peritonitis developed and claimed his life after several days. Glenn was 20 when his father died; Ray, 18; Brown, 15; Ralph, 11; Virginia, 9; and Dorothy, 7.

The family faced more bad news after the funeral. Bob Ketner had never incorporated his businesses. And worse, he died without a will. The five stores would have to be auctioned off, one by one, to settle the estate. Glenn and Addie, with the help of her father, James Glover, purchased the Kannapolis store Glenn had been managing. Respecting the business record of his late father, suppliers were happy to sell to Glenn, even though he wasn't old enough to sign contracts.

Ray Ketner bought one of his father's stores in Salisbury but soon left the grocery business. He later became National Youth Administrator for Rowan and Cabarrus counties and was one of the first three men from Rowan County who volunteered for military service on November 21, 1940. After 20 months overseas in the war, Ray returned to North Carolina to sell insurance.

Glenn pressed on. Supported and assisted by Addie, he purchased his second grocery store three months after his father's death. It too was in Kannapolis, in the Centerview section. In September 1933, he opened a third Kannapolis store at 810 North Main Street.

"It was a lot of responsibility," Ketner acknowledged much later. "I guess if you were of the Depression, you didn't have much time to stop and figure out why you couldn't do something. You just thought you could and tried to do it."

Kannapolis was a large, unincorporated community dominated by Cannon Mills, the giant towel maker that virtually owned and paid for everything in the "Towel City." The large population, most of whom rented their homes or businesses from the mill, straddled the Cabarrus and Rowan County lines.

The early Glenn Ketner stores faced competition from A&P and the D. Pender Grocery Co., which later became the Colonial grocery chain. The Kannapolis stores still used the single checkout counter where the customer would tell a clerk what he wanted, the clerk would retrieve it and pile the items on the counter, where they would be checked and bagged. A clerk needed a good memory, because he had to remember the prices on 700 to 800 unmarked items. A clerk also had to be quick at arithmetic.

Glenn's small Kannapolis stores continued to use his father's "live and let live" slogan. And he was itching to bring the philosophy back to Salisbury.

3. Working for big brother

Tommy Eller walked the streets of Salisbury in 1947 looking for a job as an auto mechanic. Like his father, he loved to tinker and he thought being an automobile mechanic would satisfy that urge.

Eller poked his head into every garage in town, but nobody had a job. And he needed one. His wife was pregnant, and he had no money to speak of after his stint of two years, five months and 19 days in the U.S. Navy. Born April 24, 1927, in China Grove, Eller was one of nine children. His father was a textile worker. His mother raised the family and always had one or two odd jobs on the side.

Tommy Eller's first job, at age 12, was stocking shelves at the A&P in the little town of China Grove, in southern Rowan County. He eventually took the job full-time, working before and after school. In the summers, he worked in the cotton mills for better pay and better hours.

"You worked 40 hours a week and made 15 cents an hour," he said of the mills. "At A&P, you worked 50 hours at 10 cents an hour."

A strong, stocky man, Eller once entertained hopes of becoming a bricklayer. Three of his brothers were bricklayers, and they made good money. But he tired of shoveling rock for his uncle and saw no connection between that backbreaking job and laying brick. The uncle kept stalling on his promise to teach Eller the profession, so he walked off a job one day and never went back.

World War II ended soon after Eller joined the Navy at 18. He spent much of his stint in a task force testing atomic bombs in the Pacific.

Finding nobody in need of an auto mechanic that day in 1947, Eller decided to seek an employment agency's help.

"Glenn Ketner has the ideal job for you," a young woman told Eller. "He's got openings right now."

"Well, I don't want to go back into the grocery business," Eller replied. "That's all I've ever done."

Nonetheless, Eller went to see Glenn Ketner and was hired as a produce clerk at $25 a week. The government also paid Eller $90 a month on the GI Bill, designed to help veterans get back to work. Eller began unloading trucks of fruits and vegetables and taking the crates to coolers for storage. He trimmed lettuce, carrots and cabbage. Potatoes arrived at the store in 100-pound bags. It wasn't uncommon to handle two or three tons of potatoes a day, picking up the big bags, carrying them to a dumping spot, and repackaging them into ten-pound bags. Apples came in heavy wooden crates. Carrots came six dozen to a box and packed in ice. Lettuce came 48 heads to a crate, again with ice on top. The work was not unlike throwing rock into a wheelbarrow for his uncle, the bricklayer, Eller realized. But he liked Glenn Ketner, who quickly rewarded him through promotion.

"He was a first-class gentleman," Eller said in later years of Glenn Ketner. "I had a great deal of respect for him. He was the type of guy that we could have a sales meeting, for example, on a Saturday morning, and he could chew on you, and you wouldn't realize he was chewing on you until you got to your car. He was just that nice about doing it. He was a super guy to work for, very considerate, fair."

Despite the Depression, by June 1936 Ketner had returned to Salisbury with a store at 128 East Innes Street. His first day in Salisbury, Friday the 13th, was what he considered "the opening of all times." He took in $600, a phenomenal amount. The store went on to do 10 to 12 times the volume of the average Mom and Pop groceries of the day.

In 1937, Ketner sold his Kannapolis store on North Main
Street. Cannon Mills Co. built another store for Ketner in 1939 at
A Street and West Avenue. In the same year, Ketner sold his two
other original Kannapolis stores and bought the Community Food
Center in Albemarle, about 25 miles southeast of Salisbury.

Ketner's Inc. kept plugging along, quietly developing a
reputation for promotion and innovation. The small chain purchased
Dry's Cash Market on North Main Street in Salisbury in November 1941 but closed it within two years. Glenn started his own
warehouse, the Excel Grocery Co. on North Lee Street, and sold
groceries wholesale to other area stores.

Glenn discovered that he had better control of his stock and a
quicker turnover in supplies with the warehouse. Fruits and
vegetables came directly from fields and orchards as far away as
Florida and Georgia. Other produce came from local distributors
such as Eli Saleeby on Council Street in Salisbury. The warehouse
had a railroad siding to handle whole carloads of goods if the price
was right.

In April 1942, Ketner's Inc. moved its East Innes Street store
to an adjacent corner, filling the spot vacated by Haden's Tire and
Auto Supply. The tire store had burned. Here, Glenn Ketner set up
his first self-service supermarket and advertised his low prices and
good service. A radio jingle for the Ketner stores from 1942 was
sung to the tune of "Comin' Round the Mountain":

"They'll be comin' down to Ketner's every day,
For their groceries are the best in every way!
Ketner's market is so super –
Ketner's costs are super-duper!
Ketner's market is perfection, housewives say."

"One thing I remember about working for Glenn Ketner,"
Eller said years later. "He made a statement one time about
refunds. He said, 'If you're going to make it good, don't make
them mad.' Years ago, chickens weren't nearly as chilled as they

24

are now when they came in. When you took them off refrigeration, you better get them back on refrigeration fast. Well, this lady had left one in the car probably too long, and it got hot and it was bad. She brought it back. Well, the first thing the kid said was, 'If you had put it in the refrigerator when you got home, it wouldn't have done that.' It was downhill from there.

"Hell, if you're going to get them their money back, don't tick them off."

By 1948, the silver anniversary of Bob Ketner's first meat market, Ketner's Inc. had three stores, plus Excel Grocery Co. Glenn Ketner was poised for expansion to 100 percent self-service supermarkets. By now, Wilson Smith and Brown Ketner played big roles in the Ketner operation, helping it become the first chain in North Carolina to offer pre-packaged produce and one of the first with pre-packaged meats.

• • •

Wilson Smith was destined to be a grocer. Born the son of a meat cutter in Spartanburg, South Carolina, in 1917, Smith moved to Winston-Salem, North Carolina, with his family when he was 2 years old. His father sent his boys, Julian and Wilson, to stay with their aunt Ada in Salisbury when their mother died. Ada West raised the boys from the time Wilson was 8. By that age, he was delivering groceries in a wagon for pennies, nickels and dimes. As he grew older, the small delivery wagon led to more steady hours with Carolina Stores in Salisbury. After high school, he transferred to Charlotte where he made $9 a week for what became Allen Stores – a distant forerunner of Winn-Dixie. But Smith made his way back to Salisbury, and a store closing led him to take an assistant manager's job with Glenn Ketner in 1938.

Only World War II interrupted Smith's grocery career. He joined the Army Air Corps in 1940 to begin a five-year stint that would see him go from private to captain and earn five combat ribbons and the Bronze Star. He and his unit set up air bases behind

25

the advancing Allied troops through France and all the way to Frankfurt, Germany. Ketner saved Smith his job, and by 1948 Smith had become advertising manager and produce supervisor. He considered Glenn Ketner his mentor and learned from him that the two most important people in the grocery business are the customer and the employee. A workaholic, Smith decided to lead by example.

"If they could see me mopping the floor, wearing a store apron, sweeping, dusting – if they saw me doing it, they knew I wasn't asking them to do something I wouldn't do," Smith said. Smith possessed a special talent, that of a sign man. Grocers used to buy drop chalk from drugstores, mix it with water and use the solution as paint to advertise the sales of the day on windows. It washed off easily. Smith did it all quick, neat and freehand.

"He was just a fine fellow," Glenn Ketner says, "and the kind of guy the longer you knew him the more you liked him. He was an excellent sign man also. Oh, he was terrific on that. And fine in the store. So he became the sign manager, and then we were expanding on it, and he was drawing the ads."

Occasionally, Ketner sent his men to seminars or asked them to accompany him to conventions of the Supermarket Institute or other industry groups. Wilson Smith returned from a school in Boston in the late '40s bent on pre-packaging as a means of providing cleaner, neater produce. He started experimenting with it.

"Well, here's what we're going to do," Glenn told Smith and Eller one day. "You're either going to go all the way, or you're going to quit. If you're going to pre-package, you're going to pre-package all of it."

Smith and Eller jumped at the chance. Green beans, celery, corn, lettuce, squash, cucumbers, peppers – they wrapped all of the produce except cabbage in plastic, protecting it from human touch.

"It was mostly trial and error," Eller recalls. "You did whatever the customer wanted. You just hoped you had it the size they really wanted. You had to take cellophane sheets and heat it, turn it over and seal it. It wasn't nearly as sophisticated as it is now. Cut the corn, put it three to a tray, four to a tray or five to a tray, wrap it. I always preferred pre-packaging."

"In those earlier days, there was a lack of space in stores," Glenn Ketner says. "They weren't large enough, and the manufacturers, as they are today, were always trying to get more of their products on the shelf for displays. I think pre-packaging fruits and vegetables and meats really became a very smart thing to do. Not just because we were the first ones to do it, but it helped save fruits and vegetables from tumbling around and people always trying to get the largest ones. And meats, you used to walk up to the meat case to look at the steaks and then tell the butcher, 'That's what I want, and I want it cut right now.' People were pretty hard-headed about that."

In the beginning, a lot of experimenting went on with the plastic film to cover the meats. A store had to have a film that allowed the customer to inspect the meat visually, and allowed the meat to breathe. Red meat needs enough oxygen to keep its color. Brown Ketner went with a DuPont packaging process, and Ketner's Inc. unveiled its self-service meat and produce sections in its Salisbury store in 1948. *The Salisbury Evening Post* proclaimed the "revolutionary self-service meat department" one of the first 200 in the United States. It boosted the already considerable reputation Brown had as a meat man.

Brown Ketner had a knack for looking at 100 head of cattle butchered, quartered and hanging in a meat locker and knowing immediately the grade of beef, how much fat was in it and if it had been corn fed. He routinely went to cattle sales in the Midwest or to the Armour Co. in Chicago to get Ketner's the best quality meats.

After high school, Brown became his brother's market manager and ran the meat departments in the Kannapolis stores until Glenn sold two and moved into the Cannon Mills-built store. One day before the move, Glenn approached Brown and handed him some money. He gave Brown two weeks to learn as much as he could about the way other grocery chains did business. Brown took the peculiar assignment and made the most of it, working various jobs for A&P, Dixie Home and as far south as Publix in Florida. Even though times were hard, no one ever turned him down when he asked for a job, and he would begin immediately. Later the same day, Brown would walk up to the manager and quit, saying, "Look, I think I made a mistake. I've got another appointment."

Where the appointment was, Brown didn't know because he wasn't sure where he was going. But within a couple hours or a whole day in the stores he visited, he could tell whether they had anything new that Ketner's could use. "One after another," he said, "I'd pick up a few tips here, a few there. So I headed home."

Brown didn't know what his job would be with the new Kannapolis store. His uncle Charlie, the butcher at the old Franklin farm, was joining the operation. Brown expected him to be the meat manager. Brown doubted he would be a produce man, and Baxter Whitley seemed the likely candidate for store manager. But Glenn called a meeting and announced that Brown, then 24, was his choice to run the store.

"I said, 'Oh, my God.'" Brown remembered many years later. "So I took it. Every damn body was older than I was. Try that on for size. But it worked out very good. I was just mean enough and lucky enough that it worked out."

Brown's assistant manager never made the connection that Brown and Glenn were brothers. In fact, he assumed "Brown" was his boss's last name. The assistant manager complained to Glenn one day that he should get rid of "Mr. Brown."

"Women come in here and he'll grab them and kiss them, even if they've got a mouthful of snuff," the man said. "And it's running down his chin, and he won't even wipe it off until they're out of sight. He's crazy. He'll carry their babies while they're shopping. You don't want a man like that."

But Glenn did, and the assistant manager soon lost his job.

As store manager, Brown demonstrated a knack for thinking under pressure. Customers started to gather on the morning of a big sale, and the growing crowd began to press against the store's doors and windows. The police weren't able to pull them back, and Brown feared that someone was going to get hurt. Finally, he grabbed a handful of silver dollars and threw them over the crowd onto the sidewalk and parking lot. Those in back raced to pick up the coins, easing the pressure on the ones in front and allowing the doors to be opened. Ten people were admitted at a time.

Brown, a burly man, liked to joke and poke fun. A Dixie Home store (what would become Winn-Dixie) competed for business across from the Ketner store on West A Street. One day Brown noticed his uncle Charlie putting up a sign, "Fryers, 25 cents a pound." Brown couldn't believe it – fryers were costing about 35 cents a pound delivered to the store.

"Charlie, what the hell?" Brown screamed.

"Those sons of bitches over there think they can sell them cheaper than I can," Charlie Ketner answered, motioning across the street to the Dixie Home store, where clerks already were taking down their sign, crossing out "25" and marking the price of fryers at 23 cents a pound.

Charlie Ketner immediately went to 21. Dixie Home went to 19. Brown Ketner stood and watched the battle go on for about an hour.

"The next time you take that sign down, Charlie, I want you to put 'Wings of' in small print above the word 'fryers,'" Brown finally instructed.

"Why?"

"It'll be evident to you in a minute."

Charlie affixed the words "Wings of" to the sign, and the price war continued, with the price of fryers dropping as low as 13 cents a pound. At least that was the price at Dixie Home. Ketner's was selling wings at 13 cents a pound. About an hour after the sign war waned, Brown Ketner spied the store manager from Dixie Home walking the street, nonchalantly trying to get a closer look at the

Ketner store. When he strolled close enough to read "Wings of" on the sign, he stopped. Brown had waited to see this, so he calmly walked out to exchange greetings.

"Brown," the Dixie Home manager said, "I hate to ask you, but what are you selling fryers for?"

"Thirty-nine cents a pound," Brown said with a straight face.

"You know what those ignorant sons of bitches that work for me think you're selling them for?"

"Thirty-nine cents a pound?"

"No, they think you're selling them for 13 cents a pound."

"No, no. That's the wings," Brown said, a smile invading his lips.

The Dixie Home manager stormed away, and in a few minutes his sign was down, and fryers at Dixie Home returned to 39 cents a pound. Brown and the man went out later for a cup of coffee and a good laugh.

Close to the end of World War II, Glenn sent Brown to the Pee Dee Avenue store in Albemarle to see whether he could salvage it. The store had lost a good manager to the service and his replacement had done a terrible job. The store's lack of customers made it like a mausoleum, and Brown racked his brain to find a way of getting back the lost business. He soon noticed that schoolchildren had to pass his store on their way home. He started throwing pennies on the sidewalk and, not so mysteriously, the pennies led into the store. Children picked up pennies and went all over the store finding them. After two days of the same routine, parents started coming into the store wondering what was going on.

"I need the business," Brown explained. "You all haven't been back. I know the people who have been here disappointed you, or you would have never quit."

The parents promised they would be back, but Brown kept up the little gimmick for a couple of more days. The store returned to healthy sales, good enough that Glenn Ketner agreed on another Albemarle location to stay ahead of the competition. Glenn eventually made Brown vice president and operations manager – the company's chief trouble-shooter.

• • •

When Ralph Ketner was still in high school, he hitchhiked the 16 miles from Salisbury to work in one of Glenn's stores in Kannapolis. On some weeknights, he would work until 9 or 10 at night, then catch a ride back toward Salisbury with the 11 p.m. shift change at Cannon Mills.

On Friday nights, Ralph would sleep at Glenn's house because the stores would open at 5 a.m. Saturdays and stay open until 2 a.m. Sundays – 21-hour days. "And that was back when you walked," Ralph recalled years later. "If a customer wants a box of matches, you walk to get it. You get back, and they want a box of soda that was right beside the box of matches a hundred feet away. You walk to get that. Boy, your tail is dragging after 21 hours of steady walking.

"Glenn had one rule he would never violate: He wouldn't let anybody work over 24 hours a day. That's to let you know you belong to him. He was extremely tough. He was sharp. He is the sharpest man I've ever seen. We always called him the smart Ketner because he's the only one who ever had any money."

Owing to his incredible gift with numbers, Ralph went to college in Indiana as an accounting major. After a stint in the service, he returned briefly to work for Glenn to run his warehouse.

"That's when I got up with this rule of not working over 24 hours a day," Ralph says. "I would have a date at 7 or 8 at night, but I had to wait until all the salesmen came in and all the trucks came back at 9 o'clock, 10 o'clock. So finally I told him I just wouldn't work for him. I quit." By 1950, he would return.

• • •

In July 1949, Ketner's Inc. opened a store in Lexington, North

31

Carolina, a part of Davidson County on the north side of the Yadkin River. It became the company's first entirely self-service supermarket and one of only a half-dozen in the state. The same year Ketner's moved into a large new store in Kannapolis. Located at West Avenue and Oak Street, the store had entrances and exits on both streets.

The promotional side of Glenn Ketner gave Kannapolis residents a sale on a train carload of sugar in 1950. In Salisbury, cheese drew top billing as it had in the days of Bob Ketner's big cheese. Glenn sold 50,874 pounds and 36 varieties of cheese during a week that featured the appearance of Miss Wisconsin.

In 1951, Glenn entered the real estate investment business by constructing a new supermarket at the corner of West Innes and North Fulton streets in Salisbury. He incorporated the new venture as Rowan Investment Company and became his own landlord. The store was his biggest and most modern, with 26,250 square feet on two levels. The basement level was used for storage. The store's opening marked the first appearance in Salisbury of S&H Green Stamps. Ketner's also gave away a 1951 Chevrolet sedan as part of opening-day celebrations.

From 1948 to 1951, Ketner's more than doubled its employees to about 200. The chain now had five stores, plus the Excel Grocery warehouse. Officers were Glenn as president and treasurer, Brown as vice president, Addie Ketner as secretary and Wilson Smith as advertising and produce manager. The growth continued with the opening of a Mooresville store in neighboring Iredell County in November 1953. A second Lexington store opened in October 1954, and it was the first time Ketner's offered parcel pickup. Two months later, Ketner's moved into the second Albemarle store, built for the company by Wiscassett Mills.

The promotions continued. Glenn's monthlong campaign to sell Campbell's cream of mushroom soup landed his picture on a full-page Campbell's advertisement in national trade publications. Glenn teamed with an appliance company to sponsor a cooking school in Lexington in 1953. He put floats in two Rowan

County bicentennial parades in 1953. President Dwight D. Eisenhower visited Salisbury for one of the celebrations. In 1955, Ketner's gave away $50 spending money and free one-week vacations to Florida. Another new Chevrolet was given away that year, too.

Each year, the growing company reported record sales.

"Glenn Ketner will always be tops with me because of his way of going about things," said Jim Berrier, who became Ketner's office manager. "He would come in on Saturday morning and he'd say, 'Give me a list of all the new people that have been hired during the week.' And he'd go out to the stores and he'd walk through, and if he knew there had been a new man hired in the produce department, he'd go by the produce department and he'd say, 'Hello, Bill Smith' or 'Hello, Jim Jones,' and they'd think, 'He even knew my name.' He was that type of fellow. He'd make you feel good."

Berrier was the son of a farmer in Davie County, a small, adjoining county carved out of Rowan's original territory. He worked briefly in a five-and-dime store before a World War II stint overseas in the Army. He majored in business at Salisbury's Catawba College after the war and was hired by Glenn at age 26. He never classified himself as a true accountant, though he became quite proficient at handling the books. He supervised the accounting done in the office, checked up on all the clerical work and performed various administrative duties – from paying the bills to figuring the taxes on employees. He discovered that Glenn Ketner ran a tight ship.

"He always taught you to keep the lights off when they're not needed, Berrier said, "One day, I went back to get me a drink of water, and I walked past the girl's restroom. I saw that the light was on – there was just a crack in the door – and so I reached my hand in there and turned the light out. When I did, there was a girl sitting on the commode, and she let out a yell, and everyone came running back saying, 'What's wrong? What's wrong?' But it's just an example. I did that automatically, reached in to turn the light off, thinking if someone was in there, they would have shut the door. Every time I see that lady today, I think of that."

Frank Hinds moved to Salisbury from Vermont in 1953 at age 30. He had several years experience with an independent grocer and figured he could work three or four years for a small chain in the South before going into business for himself. Glenn Ketner hired Hinds, and the Yankee transplant was surprised to discover the sophistication of Glenn's operation.

"They worked hard, every one of them," he said of Glenn and his lieutenants. "I came down here and saw that Ketner was way ahead as far as self-service, the meat operation and produce. They were bagging produce for self-service before anyone else."

Hinds began his Southern training as an assistant manager, then shuffled to the produce department at the new, large store at Innes and Fulton streets. Next came a couple of months in the meat department, then a stint on the grocery side in the Kannapolis store. He filled in during sickness and vacations as store manager in Mooresville, Albemarle and the East Innes Street location in Salisbury. When the manager at the premiere Ketner's supermarket at Innes and Fulton streets became ill, Glenn Ketner installed Hinds as store manager. Little did Hinds know that his store would be a central player in a price war to be fought against some of the Ketners before the end of the decade.

• • •

One Saturday morning, the staff at Ketner's had a sales meeting. The group learned that Glenn Ketner wanted to go into the produce business. At the time, Glenn already was running Tommy Eller ragged in efforts to find the best bargains on produce – a truckload of apples here or a truckload of peaches there.

"OK," Eller asked, "who's going to be in charge of this? Go into Columbia and buy produce, bring it back, deliver it to stores and all that?"

"You are," Glenn answered.

Eller was upset. If he was going to be responsible for it, he wanted someone good doing the buying. On the way home that day, he stopped by the home of Clifford Ray, who had a wholesale trucking business in China Grove. Ray was a tall, thin man of few words – a mountain boy from Watauga County. His family had raised produce and he had grown up behind a plow horse, preparing the land for potatoes, cabbage and tobacco. He started his own wholesale produce operation in Deep Gap in 1941, and later added friend Jake Moretz as a partner to expand the business. By 1954, Ray bought out Moretz and moved his operation to China Grove, where his main customer became Ketner's.

Ray had never worked for anyone but himself.

"Cliff, Mr. Ketner is going into the produce business," Eller said. "I always told you that if he decided it, I would come by and tell you."

The pair took a seat on a nearby rock wall and talked for two hours.

"How about you coming to work for Glenn?" Eller finally offered.

"I've never drawn a salary in my life," said Ray, then 43. "I'm not sure I could work for someone else. Besides, they probably won't pay me what I'm making."

"Well, Cliff, I don't care what you're making. All I want is somebody who will haul produce, shoot straight and be fair and can handle the money and I don't have to worry about it. I know you can do that."

Eller set up an appointment between Ray and Glenn Ketner. When they emerged about an hour later, Glenn had hired Ray and bought his truck, without ever having seen it.

"But the guy was honest," Eller said later. "Glenn felt comfortable with him. So we had a beautiful deal. Cliff had a lot more knowledge about produce than I did. He knew how to buy it. I didn't know how to buy it. I knew how to sell it."

Eller and Ray developed a lasting friendship.

Lion's Share

A turning point for Eller's reluctant career in the grocery business came in 1953. By then he was a supervisor, going from store to store, but still he was questioning whether he wanted to stay. He attended a seminar in Washington, D.C., and found himself paying close attention to a speaker whose topic was jobs and job performance.

"If you don't like what you're doing, then get out of it and find something you like doing," the man said. "If you can't find something you like better than what you're doing, then find something good in what you're doing."

Eller returned home with the speaker's words still bouncing around in his head. As he shaved one morning, he looked in the mirror and thought, "You know, the grocery business isn't too bad. It's regular. You work six days a week. You get paid every week, and everybody's got to eat. You meet a lot of nice people."

Above all, Eller decided, he enjoyed meeting the people. If he was going to stay in this business, and that was the one aspect of it he enjoyed the most, then he was going to concentrate on making customers happy.

"I learned to like the grocery business," Eller said. "I'm glad the Good Lord didn't let me be an auto mechanic."

4. 'I quit'

The walk home from school on days like this seemed especially long for young Ralph Ketner. He'd gotten a licking and knew there would be another waiting for him as soon as his father, Bob, got the news.

School wasn't high on Ralph's priority list. He disliked it so much that in the first grade, he ran away and hid under the house.

Ralph only hoped that all would blow over with his dad before it was time to go bowling. Ralph was a crackerjack bowler, so good that his dad bet on him against grown men. The boy inherited that gambling spirit, though it would take different forms in his adult life, as would a tenacity bordering on obsession. For now his obsession was bowling. Salisbury had three duck pin bowling alleys in the '20s, and Ralph played every minute he could.

After work one Friday night years later, Ralph went to the bowling alley at 7:30 and bowled 45 games over the next 12 hours. He went straight to work Saturday morning at the grocery store, worked all day, then entered a bowling tournament that night in Charlotte, bowling until 3 a.m. Sunday.

As a boy, Ralph had only one other passion that came close to bowling: the challenge to earn spending money. In addition to working for his father's grocery business, he peddled ice cream for local entrepreneur Dan Nicholas and hawked newspapers on Sunday mornings at the square in Salisbury.

Ralph was both a gifted and troublesome child. When a Ketner's Cash and Carry needed an extra clerk, someone would send to school for Ralph, who would leave class so he could add up the prices of merchandise for customers. He beat adding machines every time.

He especially enjoyed trips to the family farm in Rimertown. It wasn't unusual to allow a group of 10-year-olds to walk a cow the 16 miles to Rimertown in those days, and Ralph always begged for the opportunity.

One day Ralph asked his father for permission to lead a newly purchased cow to Rimertown with his buddies. "No, I don't want it to go to the farm," Ketner told his son as he got into his car. "Take it out to White Packing Company and get it killed."

Ralph asked his father where he was going.

"Spencer," came the reply.

"Can I go with you?"

"I don't care what you do."

"I don't believe I want to go," Ralph answered with a grin that grew wider as his father drove away.

"Let's head for Rimertown," Ralph told his friends.

"But your dad just told you not to take the cow," he was reminded.

"He changed his mind," Ralph declared. "He said he didn't care what I did. Let's go."

It was 2 a.m. when Bob Ketner pulled up at the farm in Rimertown in a truck to pick up the wayward boys. He told them the FBI had been alerted and that the sheriff was out looking for all of them. Why had Ralph brought the cow here, his father wanted to know, when he had specifically told him to take it to the butcher?

Ralph reminded him that he had said he didn't care what Ralph did. The son had his father on a technicality.

Employers, salesmen and competitors in Ralph's future would learn Bob Ketner's lesson the hard way.

Losing first his mother, then his father by the time he was 11 cut Ralph loose from his strong family moorings and allowed him to drift. He tried living with his stepmother in Florida after Bob

Ketner's death in 1932, but it didn't work out. Ralph was used to hustling for spending money.

"Down there I had to ask for every nickel I got, and boy that didn't go good," he recalled. "I told my stepmother I was moving back to North Carolina."

She gave up and moved the family back to Salisbury. Ralph picked up his various business interests where he'd left off.

In Glenn's stores, Ralph couldn't stand for any other clerk to have more sales cash in his drawer than he did at the end of the day. He'd run to get the matches and soda. He'd work through lunch. It wasn't worth a penny more to him, but Ralph craved the approval of big brother Glenn, nine years his senior.

In school, Ralph took easy courses and fast-talked his way along. In business arithmetic, the teacher put a problem on the board and explained how to add the columns of figures.

"That's not the way to do it," Ralph called from his seat.

"Can you do it better?" the teacher asked him.

"Yes, ma'am. Much better."

Ralph took the chalk, made a few strings of figures on the board and added them up in his head, just the way he'd done at Ketner's Cash and Carry. It was like a carnival magic trick.

"OK," the teacher said, "Ralph can add it any way he wants to, but the rest of you have to do it this way."

One day the teacher wrote a math problem on the board and Ralph immediately yelled the answer. The teacher wrote another problem on the board. Ralph called out that answer, too. Finally, the teacher made a bargain with Ralph. If he would leave her class and never come back, she would give him an A.

Ralph sought out courses he found easy: woodworking, business arithmetic, algebra, advanced algebra. Everything was going great until he stumbled into geometry. Where he had been averaging around 98 percent, his average for geometry was 25. As the semester wound to a close, Clifford Beck, his geometry teacher, told him to prepare for a failing grade. Ralph wouldn't be able to graduate if he failed geometry.

DAVIE CO. PUBLIC LIBRARY
MOCKSVILLE, NC

"Mr. Beck, have you thought how it's going to look on your records if I fail under you?" Ralph asked with a straight face.

"What do you mean?"

"Last year," Ralph said, "I had Miss Groves, the principal of the school, and had a 98 average. Now, you fail me. If I fail, she's going to wonder about your teaching abilities. First year you've ever taught. You owe it to yourself to pass me so it doesn't become an issue."

"Let me think about it," Beck said.

The next day he called Ralph in and said he would be giving the boy a C-minus, the lowest grade Ralph could get and still graduate.

With his share of his father's estate, Ralph looked around for a college to attend in 1937. He settled on Tri-State College in Angola, Indiana: "I got a catalog from there and it appealed to me because you start your major the day you go. You go to school 48 weeks a year, and you were out from August 20 to September 20 or thereabouts."

Tri-State had students from 48 states and a large Chinese student population, and Ketner was, in his words, "a wallflower."

"They didn't have dormitories," he said. "You lived in private homes. Hell, I just didn't mess around at all, didn't date or anything. I worked all the time and didn't do any studying. I think in four years of high school, I've yet to take the first book home. I had no foreign language, no chemistry. The things I didn't take would fill 10 books. If it was hard and required homework, I didn't want to touch it.

"What was unique about their school was they started a new curriculum completely every three months. So kids could drop out, work for three months, get enough money to come back, and go to school. And so I majored in accounting, got through advanced auditing because I picked up extra courses in accounting trying to get through."

Worse than the fear of foreign language for Ketner was the fear of speaking in public. "I was so nervous I wouldn't tell you my name in public for $10,000," he says. "I took public speaking five times at Tri-State. I would have graduated, if I hadn't screwed up on public speaking. Every time it was my turn to make a talk, I would drop the course. I laid out of business law. I loved it, but I'd lay out because I had the feeling they'd call on me that day to read the case and there'd be some names I couldn't pronounce."

Ketner actually lacked the six months he needed to graduate because he ran out of money. He returned to work for brother Glenn's store in Kannapolis.

Cannon Mills employee Joe Ridenhour, who used to share the 21-hour days at Ketner's with Ralph, stopped by and asked if he would like to work for Cannon Mills. As he feared, Ralph was nervous at his appointment with Gray Bostian, company treasurer, and Steve Miller, head of accounts payable. It was public speaking all over again. He stumbled and bumbled. Finally the question came: "How are you on arithmetic?"

Without hesitation, Ralph said, "I'm damn good."

They laughed and said they had finally found something he didn't mind saying. Ralph had the job.

Two weeks later he told his boss that he was quitting.

It was a big office with 50 people in it. A clock hung on the wall at the far end. Employees were told that they would sit down at 8 and remain at their seats working until the bell rang at noon. They could only get up to go to a filing cabinet.

"You had to call Mr. Lipe in the building department if you wanted to go to the bathroom," Ralph said. "That's how strict they were, and he timed how long you were gone. One morning I was determined that I wasn't going to look at that bell till the damn thing rang. I just had that much willpower. Well, I worked for what seemed like 10 hours and the bell hadn't rung, and worked another 10 or 20 hours and the damn bell hadn't gone off yet, so I couldn't resist it any longer. I knew it had to be one minute to 12. I looked up and it was 10 o'clock.

"When I resigned, I told the boss, 'I just worked 40 hours and got paid for two.' And he said, 'What do you mean?' Hell, it seemed like 40 hours and I said, 'I'm just not going to work at a job I hate this much. Any fool can do what I'm doing. I'm just going to quit.' He asked me to try it two more weeks and I said I wouldn't try it two more hours. I quit."

Would he consider a different job?

"You put me on something that requires a little intelligence, yes, I'll try it. I won't guarantee I'll stay, but I'll try it," Ralph said.

Ketner got along fine at Cannon Mills for a time. He enjoyed his new work much better, but periodically he told Joe Ridenhour that he was going to quit. He always spoke his threat to Ridenhour because his friend had the ear of Bostian, the treasurer.

"I'd get a raise every other week or every other month because Joe was going to report that I was thinking about quitting," Ralph recalled. "I knew that was what he was doing."

Ketner was sent to the vault one day to look for an invoice and noticed another invoice that said "two percent, 10 days." Cannon Mills had failed to take its discount for paying on time. "So I pulled three years of invoices without them knowing it, and they had not taken a discount in three years and paid every damn one of them on time. So I told the boss, 'You write this letter to Buffalo Chemicals and you get a $3,500 discount.' Five years' salary he got back just because of what I found.

"And other things. They were buying something at 19 cents each and they got 12.5 percent discount. Well that's one-eighth, so one-eighth of 19 is two and three-eighths. Everybody knows that, hell, but they were dropping the three-eighths because it's less trouble. That's all right on one. You only lose three-eighths of a cent, but if you buy 10,000 of those damn things, you lost three-eighths cent on 10,000. That's $37.50. So I told the boss about that. I researched all that and got all that money back. So it's a wonder they ever survived."

Ketner was feeling pretty good about himself, and when he saw his buddy Joe Ridenhour he asked for another raise. Ridenhour said he had figured out that Ralph had been using him to get raises. He wasn't worth another raise, he told Ralph.

"I've got to quit then," said Ketner. "Hell, I can't work for a company that overpays me. It's against my feelings."

Ridenhour said that he didn't think Ketner was overpaid.

Like delivering one of his brother Ray's counter punches, Ketner went for the kill. "Joe, you just said that they're not underpaying me, now you're saying they're not overpaying me, so you're saying that out of all the money in the world, they've chosen the right payment to pay me. That automatically can't happen. Either I'm overpaid or underpaid, one way or the other." Ridenhour just threw up his hands and walked away.

When World War II broke out, Cannon landed lots of military contracts and all employees were given a 5 percent raise on a Friday. Ketner marched into his boss's office on Monday morning and asked for another one. Ketner remembers the conversation: "The boss looked at me and said, 'I've seen everything in my life. I thought you would never surprise me, but I've never seen a man get a raise on Friday and ask for one on Monday.'

"I said, 'Oh my God, did I get a raise Friday? Mercy, I apologize. I just didn't mean this. How much was it?' He said it was five percent. I said, 'You're not talking about the five percent increase?' He said, 'Yeah.' And I said, 'My God, that's not a raise. Everybody got that. I've worked my tail off; I was entitled to a raise. Now because everybody else gets a five percent increase, you're counting that as my raise?' I said, 'Uh-uh, I can't do that. I quit.' "

But Ketner had a hard time leaving Cannon Mills. He broke most of the company's rules and got into a fist fight with a relative by marriage of the owner – and ended up better off every time.

The company had a rule that if an employee was kicked out of the local boarding house, Merrill Hall, he would be fired. Leave it to Ketner, but he raised a stink about how bad the food tasted and demonstrated with invoices how the boarding house was paying too much for groceries. The head man failed to appreciate Ketner's insights and told him to get out. Ketner broke the news to his boss, who gained him a reprieve from Bostian. "Well, we're not firing

43

you," his boss said on returning, "but for God's sake, wherever you go when you move out, calm down a little bit.' "

Ketner changed boarding houses and began rooming with Alan Hayes, the brother-in-law of mill owner Charles Cannon's daughter. Cannon not only ruled as king over the company but was king of Kannapolis. Hayes and Ketner got on each other's nerves, and the room became a tinderbox waiting for a match. It erupted one night with Ketner earning a healthy cut on the eye and a fat lip. He quit to stop the bleeding but vowed to finish the fight later. One day after lunch they met back in their room at the boarding house.

"Are you ready to finish it?" Ralph wanted to know.

"Yeah," Hayes said with contempt. "Let's go."

The ruckus that followed prompted the boarding house maid to call the police, who decided not to press charges.

An exhausted Ketner returned to work the same afternoon fully expecting to be fired. For sure, the company officials didn't want any more trouble. Somebody had to go. Ralph gladly transferred to the auditing department.

Ketner finally left Cannon for an auditing job in Pennsylvania for six weeks, before returning to North Carolina to join the Army. Thousands of young men were enlisting, and Ralph signed up with his friends. They were shipped to Casablanca to assemble auto parts, and Ketner became head auditor. He was an enlisted man but found out that head auditor was supposed to be a commissioned officer. He tried writing home to get promoted to second lieutenant, quoting the regulations word for word. The Army never answered.

Ralph spent 45 months in the Army and came home to work again briefly for brother Glenn at his warehouse, the Excel Grocery. Soon he was off again. He spent a year as auditor and assistant office manager for Central Motor Lines. During that time, he married Ruth Jones.

Ruth had a friend visit from San Francisco and Ralph began explaining the shortcuts he had put in at the trucking firm. "Things they were doing were unbelievably wrong, just idiotic," he explained. "I had to fight like hell to ever get them to accept my ideas."

Ruth's friend liked Ralph's attention to detail and asked him if he would be interested in a job that would double his salary. "I'll take it," he said.

Ralph and Ruth and two friends drove across country to San Francisco and Ralph started a new, short-lived career. After seven months, Ruth got word that her father was ill. She wanted to return home, and Ralph landed a job with the Internal Revenue Service.

Ralph bounced from one job to another – 10 in three years. "I never got fired," he said later, "but I found nine things I didn't like to do." He worked as an auditor for the Army Exchange and as an appraiser for a company in Philadelphia. The firm sent Ralph to help appraise the Ben Franklin Hotel. "They had a fellow that could tell whether their fancy paintings were authentic or not. I told my friend, 'Hell, I can't work here. This thing's over my head. I don't know anything they're talking about.'"

Ketner decided to test an idea that had simmered a long time in the back of his mind: home delivery in Salisbury of the *New York News* and *The New York Mirror's* big comic sections. "Joe Palooka sold for a dime and Dick Tracy sold for 15 cents," he said. Ketner figured that he could make half as much for one delivery of those newspapers as the hometown *Salisbury Evening and Sunday Post* made for seven.

With typical persistence, Ketner went to New York and sold the national sales managers of the two newspapers on his venture. *The Mirror* promised to ship him 2,000 papers, the *News*, 3,000. Ketner lined up some needy kids as delivery boys and worked out routes around Salisbury and Kannapolis. After weeks of preparation, he sent word to New York that he was ready. The papers arrived at the Spur service station on North Main Street, but they proved more trouble than Ketner had bargained for.

"You've got the comics in one section, you've got the colored parts in another section and you've got the news in another pile," Ketner recalls. "I've got 15,000 pieces of paper to assemble

Lion's Share

between Friday when they dropped them off and Monday when I put them in the kids' homes while they were in school. Well, two or three of the boys sold 100 percent of their allotment. Some of the others would cut the strings and read the funny papers. Half went unsold. So, boy, I called them, 'For God's sake don't ship me any more.'"

The Mirror sales manager was impressed that Ketner had succeeded in selling half. He encouraged him to stick with it. But Ketner had soured on the newspaper business. He quit, again.

Ketner soon landed a job with the State Revenue Department. Once, while he and a partner were auditing a bank, the partner noticed that Ketner was working without a scratch pad for his calculations.

"You'd better get to work there," the man told Ralph.

"I'm through with all mine," Ketner replied.

"Through? Hell, you haven't even made a damned note."

Ralph offered his figures, and they were different from every one of his partner's.

"Well you ain't got the right answers," his partner sneered.

"Yes, I have," Ralph answered. "This one is interest accrued until 1 o'clock; this one was to 1:30; this one was to 2." And he was right.

But the state revenue job proved to be just one more that Ketner didn't like. Then came the exciting yet sobering news from Ruth that she was pregnant. Ralph phoned his brother Glenn. "Look," he said, "I'm ready to settle down."

The impulsive Ralph Ketner was back in the grocery business. It was anybody's guess for how long.

5. Opportunity knocks

It was obvious to anyone who worked for Glenn Ketner in the mid-fifties that his grocery store chain was on the move, but few foresaw the dramatic change that came in 1956.

For Frank Hinds, the manager at Ketner's biggest store in Salisbury, the spring of that year held two fateful meetings. At the first one in March, Glenn called his store managers together and said the Ketner's chain had an opportunity to grow faster than anticipated. In the next few days, he said, Ketner's would merge with the Milner Piggly-Wiggly stores in eastern North Carolina.

The Milner organization began in 1921, founded by brothers H.H. and P.C. Milner. Their partnership was known as the Piggly-Wiggly R and D (Raleigh and Durham). H.H. Milner came to Raleigh in 1921 after operating various Piggly-Wiggly stores in Mobile, Alabama, and serving stints as district manager for the organization in New Orleans and Indianapolis. He secured a franchise for North Carolina's Wake and Durham counties in 1921 and steadily expanded his company, building a Raleigh warehouse to serve his handful of stores in 1947. Milner's more than doubled its size over the next several years before H.H. Milner died in 1955. P.C. Milner's son, John, became president of the company. He had joined his family's business in 1947 as advertising manager, later becoming the head buyer.

Like Glenn Ketner, Milner viewed the merger as a means of continuing expansion plans for more Piggly-Wiggly stores in Raleigh, Durham and the communities east of Raleigh. The new chain, to be called Ketner-Milner's, would combine two warehouses, the eight Ketner stores and 15 smaller Milner stores – seven in Raleigh, four in Durham and one each in Cary, Smithfield, Dunn and Goldsboro.

In the back of his mind, Glenn Ketner envisioned filling in the space between Salisbury and Raleigh (100 miles to the northeast) with stores in towns and cities such as High Point, Thomasville, Greensboro, Burlington and Hillsborough. The new interstate highway under construction, I-85, would provide a quick transportation link for all of these towns.

The new 23-store chain was the largest owned and operated by residents of North Carolina, employing about 600 people. Combined sales were about $20 million. With the merger, Glenn became president; John Milner, senior vice president; and Brown Ketner, Wilson Smith and R.B. Liles (from the Milner's side), vice presidents. Ralph Ketner assumed the job of director of purchasing. Addie Ketner took a seat on the Ketner-Milner board of directors, and Jim Berrier was named assistant secretary.

Soon after the merger, which was accomplished through an exchange of stock, a 24th store was added – a Piggly-Wiggly in Wilson that had been near completion before Glenn Ketner and John Milner negotiated their deal.

Within days of the Ketner-Milner announcement, Winn-Dixie came courting. Addie Ketner remembers a Winn-Dixie official calling their Salisbury home at 2 o'clock in the morning with an enticement.

Based in Jacksonville, Fla., Winn-Dixie wanted a stronger presence in North Carolina. Only a year earlier, the chain – known then as Winn & Lovett Grocery Co. – had no stores in the Carolinas. But by the end of 1955, the company had merged with three different chains, including the Dixie Home Stores, which had 73 stores in South Carolina and almost 40 in North Carolina. The Florida company changed its name to Winn-Dixie.

As the nation's eighth-largest grocery store chain, Winn-Dixie had expansion plans that made those of Ketner-Milner appear modest. Through merger and acquisition, the eight-state chain was approaching 400 stores in the Southeast and $500 million in annual sales. By 1956, the chain already was into a year in which its size would essentially double. A.D. Davis presided over the company whose officials kept wooing Glenn Ketner and making quite attractive offers in terms of buying him out and providing for his employees.

The benefits and opportunities for advancement would be better with a larger chain, Glenn agreed. Winn-Dixie would have to build a new warehouse and distribution center. Glenn, a former president of the Salisbury-Rowan Chamber of Commerce, received assurances that the center would be built in Salisbury. He knew of a perfect spot on Old Concord Road.

The Winn-Dixie people said few employees would have to move or transfer. Glenn himself would be named a vice president and become division manager. Ralph could head the division's buying operation. Brown could head meat operations. Wilson Smith would be able to stay in Salisbury and supervise the eight former Ketner stores for Winn-Dixie. Executives from the Milner side also would be given similar positions in the division.

The offer was too good for Glenn to ignore. Frank Hinds suddenly was called in May to a second meeting, this one in a banquet room at the Yadkin Hotel in Salisbury. Here, Glenn Ketner announced a pending purchase of the Ketner-Milner chain by Winn-Dixie and the end of a business he had seen grow from $10,000 a year in sales to $20 million.

"You had to wear boots to get out of the room. Tears really flowed," Wilson Smith recalled later. "We felt like we really had something going. We had the Piggly-Wiggly stores, and we had the operation here in Salisbury. We felt like the area would really grow between here and Raleigh and we could really have been a big chain."

One formality remained: the signing of the papers. Glenn, Addie and Brown, who was a minor stockholder, drove the three hours to Raleigh to affix their signatures to various documents.

Even though Glenn and Addie had controlling stock, they wanted Brown's signature to make the decision unanimous. Glenn thought he noticed a hint of hesitation with Brown.

"Brown, you'll be making more with them than you are with me," Glenn told his brother.

"Yeah, it won't be as much fun though," Brown answered.

All the papers were spread out on a table, but when the time came to sign, Brown froze. His hand would not allow him to sign the papers. The parties involved decided to call off the procedure for that day and meet back at the same place several days later. Again, at that signing, something in the message between Brown's brain and his left hand wouldn't allow him to sign the documents. Glenn, Addie and Brown got into the car for a long drive home.

"Does it mean that much to you?" Glenn finally asked.

"Hell, no, I must have been drinking too much on the way up," Brown said, laughing off his strange paralysis. "We'll try it again Friday."

To this day, Brown Ketner isn't sure anyone would recognize his signature, but he finally signed the purchase agreements.

As part of the deal, Glenn Ketner signed a non-competitive agreement, stating he would not go back into the grocery business for a minimum of five years, his employment with Winn-Dixie notwithstanding. Ralph Ketner recalls that a couple of weeks the sale, Glenn asked him to sign a similar promise.

"I thought he said it was an agreement not to go back into business," Ralph recalls.

But Ralph told Glenn he had never been in business – how could he not go back into business?

"You know what I'm talkin' about," Glenn said.

"Well, how much are you going to pay me? I'm not going to sign anything I don't get paid for."

Glenn told Ralph he wasn't going to pay him anything. The discussion ended.

"If they had given us $500, I'd have signed that thing so fast,"

Ralph said in later days. Brown Ketner and Wilson Smith also stayed away from any agreement "not to go back into business."

When the acquisition became final in June 1956, Winn-Dixie had more than 400 stores in North Carolina, South Carolina, Florida, Georgia, Alabama, Mississippi, Kentucky and Indiana. It had added more than 200 stores over the previous year through mergers and buyouts, and chairman J.E. Davis promised that expansion would continue with the construction of new stores, some in the Piedmont region of North Carolina. From Frank Hinds' point of view, he liked the chances for advancement with Winn-Dixie, and the benefits – health insurance and profit-sharing – seemed better. For Brown and Ralph Ketner, Tommy Eller and Jim Berrier, the buyout meant living and working out of Raleigh during the week. For some, the experience would not be pleasant.

Things quickly soured for Glenn Ketner and Wilson Smith, too, even though they stayed at home.

As division head and vice president, Glenn soon discovered he was wanted everywhere but Salisbury. Company planes flew him in and out of the small Rowan County airport. He liked the Davis family, but other executives in the company "drank too much strong tea – they didn't know when to go to bed," Glenn said.

Addie Ketner realized that her husband was too much of an individual not to be his own boss. He had pioneered too many ideas that were successful to be taking orders from other people. Glenn also saw his former employees moving from store to store or being asked to relocate to other states. The final annoyance came when Winn-Dixie reneged on its promise to build the warehousing and distribution center in Salisbury, opting for Raleigh instead. As division manager, the distribution center was supposed to be his baby, and Papa Glenn wanted the center in Salisbury. To him, that was part of the deal.

Wilson Smith remembers that the Winn-Dixie announcement of its decision to build in Raleigh also came while Glenn was out of state, at a Lutheran convention. In late January

1957, Glenn resigned from Winn-Dixie. *The Salisbury Evening Post* said he had agreed to stay on in "an advisory and consulting capacity." But in essence, Glenn was out of the grocery business. His non-competitive agreement said nothing about real estate, and Glenn turned his attention to his Rowan Investment Co., which a year earlier had spent $70,000 to purchase land for a new shopping center at West Innes Street and Mahaley Avenue.

Glenn planned, ironically, for his major tenant to be a supermarket. He couldn't be a grocer, but he could be a grocer's landlord. He already was Winn-Dixie's landlord at the former Ketner store at Innes and Fulton streets, where Frank Hinds continued on as manager.

Glenn wasted little time. He announced on April 19, 1957, that he would build Ketner Center. I.W. Ashburn, a trust officer at Wachovia Bank and Trust, became leasing agent for the center. By August, Wagoner Construction Co. of Salisbury started building the facility.

• • •

Wilson Smith didn't like his new job with a big corporation. The Ketner's organization had always seemed like family – a team approach for a common cause. Friends helping friends.

With Winn-Dixie, Smith began feeling more like a number than a person.

"When we were with Glenn," Smith said, "the idea was that the customer was really the No. 1 person. And we went all out to satisfy the customer. When we went to a larger chain, we found that that relationship was not there. So I think we became a little bit disillusioned with the type of service we were supposed to give our customer."

As a grocer, Smith had picked up a few insights from his new company. He learned better ways to merchandise and to provide a bigger mix of items. And he figured the experience of working for a national chain was worth something. But he watched Glenn's real estate activities with more than passing interest.

• • •

"You know," Tommy Eller said many years later, "when you work for a small company, and you see it start growing – you feel like you're a part of it, you feel like you've contributed to it. Well, there's a different feeling doing that than a guy out of high school or college has in going to work for, say, IBM. You've got a job. You're probably contributing, but you don't get the satisfaction of contributing, like working for a smaller company. There you have a relationship with the people you're working with that doesn't require memos, for example."

Throughout his career, Eller would despise memos.

"The other thing is," Eller said, "with Winn-Dixie – when you merge into a large corporation, they have a tendency to feel like they're smarter. And I don't particularly like that. I feel like you learn something from everybody. Now the guy I worked for directly in Jacksonville, Florida, the executive vice president in charge of produce, was a super nice guy. He was a first-class gentleman. We never had a minute's problem. But a lot of other people I dealt with I had little respect for."

When Ketner-Milner sold out to Winn-Dixie, it had produce warehouses in China Grove and Raleigh. A vice president from Florida came to North Carolina to visit Tommy Eller, asking him to oversee both warehouses. Eller left the China Grove warehouse operation in the capable hands of Clifford Ray and spent most of his time in Raleigh. He later realized that Winn-Dixie was moving toward a day when it would move the whole produce operation to Raleigh and close the China Grove warehouse. He knew that Ray would never move to Raleigh.

Eller lived in an apartment in Raleigh during the week. One Saturday he and his wife went house hunting and decided on a place in Raleigh. On the drive home, Eller had second thoughts.

"Don't cash that check," Eller told the real estate agent over the telephone that night.

"What do you mean?"

"I'm not going to buy that house. I'm not going to move to Raleigh. It's that simple. I just don't like Raleigh, and I'm not going to live in Raleigh. I'll rent an apartment to stay in, but I'm not going to buy a house."

Eller actually liked his job. "It was great, but all I did was drink liquor, eat steaks and politic," he said. As produce director for the Raleigh division, Eller coordinated the selling of produce, fruits and dairy products in all of the stores from Raleigh south to Conway, South Carolina, and as far west as Hickory in the foothills. Eller had an expense account, company car and private secretary, but he felt as if he weren't doing anything.

"The more I thought about it, the more I decided I wanted to come back to Salisbury," he said.

• • •

Brown Ketner had been in charge of operations and the meat end of Ketner's for so long that he was used to giving orders and expected them to be carried out. He had some run-ins with his new Winn-Dixie colleagues, including the divisional vice president who took Glenn Ketner's place. One of Brown's first directives, which raised the eyebrows of Winn-Dixie executives, told store meat managers to put the worst part of every meat on top of the package, so a customer could see it. It went back to Brown's philosophy with Glenn's stores: "You can fool the customer until he gets home, then you're the damn fool."

Ralph Ketner acknowledges that the Winn-Dixie people didn't like Brown, and Brown didn't like them. One Saturday morning the Winn-Dixie officials – Brown and Ralph included – were having a sales meeting in Raleigh, going over the specials to be featured in the coming week. Ralph gave his report on the groceries, since he was the buyer. No problem. But Brown caused a stir when he reported that Winn-Dixie's meat department would feature whole chickens for 25 cents a pound and cut-up chickens for 29 cents a pound.

"Brown," an executive said, "you know you can't charge more for cut-up chickens than you do for whole chickens."

At the time, nobody did. In fact, it was unheard of. Asinine, Ralph Ketner would say in later years.

"You're right," Brown said. "You can never charge more for cut-up chickens."

The men eventually went around the table again, restating their specials.

"Whole chickens, 25; cut-up chickens, 29," Brown announced.

"Brown, I thought we had that clarified," the executive reprimanded. "You cannot charge more for cut-up chickens."

"I agree with you," Brown said politely. "Nobody should ever do that. I just charge less for whole ones."

Frank Hinds says Brown Ketner could have made a living as an entertainer, although he sometimes lacked finesse in giving constructive criticism. Brown once chewed out a cashier for being rude to a customer, and the woman got so mad she slapped him. Brown slapped her back, and the woman stood at her cash register for the better part of the next hour crying and ringing up groceries.

And Brown was picky about the quality of his meat departments. He finally resigned after a dispute with his bosses over policy in the meat departments.

• • •

Brown Ketner had a contingency plan already in the works with brother Ralph and Wilson Smith. The plan focused on Glenn Ketner's new shopping center. The men had talked with Glenn and among themselves – mainly by telephone – about the idea of running their own grocery store. Since the Ketners were in Raleigh and Smith lived and worked in Salisbury, they decided to meet in between. They chose an L-shaped motel near Burlington

55

along the new interstate and rented a room for about five hours, staying until 10 or 11 p.m. The men were of the same mind, believing they had in themselves a strong nucleus for a new company. They also presumed they could hire many of the former Ketner employees such as Tommy Eller, Clifford Ray, Jim Berrier, Bob Roseman, O.L. Casey, Odell Casteen and others.

Meanwhile, Glenn Ketner's leasing agent, I.W. Ashburn, had been circulating word to the Winn-Dixie, A&P and Colonial chains that Ketner was building a shopping center and looking for a grocery store to be its anchor tenant. He reported back to Glenn that all three were interested. So were "the boys," Ketner's brothers and their friend Wilson Smith. Of the candidates, Ashburn reminded Ketner, the boys would be the biggest risk because Glenn couldn't borrow money on their lease. For any of the chains, a bank would be willing to lend 90 percent of the money.

Building the new store for a chain made sense. Building it for Ralph, Brown and Wilson did not.

Glenn Ketner decided he had enough confidence in them to take the risk. Eller, still on the inside at Winn-Dixie, learned that his company may have made Glenn's decision easier. At a meeting, the possibility of Winn-Dixie's moving into Ketner Center came up, and Eller offered that he thought a move from Frank Hinds' store to the new shopping center made sense. But a vice president said Ketner was asking too much rent – one-and-a-half percent of sales.

"I think they really felt that they could beat on him and get the price down and still get the store," Eller said. "Well, then, that's when Ralph and Brown and Smith kept telling Glenn, 'If they're not going to take it, we'll take it.'"

So the decision was made. Winn-Dixie would be facing a new competitor in Salisbury – one with inside knowledge of its operation. Brown left Winn-Dixie first, followed by Wilson Smith and Ralph Ketner in August of 1957. In typically loyal fashion, Smith felt obligated to work on for Winn-Dixie until a new store in Concord could be opened. He didn't want to leave anyone in a bind.

The week of the Concord grand opening, the divisional manager drove to Concord to try and talk Smith out of his decision. Smith said no, but the manager had anticipated that answer. He told Smith to turn in his reports and instructed Smith's replacement to drive Smith home. There, Smith officially turned over his company car and severed his relationship with Winn-Dixie for good.

The executive vice president that Eller liked so much said everything he could think of to entice Eller to stay with Winn-Dixie. He offered Eller a year's leave of absence with the promise of holding his job until he returned. He said Eller could transfer to the city of his choice – Louisville, Tampa, New Orleans. Eller stubbornly refused. He wanted to join his old friends and their new venture in Salisbury. He and Clifford Ray would be a package deal, of course.

"I knew we were going to have one store and have lots of fun," Eller said. "I hoped we were going to have fun."

6. Cold day, hot war

C.W. Cranford looked twice at the reading on his thermometer. It said 7 degrees, and his years of meticulous weather
watching led him to trust the measurement. He jotted down the
reading in the appropriate column beside the date: December 12,
1957.

This Thursday had dawned to North Carolina's coldest weather
in a decade.

On Mount Mitchell, the highest peak east of the Mississippi
River, the temperature had dropped to minus 18 degrees overnight,
missing the state record by only three degrees. And in Salisbury
– nestled in the Piedmont and where Cranford served as resident
meteorologist – a newspaper reporter drew the assignment of
describing the weather confronting his town. "The night was
particularly cold," he typed, "because the low temperature was
accompanied by biting winds that seemed to whistle through
every crack."

Sixteen-year-old Jeff Ketner played hooky from China Grove
High School that Thursday morning. He could see his breath
inside his father's car as they rode together at daybreak on the 10-
mile trip to Salisbury. He looked down at the new shoes he had
bought the day before, just for this occasion. When he looked at
his father, Brown Ketner was smiling.

Brown Ketner enjoyed days like this. Nothing would be easy
about it, and the cold temperature added to the challenge. He had
put his whole future on the line.

So had Brown's brother Ralph, whose 7-year-old daughter,

Linda, woke up early that morning, too. She went to her closet looking for something special to wear to the grand opening of her father's new grocery store, Food Town. She finally decided on an outfit decorated with tigers.

Ralph Ketner had some bigger things to worry about first, such as the parking lot. The three Food Town partners had enough experience to know that their grand opening would attract a huge crowd of shoppers. The parking was generous: room for 375 cars. But there was a big catch. Glenn Ketner had been waiting until the day before the store opened to pave the parking lot. On that particular Wednesday, it snowed, foreshadowing what would be a cold, snowy winter.

So for the opening, and for months to come, the parking lot remained gravel and dirt. When the temperature went above freezing, it became gravel and mud, not a good mix for women shoppers in high heels. But the men behind Food Town were impatient. Ralph Ketner hoped the morning glaze over the frozen parking lot would save the day and be a blessing in disguise.

The freezing weather had already relieved Ralph of his biggest worry about opening day: messing up the mayor's name when he cut the ribbon at the grand opening. Ralph was more scared of standing in front of a crowd and making a few remarks than almost anything – bankruptcy included. At 3 a.m. he had been ready to call brother Brown and ask if he'd take over the presidency and cut the ribbon the next morning, but somehow Ralph managed to drift off to sleep. His worst fears proved unfounded. It was so cold few people paid attention to the ribbon-cutting. They wanted to get inside.

In middle age, Ralph, Brown and Wilson Smith were gambling their savings and mortgaging their future. Their first store represented the largest supermarket in Salisbury and one of the largest in the Piedmont – more than 15,000 square feet. The long, low store stood as the anchor to Ketner Center, Salisbury's first planned shopping center.

Lion's Share

Like all good grocers, Wilson Smith knew how to move quickly through a store, and this particular morning he glided at top speed. He liked the look of this store. The all-glass front. The yellow, blue and shrimp pink on the walls. The gray tile floors. The green checkout stands.

The layout imitated a typical Winn-Dixie store of the day. The produce and frozen foods were positioned to the customers' right as they walked into the store. Self-service meats were spread in long cases along the back. Dairy products stood along the left wall. Salesmen straightened up the beauty aids, toys, medicines and specialties toward the front. Between the walls, eight gondolas, each 46 feet long and separated by 6-foot aisles, carried 5,000 items that made up the grocery stock.

Smith stepped on the Magic Carpet automatic door to make sure it worked.

Tommy Eller, produce supervisor, scanned the fruits and vegetables one more time. The cold snap eventually would mean higher prices. But for the weekend, at least, customers could get two large heads of lettuce for 25 cents and a 10-pound bag of potatoes for 35 cents. The day promised to be a homecoming for Eller, and he was looking forward to seeing familiar faces. He didn't know it then, but he would work off 50 pounds during the next eight weeks.

In the days leading up to the opening, Clifford Ray bought the produce and hauled it to the store in his truck. In North Carolina grocery circles, Ray, Eller, the Ketners and Smith were considered among the best in the business, so it was a bit unusual to see all their expertise focused on the opening of one store. So many chiefs. So few Indians.

Eller found it refreshing compared to the bureaucracy at Winn-Dixie. Here, it was, "Cliff, how about doing this while I do that," or "Bill, wouldn't this look better over here?" There was no "Mister" in front of a name among these men. And they did everything, from mopping the floors to cleaning the parking lot. Each man brought a special talent to the lone store.

Eller considered this first Food Town three stores in one. He managed the produce and frozen foods. Brown Ketner bought and merchandised the meats. Ralph Ketner purchased the groceries and set all the prices on grocery stock. Smith was the advertising man, doing all the signs in the store and drawing up the newspaper advertisements with help from the rest.

On paper, Ralph Ketner headed the company as president. But for this store, titles didn't mean much. Meetings usually meant grabbing a soft-drink crate and sitting a spell at the back of the store.

As preparations continued for opening the doors December 12, cashiers took last-minute instructions on the store's new cash registers that Food Town touted as eliminating the "manual figuring" of change and the guesswork on sales tax. Clerks also prepared to give away hostess aprons for the first 5,000 women. Free pencils, lollipops and balloons were to go to children. One vendor offered a free 5-by-7 portrait of any child under 13 with the purchase of a twin-pack of chocolate chip cookies for 39 cents. Prizes would be given: wrist watches, portable radios, coffee makers, silverware, $10 food certificates, a Green Giant doll and Swedish cocktail sets. And some lucky customer would win $100 cash each of the first two weeks of business.

Salisburians read about the new store's planned opening the night before in four full-page advertisements in *The Salisbury Evening Post:* "It's big," the ad copy began. "It's beautiful. It's bountiful. Salisbury's newest, largest and most modern food store. More than 100 years experience behind the management of Food Town Stores."

So Ralph and Brown Ketner and Wilson Smith were not so secretly planning for Food Town to be more than one store. But for now they wanted people to know of the Ketner Center Food Town's pre-packaged produce, "meats of distinction" and a new Hobart-Dayton Model 2000 scale for the accurate weighing, pricing and labeling of meats. They also thought customers would enjoy parcel pickup – a Salisbury first.

Lion's Share

Jeff Ketner realized he was facing the coldest day of his life. He was working the parcel pickup.

C.C. Owen made last-minute checks on the new heat pump he had installed for the store. Weeks earlier, after the concrete had been poured for the floor inside, constant rain hampered its drying. Stock couldn't be moved in. Owen ended up turning on the air conditioning to help the water evaporate, but it continued to worry the founders for about two weeks. When the floor finally dried and the stock was in, Owen switched to heat. He was keenly interested in how the new heat pump would respond. As for investing in Food Town, Owen had been one of those to decline because of the considerable competition Food Town faced.

Some well-known supermarkets were already established in Salisbury. The Winn-Dixie stores on East and West Innes streets advertised "low, low prices and S&H Green Stamps." The Colonial Store at South Main and Horah streets boasted that "Your total food bill is less when you shop at Colonial." The Harris Super Market on South Main claimed to be "The Friendliest Store in Town." The country's biggest grocer, A&P, had a successful store on South Main Street.

Besides the chains, Food Town faced competition from independent grocers: Earnhardt's Superette in the Chestnut Hill section, Trexler's Modern Food Market on East Innes, the E.L. Rufty Cash and Carry Grocery on North Main, the Lash Self-Service Store on Council Street and more. But the Food Town people had other things on their minds. This was opening day.

Salisburians flocked to the new store as expected, and Jeff Ketner was right, it was the coldest day of his life. The young Ketner loaded bag after bag of groceries into cars. At one point he counted 53 shopping carts lined up, waiting for parcel pickup. The wind howled on this overcast day. The temperature never rose above 30 degrees. But many of the first customers who bundled up against the cold came for more reasons than just special prices, prizes or curiosity. They were looking after their investment.

Food Town finally closed its doors at 8:30 p.m. The store was in a shambles, and the operators knew they faced several more hours of work to restock, clean and get set for Friday.

As Jeff Ketner mopped an aisle, he kept noticing something red on the floor. It was a deeper red than the Carolina clay that had been tracked in all day. He looked at his mop and in his bucket of water before he realized that blood was coming from his feet. He lifted a foot to see that the parking lot's gravel had cut through the bottom of his new shoes, through his socks and into his flesh. Outside on the parcel pickup, the frigid weather had kept his feet from bleeding, and they were so numb he hadn't felt pain. Inside, his feet were warming and slowly starting to hurt.

Brown Ketner and his son returned to China Grove about 1:30 a.m. As the light came on in the car, Brown noticed something red on the floorboard. He thought something had spilled until Jeff told him what had happened. He rushed the boy inside.

"The bottom of his foot was gone," Brown would recall years later. "Just raw. You could even see the tendons. He had worked all damn day like that."

The Ketners bandaged the feet, and later that morning Jeff Ketner played hooky again, returning to work at Food Town.

• • •

In modern day parlance, the men behind Food Town scorched the earth to open that first store by December 12. Scouring the telephone book for investors was just one of the time-consuming details. The men also had to design a store's interior – Brown laid out a plan – furnish it from scratch and order the groceries, meats, produce and other items to stock the store. They had to hire cashiers and stock boys. They needed signs of all shapes and sizes for inside and outside the store. Advertising had to be lined up. Vendors had to be contacted. They needed a warehouse and office space. They fretted over grand opening promotions.

Then there were the worries out of their control. The parking lot. The furnace. The weather.

Lion's Share

Tommy Eller left Winn-Dixie at the first of October 1957, but the Food Town founders couldn't give him a job right away.

"Well, I could not afford not to work," Eller says. "So Clifford Ray and I took his truck, and we went into the wholesale produce business just to have something to do. We would buy produce and then sell it to Winn-Dixie. I had contacts in Raleigh and I could call over and talk to the guys that bought it and say, 'Now look, John, anything I can help you with?'

"I remember one time sweet potatoes were coming in down in southern Rowan County, and he said, 'Yes, I could use some sweet potatoes.' All we had to do was go to the farmers, put them in baskets and load them on the truck. We drove the truck to Raleigh; they unloaded it; we collected the money, drove home. That's all we had to do. Easy. Very simple. But, you know, you had to know where to go. We did that twice a week. That gave me enough to pay my bills."

When Eller finally could go to work for Food Town, he took a $75-a-week cut in pay from what he was making at Winn-Dixie. Young Jeff Ketner worked about six months without being paid. Jim Berrier, who invested money with Food Town, helped with the company's books at night for no salary. He and his friends had the understanding that Food Town would hire him when things got better. During the day, Berrier worked for Greg Peeler at Bamby Bakery.

Wilson Smith went from August to December without being paid, as did the other founders, Later, he worked at half salary – half of the $12,500 a year he made at Winn-Dixie. He returned to his former salary when Food Town was on more solid ground.

Mother Nature also sided against Food Town that winter. A family history written for Glenn Ketner says that the Ketner Center parking lot was paved "in early 1958." But the Food Town founders remember the unusually bitter winter delaying the paving much longer, into the spring. Meanwhile, on seven consecutive Wednesdays that winter, it snowed in Salisbury.

"It took all of the money we had to get the lot cleared of snow so our customers could get in to us," Smith says. Snow was piled as high as the building, an abnormal accumulation for Salisbury, which has gone whole winters without even a dusting. Ever the promoters, the Food Town chiefs made snowballs and stored them in a freezer so they could have a snowball sale in July.

Food Town even resorted to valet parking in inclement weather. Women customers would drive up to the front of the store, hand over their keys and Food Town employees would park their cars. If the weather was still bad when they finished their shopping, Food Town workers retrieved their cars and pulled them up to the parcel pickup. The store continued that practice even after the parking lot was paved.

Ralph Ketner immediately discovered that Food Town's one store didn't have enough volume to justify a warehouse, and he couldn't wholesale groceries out of the North Lee Street location because competitors weren't going to buy from the Ketner-related operation. He sold the warehouse's over supply to Merchant Distributors Inc. in Hickory and began pulling merchandise from MDI's warehouse.

This adversity paled in comparison to the price war that competitors, especially Winn-Dixie, mounted against Food Town. Just the mere presence of that one Food Town store irked the Winn-Dixie officials. Consider it from their point of view:

Winn-Dixie had effectively eliminated one of its toughest competitors in North Carolina by buying out the Ketner-Milner chain. It also benefited from the immediate infusion of talented executives to run the Raleigh division. But some of those new employees, such as Brown, had rocked the corporate boat. Also, Winn-Dixie was paying rent to one of its former executives, Glenn Ketner, while he was building a store for Winn-Dixie employees who would quit and become fierce competitors. No, Glenn hadn't violated his non-competitive agreement, but how much closer could he get?

In their year with the company, Ralph and Brown Ketner, Wilson Smith, Tommy Eller, Clifford Ray and the other former

Ketner employees Food Town was hiring away had gained an intimate knowledge of the way Winn-Dixie did business.

"When we started, Winn-Dixie was really upset," Eller says. "I mean, they were ticked off."

One fact was clear to the Food Town people then and it would take on great irony years later. If Winn-Dixie had followed through on building its warehouse and distribution center in Salisbury, Food Town would never have formed. Glenn Ketner probably would have stayed with the company, since much of his travel to Raleigh would have been eliminated. His brothers and employees such as Jim Berrier and Tommy Eller could have lived in Rowan County. The produce operation probably would have remained open, allowing Clifford Ray to stay. Wilson Smith's old friends would be back in town.

"When we first opened our store, the rumor was that they had set aside a fund to break us, and they almost did," Smith says of Winn-Dixie.

"It may have been a rumor, but they made a statement and it got back to us that they had $2 million to break us," Eller says.

Frank Hinds became a key figure in Winn-Dixie's assault against Food Town. The battleground became price. As soon as the Thursday afternoon newspaper hit the streets about 1 p.m., store manager Hinds would pick up a copy and head to a meeting in the back of his Winn-Dixie store with the produce manager, meat manager and area supervisor. They spread the paper out and wrote down all of the "hot specials" Food Town and other competitors were running for the weekend. A call then went to Winn-Dixie's Raleigh warehouse where shipments would be put together to cover those specials. Salisbury's Winn-Dixie stores had the merchandise by Friday morning and it was priced the same or lower than the competitors'.

Salisbury shoppers came to realize that they could go to Winn-Dixie stores and buy all of the town's grocery specials in one place. They didn't have to go to A&P for bread, Harris for pork chops, Food Town for bananas and Colonial for Coca-Cola.

"So we did a lot of business," Hinds said. "I don't know whether we made any money or not."

Hinds says he had definite marching orders from division headquarters to match all the specials. "It might even have been from the corporate headquarters in Jacksonville, I don't know," he says. "That was only in this area. I think there was some bad feeling on the part of Winn-Dixie toward Food Town when they opened up. I think some people figured Glenn was behind all this. There's still some feeling among the natives here in Salisbury about that. I don't think he was."

The idea behind weekend specials, or loss leaders, is to draw customers into the store so they buy all their groceries. Stores won't make any money on the specials, but they do make it up on the other groceries whose prices have a built-in profit margin. Owing to their father's low-price philosophy, the Ketners hated to be beat on price by anyone. They swallowed Winn-Dixie's bait and the lines were drawn for a price war.

The biggest problem in a price war is that shoppers realize it's worth their time to cherry-pick and buy in quantity only the ridiculously low specials at one store, then go to the next. Stores fail to make any profit when that happens. Winn-Dixie could afford to lose in an isolated price war, even expected it. Food Town could not.

Bread went down to a nickel a loaf. Fryers were 15 to 19 cents a pound. Sugar was 19 cents for a five-pound bag. Coffee sold for 39 cents a pound. For its Fourth of July special in 1958, Winn-Dixie offered Coca-Cola for 49 cents, plus deposit, for 24 six-ounce bottles. Hinds' store had two huge Coca-Cola trucks parked outside, and as one would empty it would leave to get another load.

Food Town had its specials on soft drinks, too. Six-bottle cartons of Pepsi sold for 9 cents sometimes. Crates of bottles stacked up like cordwood at the end of the building, Jeff Ketner says a full-time person had to be hired just to deal with the empty bottles. To Jeff Ketner, the battle over price reached a level of insanity the Saturday he was asked to tape money to bread. Food

Town taped nickels on bread selling for a nickel a loaf, essentially giving bread away.

Jeff Ketner said it was not unusual to see customers with shopping carts full of bread or chicken. A common sight at the parcel pickup was a customer pulling up for her Food Town groceries with several bags in the back seat of specials already gathered from Winn-Dixie. In its Salisbury stores, Winn-Dixie displayed Food Town's newspaper advertisements and next to them posted a sign saying, "We meet all Food Town prices."

"I believe they wanted to make us an example," Ralph Ketner recalled in 1982, "to say to all of the personnel in the stores Winn-Dixie bought in South Carolina, Virginia, Georgia and Louisiana: 'Now don't you try this!' And they nearly succeeded in putting us out of business that first year. They threw the book at us. I expected them to, but, quite frankly, the book was a heck of a lot bigger than I thought it would be."

When it became evident that Winn-Dixie was going to match any price Food Town offered, Tommy Eller decided he would help Winn-Dixie lose money and earn extra spending money for his brother-in-law at the same time. His brother-in-law, produce manager at the Innes and Fulton streets store for Winn-Dixie, would earn bonus money for meeting certain volumes of produce each week. Eller would run a Food Town advertisement setting a ridiculously low price on potatoes: nine cents for a 10-pound bag, for example. Winn Dixie immediately priced potatoes for the same price or less and sold potatoes galore. In reality, the store was paying its produce manager to lose money.

Was Winn-Dixie really trying to run Food Town out of business?

"It would be pretty strong to say that," Hinds says. "I think they were probably trying to get them to raise some of their advertised prices or something so that everybody could make a little bit of profit."

At times, Hinds' store could hardly accommodate its booming business in 1958. "It got to where, during that time of the food war,

68

we had to have two off-duty policemen come up and direct traffic, trying to get in and out of that small lot," Hinds recalled. Glenn Ketner, the landlord, eventually cut a second doorway in one side of the building, serving additional parking created next door.

As many as 50 people waited outside Frank Hinds' store on some mornings for 8 o'clock openings. The crowds came on Thursdays, Fridays and Saturdays. The Winn-Dixie at Innes and Fulton streets had eight checkout stands where cashiers worked non-stop on many of the price war days. People lined up with their shopping carts to the back of the store.

Grocers from neighboring towns complained to the National Grocers Association because even they were losing shoppers to the Salisbury price war. In 1958, the grocery industry rated Salisbury as one of the top five competitive cities in the United States. "In fact, the government sent an investigator to check everything out," Wilson Smith recalls.

Food Town had other problems. Glenn Ketner was building the company a second store on the other side of town, at East Innes and South Long streets, but he had run into a snag. A woman refused to sell her house and property to Glenn for the store, so his Rowan Investment Co. had to build the parking lot around her. She became one of Food Town's best customers.

Meanwhile, Clifford Ray and his wife set up a produce stand at the corner and created Food Town's own version of a farmer's market.

"Hell, he made more profit off that damn little corner there than we did," Ralph Ketner recalls. "He kept us in business for the first year. It was rough. It was one of those things where you knew you were going under. You just knew it but, damn, you're going to fight every inch of the way."

Food Town had lost half of its operating capital. Ralph Ketner called a meeting in the founders' small office space beside the store. "I was president," Ketner said, "but Brown was vice president and, in fact, Ketners all were pretty much the same. It didn't make any difference what title you had. Hell, each one of them would be in charge. So Brown was calling the shots, and he didn't believe anybody ought to sell for less than we did. But hell, you'd go bankrupt.

"I said, 'Look, we've lost over half of our money, let me lose the rest of it. I'm president, let me take over and call the shots.' "

Ralph Ketner started tying in specially priced items with certain dollar figures on an order. If a customer, for example, had at least a $15 purchase of groceries, she could buy soft drinks at a nickel a carton. With a $10 purchase, Food Town customers might be able to buy Pet milk at a nickel a can.

"Hell, nobody's ever done, it," Ketner told his colleagues, "but it's our money. It's our business. We can do anything we want to."

With the new concept, tied into the bigger purchases, the people trading with Food Town bought enough so the store owners weren't losing their shirt. Food Town recovered all of the money it had lost in the first six months. Almost a year to the day that Food Town went into business, it opened its second store to an equally cold and bitter day.

Soon afterward, the price war faded away.

Ralph Ketner's theory on why: "I think Winn-Dixie figured, 'OK, with one store we couldn't put them out of business. With two now, there would be less chance."

Brown Ketner says he chatted years later with A.D. Davis, who was president of Winn-Dixie in 1958. Davis told him, Brown says, that paying the three Food Lion founders $1 million apiece not to start their new company would have been the cheapest $3 million he had ever spent.

"He was being facetious, I think, because I don't believe he would have parted with that much money for nothing."

Glenn Ketner tired of the rumor that he was the mastermind behind Food Town. He blamed Winn-Dixie people – not necessarily their top executives – for being behind the notion, which also insinuated that his was the money behind the company. With attorney Tam Shuford's help, Glenn Ketner dashed off a polite letter to a Winn-Dixie higher-up that stated Glenn had not violated his agreement, that he had absolutely nothing to do with Food Town's store beyond being its landlord, and that Winn-Dixie was welcome to prove otherwise. He received a cordial letter back stating for the record that Winn-Dixie believed he had nothing to do with Food Town.

7. Me, too

The doors to the tractor-trailer swung open, and Jeff Ketner confronted a load of sugar that he knew would have to be stacked somewhere in the back room of the No. 1 store in Salisbury. Brown Ketner motioned to where the sugar should go, telling Jeff and a co-worker to carry the awkward bags to the spot. Brown left.

The two employees were almost finished when Wilson Smith pushed through the doors and instructed them to move the pile across the room. That accomplished, Ralph Ketner walked in and determined that the sugar would be better in a third place.

"What's it doing over here, when I told you to put it over there?" Brown demanded on returning later. Jeff gave up and told his father that the three founders should get together and decide where they wanted the sugar. He was tired of spinning his wheels.

For the first 10 years of Food Town's existence, the company did a lot of wheel spinning.

"We were just another grocery store," said Wilson Smith. "We weren't doing anything. We were buying stores. We would run them awhile, close them."

Because of a low profit margin traditionally running between one and two cents on the dollar, success in the supermarket industry means growth. After 10 years, Food Town was hardly growing. It had erected its blue and gold Food Town signs on as many as 16 stores, but by 1968 had sold or closed nine. Sales in 1963 were more than $7.25 million, and the company earned almost $89,000. But by 1967, sales had decreased to $5.8 million; earnings to $36,061 – with the same number of stores, seven, as in 1963.

Food Town's situation was not the industry norm. From 1958 to 1967, in a period of consistent food price inflation, the supermarket industry increased its sales by 50 percent. The top 10 grocery chains in the United States during much of the 1960s were, in order, A&P, Safeway, Kroger, National Tea, Acme, Winn-Dixie, Food Fair, First National and Grand Union. A&P's sales in 1963 alone were $5.311 billion.

Ralph Ketner was becoming disgruntled and restless. To him, it seemed as though Food Town couldn't work any harder for business, yet the company remained the grocery chain of last resort for developers building new shopping centers. Food Town took the leftovers, the locations no other chain wanted. Ketner could find no fault with the developers' reasoning.

Food Town also had tried every gimmick and promotion under the sun. It experimented with various pricing schemes, but basically had relied on traditional approaches, such as weekend specials. So had other grocery chains. That's what bothered Ketner the most.

"We didn't deserve to succeed," he says, "because all we were was a 'me, too,' and when you're a 'me, too,' you've got no reason to succeed. You make a car as good as somebody else, you haven't offered anything to the public they didn't already have."

The only price difference in stores of the era came down to those weekend specials – what each store chose to feature as its "suction" items to draw people into the store. Prices on other grocery items were remarkably the same or within a few cents. It was by design.

"All supermarkets used to follow A&P," Tommy Eller recalls. "If A&P had 79 cents on Tide, most everybody else put 79 cents on Tide, or 83, or 81. That was just the common thing."

Like Ralph Ketner, some of the original stockholders were becoming restless, too. Many lost faith and sold their shares back to one of the founders or traded them privately to someone else in Rowan County.

Ketner avoided R.O. Everett whenever he could. Everett, a likable, easy-going vice president at Wachovia Bank and Trust Co., called Ketner one day.

"You've got to put up more collateral," Everett said.

"What are you talking about?" Ketner shot back.

"Well, your stock's down to five dollars."

'Who said so?"

"Ernest Hardin, the only broker in town."

"It's not down to that," Ketner said. "I'll tell you what I'll do. I'll buy every share you can get your hands on and I'll give you $6. If you buy it for $5, you make 20 per cent, just like that."

Everett didn't bite, and Ketner breathed a sigh of relief. Things were so bad he wasn't sure he could have scraped together $60 for even 10 shares. While a couple of postal worker friends around him unloaded their stock, Paul Ritchie hung on to his 10 original shares that he had bought for $100. Archie Rufty, an attorney and friend of Ralph Ketner's, also kept his stock out of loyalty to Ketner. Rufty even started buying up shares of many of the people getting cold feet. William Alsobrooks, the Spencer Shops machinist who invested $1,000 in 100 shares in 1957, probably could have used the money in 1960. At 11:15 on a Saturday night, July 30, 1960, Spencer Shops closed for good.

But Alsobrooks never came close to cashing in. He moved his family to Asheville, North Carolina, in the mountainous western part of the state, where he got a new job with Southern Railroad. Meanwhile, leaders in Rowan County began looking for new industries to take the place of what had been the county's largest employer.

The company founders squirmed as the stock's declared value sank as low as $5. They didn't have any more collateral to put up. Reflecting its very modest expansion since 1957, the stock split four-for-one in 1963, a year when sales and earnings had increased 7 percent and 6.1 percent, respectively, over 1962. If the shares

74

had decreased in value to $5, the early investors had still realized a 100 percent return on their investment. Many considered it a good time to bail out. A post office friend of Ritchie's took $200 for his original 10 shares, declaring, "Anytime you can double your money, you'd better take it."

Food Town faced an uneasiness of a different kind in its first decade. On Jan. 2, 1964, Food Town accepted the resignation of C. Brown Ketner.

"My reasons for leaving this fine company are purely personal and involve my plans for the future," he told *The Salisbury Evening Post*. The local newspaper continued that the departing vice president and operations manager would not disclose his plans: "He would not say whether his future plans include entertainment or business," the story said. "Ketner is noted as one of the wittiest and most humorous after-dinner speakers in the area."

Theories abound on why Brown left. In an interview, Brown said that after a vacation out West he returned to pursue an end of the food business he had always been interested in – restaurants. More specifically, he became enamored with the Reynolda Manor Cafeteria, a place where his family ate when they went to visit Jeff when he was a student at Wake Forest University in Winston-Salem.

"It feeds a lot of people for less cost than you can do table-setting," Brown said of the cafeteria business. "I asked the fellow where he bought his tables, where he bought this and that. I got as much information as I could. And then I ended up buying the damn thing."

Brown Ketner immersed himself in another career. He would eventually draw son Jeff and veteran Ketner-Food Town employees Robert Roseman and Odell Casteen into the business with him. But it wouldn't be the last time Food Town heard from Brown, the largest stockholder in 1964.

Some Salisburians speculate that Brown and Ralph Ketner didn't see eye to eye on the company's direction, and a time bomb exploded close to New Year's Day 1964, leading to the resignation.

"As a family, I think they are close," Paul Ritchie says today. "They respect one another. They aren't mad at all.

"The story you see is what brothers can be. And I think, really, that's the crux of it. It's not a matter of not liking one another at all, but it's just a matter of the difference in the whole philosophy of things. And, in this case, it's a business philosophy."

An unfortunate incident also preceded Brown's departure. In May 1963, he spoke on "Ethics in Business" at the Salisbury Civitan Club. The talk featured comments that George Raynor, managing editor for *The Salisbury Evening Post* and a member of the club, thought should be included in an article about that meeting.

In his talk, Brown Ketner criticized the U.S. government for the role it was taking in settling racial disputes. He referred to an incident in Raleigh the same week in which the Liberian envoy to the United Nations was denied service at two restaurants because of the color of his skin. According to the newspaper account, Brown Ketner said that instead of apologizing to "the Negroes" the government should tell them that these restaurants were private enterprises in business for themselves. "Negroes have lost more," he said in reference to racial pressure, "than they'll ever gain back."

The Negro Civic League didn't take kindly to Brown's remarks. Neither did Wilson Smith. Ralph Ketner, who heard about the incident on his return from an out-of-town trip, wasn't happy about it either. They called Brown into a meeting and said future speeches should get their approval first. That angered Brown. Meanwhile, the Negro Civic League encouraged its members to boycott Food Town's three stores in Salisbury.

"I know it lasted long enough to be effective," says Doris Jones, who at the time was a counselor at Salisbury's black high school, J.C. Price. She remembers Food Town officials eventually contacting black leaders and stressing to them that Food Town would not discriminate against the "Negro" community. "They did do an about-face, and they did hire a lot of blacks,"

Mrs. Jones says. A&P had been the first store in Salisbury to hire one of her students from Price High, Mrs. Jones recalls. He was an honor student whom she dressed in a white shirt and black tie for his first day on the job as a bagger.

There were other changes coming for Food Town. In February 1964, Food Town hired W.R. "Bob" Barrier, a manager of the Bi-Rite chain, as assistant vice president in charge of store supervision. In essence, he took Brown Ketner's place. A native of nearby Albemarle, he came to Salisbury from Greensboro with 30 years of experience in the grocery business. Wilson Smith became vice president, assuming Brown Ketner's former title. Food Town also expanded its board from three to five. Wilson Smith, Brown and Ralph Ketner made up the original board. With Brown's departure, the company added Barrier, produce man Clifford Ray and attorney Archie Rufty as directors.

Barrier lasted about a year with Food Town. His responsibilities then fell on Wilson Smith.

Not long after the company had established its second store, Ralph Ketner looked into the possibilities of getting a loan for small businesses. An employee for the Small Business Administration office in Charlotte told him, "It's people like you we're trying to protect small businesses from."

"My God, man," Ketner said, "you are equating us with A&P? We got two stores and we are in the classification of A&P?"

"Yeah, we can't loan you a penny," came the answer. Ketner said he learned then that the best place for a person to find a helping hand is at the end of his arm. In these early days, Food Town tried everything to lure customers and, once it got them into the store, did everything to keep them coming back.

Tommy Eller used to keep his car parked at the back door of the No. 1 store. If a customer came in and wanted to buy something that Food Town didn't carry, and A&P had it, Eller would get into his car and speed away to the A&P, buy the item, repackage it back at Food Town and sell it to her at the A&P price, or less. Once a woman came in complaining because she had bought a bad pack

77

of fish sticks. Eller asked what brand of fish sticks and found out it was a private label sold only in A&P stores. Eller remembered the schooling he had received from Glenn Ketner: "If you're going to make it good, don't make them mad."

"Well, you know we've had an awful lot of trouble with that particular brand," Eller told her, "so we've quit carrying it. We have Gorton's fish sticks over here. I'm going to give you a pack of Gorton's fish sticks to replace yours. You take these and see what you think about them."

Food Town had a good working relationship with Charlie Roakes, who ran a little grocery across the street from Salisbury's No. 1 store. He carried a small line of groceries, specialty foods and fancy wines. He came in handy when a Food Town customer requested something that was out of stock or a bit unusual for the store to carry. A clerk would be dispatched to Roakes' store to buy the item. Roakes had a reciprocal arrangement with Food Town.

Eller and other Food Town employees also delivered groceries on several occasions. If orders had been mixed up, or if a customer arrived at home and called back saying, "I'm missing my potatoes," Eller would load the items in his car and deliver them personally.

From opening day for about two years, Food Town stores offered free coffee to customers. The small chain was one of the first to advertise the buy one, get one free sale. Stores had "Come As You Are" nights when customers were invited to shop in any attire they chose. Several people came in their night clothes and bedroom slippers. For one promotion, Food Town placed huge bags of roasted peanuts near the front doors and told customers to grab a handful and enjoy their shopping – "Don't worry about throwing your shells on the floor."

Food Town kicked off the local Little League in Salisbury every year with nickel hot dogs and drinks at McDaniel Field, right behind Store No. 1. At Newman Park on the Catawba College campus in Salisbury, Food Town sponsored baseball nights for Salisbury's minor league team. "Anybody who came

78

could get in free, and we'd give away hot dogs, had watermelon-eating contests, stuff like that," says Wilson Smith. Clifford Ray, who had taken up horses as a hobby, would perform with his trick horse at the games. The baseball promotions drew overflow crowds in the thousands.

The No. 1 store had a parking lot pancake breakfast. For a Quaker Oats promotion, Food Town served breakfast in the parking lot from 5:30 to 7 a.m. The stores had ice cream suppers and cooking schools in the parking lots.

Brokers helped on a lot of the promotions, such as Hunts Foods' "Redskins Day." Many North Carolinians have a rabid interest in the fortunes of the Washington Redskins. All of the Hunts sales people visited stores dressed as Indians. Store employees erected tepees outside. Redskins quarterback and Wake Forest graduate Norman Snead made an appearance to sign autographs.

The stores gave away new cars, silver dollars and television sets. For kids, the company sponsored Saturday morning movies at the Center Theater in Salisbury. Once, Food Town paid for the appearance of an actor who played Tarzan. The company brought in Miss America and Miss North Carolina for other events.

Winn-Dixie had the market cornered on S&H Green Stamps, the most popular trading stamp of the day. Offering stamps was a costly endeavor, but Food Town finally gave in, going with Family Stamps in the early 1960s. The stamp companies charged a percentage on sales, and Family Stamps charged 2 percent. A Family Stamps redemption store, where customers took the books of stamps they had saved and redeemed them for gifts, leased a space in the Ketner Center next to the No. 1 store in Salisbury.

The preparation and follow through on all of the promotions only added to the long hours the Food Town management was putting into their small chain. Ralph Ketner, Wilson Smith, Jim Berrier and a few others in management routinely took store inventories in the early-morning hours before the stores opened, then worked a full day.

The company began profit-sharing for its employees in 1960 and added hospital insurance, paid vacations, sick leave and annual bonuses. But there was little profit to share. Neither was there much promise of promotion.

Tom Smith, a high school student, started as a bagger at Food Town in 1958 and showed enough drive and ambition that he later became a store manager in Kannapolis while attending Catawba College. But Smith, no relation to Wilson Smith, recognized Food Town was struggling and set out on a career with Del Monte Foods in 1964.

Food Town expanded beyond Salisbury for the first time in October 1959, with the purchase of a small shopping center, grocery store included, in North Wilkesboro in the foothills of the Blue Ridge Mountains. In February 1960, the company bought the former Harris store on South Main Street in Salisbury. Then came the building of stores in Jonesville, Kannapolis and Rockwell and the purchase of stores in Marion, Statesville, Hickory and four stores in the Asheville area – all by September of 1964.

Food Town built its first warehouse when it appeared that sales volume would justify the expense. Ralph Ketner was ready to sign the lease for the warehouse's construction in the Hedrick Industrial Park when the matter of a $3,000 fee for testing the soil came up. Ketner refused to pay it, telling developer Enoch Goodman that it was his responsibility. Within two days, Ketner found another piece of property on Julian Road, and Food Town signed a deal. Enoch Goodman soon called back to tell Ketner he was right – the developer should pay for the soil test. But he learned quickly that Ketner had closed a deal on the other site.

"Glenn would have argued with me for 30 days," Goodman complained.

'Yes," Ralph agreed, "but he's got money and he can argue. A person who's got no money can't argue."

Later, after Food Town sold its four stores in the mountains, it didn't have enough volume to justify the warehouse. Again, Ketner turned to Merchants Distributors Inc. in Hickory and offered to sublease the warehouse to MDI in return for Food Town's buying again from the Hickory company. This arrangement lasted until Ketner decided that MDI had some built-in handling charges that went beyond his agreement to pay cost plus 3 percent. Ketner called a meeting of multiple store operators in North Carolina, about a half-dozen, and proposed that they start their own warehouse. All were using MDI at the time. Only two men showed an interest: Russell Walker, who had six stores in the Asheboro area near the center of the state, and Oren Heffner of Mocksville in neighboring Davie County. Heffner had only three stores.

In early 1967, the men formed a separate company Ketner named Save-Rite, and the Julian Road warehouse Food Town built almost five years earlier began serving the three small chains with a total of 16 stores. Food Town also maintained its offices at the Julian Road location. Walker became president of Save-Rite; Heffner, vice president; and Ketner, secretary-treasurer.

As Food Town itself tried to branch out, it learned quickly how folks viewed business a bit differently in other regions of the state. The company bought its store in North Wilkesboro from Tal J. Pearson days before Pearson began serving a prison sentence for selling sugar to bootleggers. Wilkes County fostered generations of moonshiners. Ralph Ketner found Pearson, a man with a third-grade education, to be a trustworthy businessman.

Ketner told Pearson how Food Town was struggling and it wouldn't be able to pay him any money down, although the company could pay him a certain amount per year plus interest. It sounded good to Pearson.

"Can we let you know Wednesday afternoon?" Ketner asked on Monday. Pearson agreed.

Meanwhile, J.C. Faw, head of the local Lowe's Food Stores, had planned to wait until Pearson went to prison before making his pitch for the grocery store. When he heard of Food Town's involvement, he went to Pearson with a certified check for $25,000 more than Food Town's offer.

Lion's Share

"I told them they had until Wednesday afternoon," Pearson told Faw. "My handshake is worth more than your $25,000."

Minutes after noon Wednesday, Faw told Pearson that the Food Town people hadn't showed up, meaning Pearson had kept his promise to wait until Wednesday afternoon.

"Where I come from, Wednesday afternoon is until sunset," Pearson said. Meanwhile, attorney Tam Shuford in Salisbury was drawing up a purchase and sales agreement for Food Town. About 3 p.m., Ralph Ketner strolled into a cafe in the little shopping center to meet with Pearson. An attorney for Faw was sitting next to Pearson waiting for the Food Town people to arrive.

"Did you come prepared to close the deal or with a purchase agreement?" the lawyer asked Ketner.

"No, we've got the closing agreement," Ketner answered.

"If they've got the closing agreement, it's theirs," Pearson said, signing the papers for Food Town and turning his back on an extra $25,000.

The company made the initial mistake of trying to convert what had been Pearson's country store, complete with fish bait, into a modern grocery. "We went in and cleaned it up so good that business dropped off," Wilson Smith said. "So we had to go back and mess the store up so people would come back." To make room in the store's warehouse for more groceries, Food Town had a parking lot sale of all the items Pearson had accumulated in his storeroom. Folks gobbled it up.

Later, Food Town sold the shopping center to J.C. Faw, who wrote into the contract that Food Town could never locate within five miles of the store as long as Lowe's operated it. For years, although Ketner believes Faw lost his shirt on the store, the agreement effectively kept Food Town out of North Wilkesboro.

Food Town bought a country grocery from a man in Marion, North Carolina. The guy was a proud hunter, who had placed mounted heads of his kills all around the store. About a week after Food Town took over, a health inspector walked in.

"You can't have those heads up there," he said.

82

"Why?"

"Well, it's unsanitary," the inspector said. "The hair can fall down in the food." Food Town took down the heads, even though they had been on the walls for 10 years.

Cannon Mills built a store for Food Town in Kannapolis, as it had for Glenn Ketner. When Food Town bought the Marsh Supermarket in Hickory, the 19,000-square-foot store became the largest in the chain. By May 1965, Food Town sold both the Hickory and Statesville stores to J.C. Faw.

In Hickory in 1962, Food Town tried a new concept: cost, plus 10 percent, and changed the name of this one store to Cash and Carry. Every item in the store was priced at what Food Town paid for it wholesale. When a customer reached the checkout stand, the prices were tabulated and 10 percent of the sale was added to the total.

During the first couple of weeks, customers gutted the store. Jeff Ketner, who was working his summer job there, said the Hickory Cash and Carry did five times the sales volume Food Town expected – all because of the new pricing concept. Jeff, his father and three other employees shipped in from Salisbury worked day and night without sleep to keep the store stocked. They stayed at a nearby motel and only went there to shower and change clothes. Two tractor-trailer loads of groceries had to be unloaded in the parking lot because the stock room was full. The men called for a couple of hundred more shopping carts from other stores. Aisles were jammed so tight at times, shopping carts could not move. Workers dropped from the push of keeping up. Jeff Ketner's best friend from college quit after a week.

The store opened on a Monday, and the five men from Rowan County did not sleep until after their long drive home late Saturday night. Jeff Ketner slept all day Sunday until 2 a.m. Monday before heading back with the men to Hickory for a second identical week. By Saturday, Jeff Ketner's head felt as if it were ripping open with each step in the store. He couldn't believe it when he saw his father come by whistling, "Zippety-do-da."

"That's when I learned what kind of guy my dad was," Jeff Ketner said later. Indeed, his father had worked similar hours during the Depression at his brother Glenn's old ballpark store in Kannapolis, selling groceries by day and cutting meat at night. Sometimes while cutting meat, Brown would fall asleep, so he learned to put a cigarette between his fingers to serve as a painful, periodic alarm clock.

The stampede on the Hickory store soon abated when customers began questioning the "add on" of 10 percent. The competition exploited their confusion, suggesting that when they shopped at the Cash and Carry store it was adding 10 cents (not 10 percent) to every item. Even though they were still experiencing considerable savings at cost plus 10 percent, customers began distrusting the practice. Sales fizzled, as did the concept. Years later, wholesale clubs such as PACE and Sam's would work on much the same principle, but they *deduct* a percentage at the checkout – a practice much easier to swallow.

In September 1964, Food Town made its biggest purchase by buying four Big Giant stores in the North Carolina mountains, a good two-hour drive west from the Salisbury headquarters. The stores were located in Asheville, Enka, Black Mountain and Fletcher and had belonged to Harry L. Giezentanner of Asheville and his brother. Wilson Smith supervised the mountain stores for a brief period by spending one day a week in the area and driving home the same night. The store managers quickly figured out his schedule and developed a network of calls to warn each other when Smith was on his way to a particular store. During the rest of the week, the stores "ran loose," as Tommy Eller describes.

Ralph Ketner called Eller one day and asked him to take a trip with him to Asheville to visit a supervisor Food Town had hired for the region. They met the man at the Black Mountain store. Ketner called the supervisor out to his company car and asked him to open his trunk. The supervisor had several cases of coffee without a transfer slip showing where he had gotten the coffee and where it was going. Ketner held out his hand for the man's car keys and fired him on the spot. The Food Town president eventually asked Eller to move to Asheville and supervise the troublesome stores. Eller refused to move, but he stayed in the area from Monday until Saturday, and the store managers never knew when to expect him.

In the first four months, Eller fired four store managers and a wide assortment of cashiers, meat managers and produce managers. Some employees were stealing from the stores. One group of employees was having cookouts with Food Town steaks they had taken from the store. On his first inspections, Eller confronted terrible conditions in the stores. The rats at one store were big enough to carry loaves of bread off the racks at night. Eller eventually had the stores cleaned up and put better management in place. He came to supervise five stores and kidded Ketner one day that he had found a house on Beaver Lake and was going to move to Asheville.

"Don't buy a house up here, we're trying to sell these things," said Ketner, who realized the purchase of the mountain stores had been a big mistake.

Food Town sold the stores to Frank Outlaw, former head of the Winn-Dixie meat operation before he fell out with the top echelon of the company. He started a chain called Bi-Lo. In July 1966, Outlaw traded 40,000 shares of Bi-Lo stock valued at approximately $2.50 a share for the Food Town stores in the mountains. Many years down the road that stock would pay generous returns for Food Town shareholders, but no one paid attention to it in the summer of 1966.

Food Town tried something else of Outlaw's: his pricing concept. The company experimented with it in the Salisbury store on South Main Street. Outlaw had taken about 50 items in his stores and marked them down to cost or less. Ice cream sold for 39 cents a half-gallon when it normally might be 79 cents. Bread was 25 cents a loaf when the regular price might be 59 cents. He also offered less expensive baby beef instead of veal and re-established the old-fashioned service meat counter where the customer could point out a particular cut. All of this was tried at the South Main Street store, which was changed to "Save-Rite" so customers wouldn't be expecting the same prices and service in the regular Food Towns.

The store, long in the shadow of a successful A&P across the street, saw its sales rise from about $8,000 a week to $35,000 a week. Despite the sharp increase in volume, the store wasn't really making money, however. Ralph Ketner chalked the experience up to what he called the "research and development" of the first 10 years.

But the initial crowds at the Hickory Cash and Carry and the turnaround in volume at the Save-Rite store presented strong hints to Ketner and other Food Town employees that price was the key to more business, just as it had been in the days of Ketner's father, Bob.

By the time he read an obscure article in a trade journal in the fall of 1967, Ralph Ketner was ready to make a change. He figured he either had to change or quit one more job. It was time, he decided, to bet the company.

8. LFPINC

The bellman hesitated for a moment when he saw what was on the back seat of the motel guests' car. He usually retrieved luggage, or clothes hanging in a travel bag. But this couple opened the door to five big cardboard boxes, the kind that toilet paper is shipped in. Strange luggage, the bellman thought. On swinging a box up toward his waist, he realized it was full of papers, not clothes, and as he retrieved each box and lugged it to the couple's second-floor room, the bellman's suspicions grew. He noticed that the husband also had carried a card table and adding machine inside. The man seemed especially anxious to begin work on whatever information those papers contained.

What was this guy, the bellman said to himself as he closed their door behind him, a bookie?

Ralph Ketner *had* traveled to the Manger Motel in Charlotte that November morning in 1967 to make a bet. The cardboard boxes contained six months' worth of invoices from Food Town's seven stores. With those numbers, Ketner planned to install a formula for cutting prices on all 3,000 grocery items in his stores at the risk of running the company into bankruptcy. His cost-cutting theory relied on one big assumption: that customer excitement over lower prices across the board would lead to a dramatic increase in sales, big enough to compensate for the lost margins. Back in Salisbury, Ketner had told Wilson Smith he wanted to leave town for a couple of days to work on an idea. He didn't know how long it would take or when he would be back.

Ketner also explained to his wife, Ruth, that he would not be good company on this sudden trip to Charlotte. She could go shopping uptown or read a book, but Ketner would be working and, please, he said, no interruptions. For Ruth Ketner, the motel room's TV was useless in this serious environment. She left her husband alone, realizing he was on a mission. A new obsession.

Ralph Ketner had been on edge since returning from Dayton, Ohio, a few days earlier. Paging through a trade publication one fall morning, he stopped at a brief first-person article written by Robert Stragand, a small grocery operator in Dayton. With a subheading of "Turns loser into winner," the article's main headline read "How to build volume and make money with low-low prices." Stragand believed in the theory that somebody knew the price of every item in his store. Not one individual alone, but all of his customers taken collectively. So he cut the prices on all his groceries, not just selected specials or narrow categories. A customer finds that kind of cost-cutting believable and exciting. She doesn't feel cheated on most of the routine items she is piling into her shopping cart.

"This fellow here has got what I've been looking for," Ketner said out loud. "I'm going to Dayton, Ohio."

On a Monday, Ketner called Stragand, who warmly agreed to have the Food Town president visit him the next day. Oddly enough, Stragand's own operation was called Food Town. Ketner arranged a flight and spent about three hours talking with Stragand on Tuesday.

"What motivated you to do this?" Ketner asked him

"Well," Stragand said, "I noticed a lady in church one Sunday and recalled she hadn't been in the store for two or three weeks, so I said, 'I haven't seen you lately.' She said, 'No, I quit trading with you. Your prices are too high.' "

Stragand explained to Ketner that he thought he had about the same prices as everybody else.

"Zwieback," the woman told Stragand. "You're two cents higher on that."

Stragand couldn't believe his ears. "I don't move five Zwieback a week," he told Ketner. "I could give them away and it wouldn't cost a nickel. I just started thinking that if somebody knows that price, then 5,000 people know 5,000 different items. So I just cut prices on everything." He went on to tell Ketner that even though he cut into his bottom line by reducing prices, he made up for it by selling more groceries. The reduction in price, he continued, had to be significant enough for people to take notice, meaning some items would have to be sold at cost or below cost on a consistent basis. Coming up with the right mix was crucial.

On his flight back from Dayton, Ketner thought that maybe he could move groceries even better than Stragand's small operation. He felt sorry for Stragand because he realized the Ohio grocer was at the mercy of his wholesaler. When a store owner buys from another source of supply, he's buying that supplier's inefficiencies. But Food Town's association with Save-Rite gave its stores their own warehouse and, because Save-Rite was buying for 18 stores, it could buy in sufficient volume to purchase groceries as cheaply as anybody.

Ketner liked Stragand and appreciated his input, but subconsciously he didn't understand why Stragand had written the article and given himself away to his competitors. "You know," Ketner said years later, "Coca-Cola doesn't say to Pepsi, 'Here's our formula – use it.'"

Days later at the motel room, Ketner began cutting, on paper, every grocery price in the stores. If an invoice showed that Food Town moved 100 cases of peas, and he cut the price 3 cents a can (with 24 cans to a case), then he had to subtract $72 from Food Town's bottom line. He did essentially the same procedure for 3,000 items.

Ketner scribbled down figures, punched madly at his adding machine – there were too many calculations for him to do this in his head – and littered the motel room with paper. He lowered the price on pet foods to below cost – in fact, he cut prices on about 10 categories of food to cost or below, including cereals, coffee, shortening, rice, grits and detergents. Ketner figured that roughly one-sixth of everything in the warehouse could be sold at cost or less. Overall, he would be selling all of the groceries for between 6 and 10 percent less than competitors.

The concept wouldn't work with meats. In the prior decade of "research and development," Ketner had once tried to have Food Town stores sell meat at absolute cost. "People started equating low price with low quality," he recalled. "It took a month or two, and it was pretty obvious that we were on a wild goose chase."

Cutting prices on nationally advertised brands of groceries, however, offered an advantage. Shoppers already perceived those products as being of good quality. And they could easily compare the brands from store to store. It was a blessing of sorts that Food Town did not have a private label whose lower prices would be confused with poorer quality.

The low-price concept wouldn't work with produce, either, because of fluctuating markets. Tomatoes might be 99 cents a pound one week and 33 cents a pound the next. Food Town stores wouldn't be able to offer consistent, low prices on all produce. So meats and produce would be some areas in which to make profit.

But Ketner clearly realized from his numbers that the overriding principle was volume. "I'd rather make five fast pennies than one slow nickel," he said years later. "It separates the men from the boys. We'd rather sell five cans of beans at 2 cents profit and make a dime, where our competitors would rather sell two cans at a nickel profit each and make the same dime."

Ketner shaved off three, five and six cents on many items, and as much as 50 cents on more expensive goods such as dog food and detergents. He finally added up all of his cuts and determined that he had decreased his gross profit by approximately 60 percent. Wanting to push on, Ketner didn't even double-check his math.

The hard part came next, figuring how much increase in volume – how many fast pennies – Food Town stores would need to offset a 60 percent loss. Ketner could make some assumptions: Expenses such as his electric bill, rent and depreciation would stay the same. Supplies would go up in proportion to sales – Food Town would need more paper bags, for example. Employee costs would probably go up commensurate with sales: If sales doubled, so would the staff. The store managers' salaries would stay the same. He went back to figuring.

At the end of three feverish days of cuts and calculations, Ketner had an answer: Food Town stores could break even with the across-the-board cost-cutting if sales increased 50 percent.

As he and his wife drove north on Interstate 85 toward Salisbury, Ketner lacked some of his normal confidence. Asking Food Town stores to increase their business 50 percent against the likes of A&P, Winn-Dixie and Big Star seemed suicidal. "You've heard the expression, 'Build a better mousetrap and the world will beat a path to your doorstep?' " Ketner says. "That's for the birds. You build a better mousetrap, you'd better learn to sell it." He had some selling to do to his board of directors.

Ketner came to the next board meeting with several charts and explained to the directors that he thought he had found an approach that would lead to more people shopping at Food Town. One chart showed that if volume could be increased 50 percent in 1968 to $8 million in sales, operating expenses would be reduced from 16.6 percent (registered in the first six months of 1967) to 13 percent. As a percentage of doing business, the cost of salaries, rent, advertising, utilities, store expense and administration would decrease while the cost of supplies would increase slightly. Ketner also reviewed how the stores would have to sell more to make up the losses from reduced prices. Archie Rufty, the attorney friend of Ketner's, immediately liked the everyday low-price concept.

"I vote with you," he told Ketner before the board had really discussed it.

"Just like that?" Ketner asked.

"Wait a minute," Rufty said. "Let me back out. Cancel my vote. Now, do you have anything in the world other than your investment in Food Town?"

"You know I don't," Ketner said.

"OK, I vote with you," Rufty repeated. "You're voting your livelihood, your life's work. It doesn't mean that much to me, so I'd be a fool to try to baby you along when you're willing to gamble everything."

Wilson Smith had deeper reservations, however.

"Let's try it in one store," he said. "If it doesn't work, at least we won't bankrupt the company."

"Bill," Ketner said, "we've had some great ideas and they haven't worked because we've tried them in one store. Rather than try it in one store, I quit. Hell, I'm ready to wash my hands of the whole thing. But I think I've got a good idea. If it works, it will be great."

"What happens if it doesn't go?" Smith asked.

"Well," Ketner conceded, "we're out of business."

Smith gave in and, characteristically, became the concept's chief cheerleader along with Ketner. The first two weeks of January 1968 further persuaded the Food Town executives that a change was needed, a big change. Sales had been $98,000 each of the first two weeks. Ketner annualized those numbers to predict a 15 percent drop in sales for the year down to $5 million and a loss for the first time in the company's history. Trumpeting low prices and continually trying to undercut other stores by pennies per advertised item, a new Big Star Discount Food Center also posed a threat to business in Rowan County, where Food Town had five of its seven stores.

The men faced several more difficult selling jobs, however. They had to persuade employees, salesmen and customers that the concept was for real. Some other things would be changing, too. The stores had eliminated trading stamps. There would be no more weekend specials. Giveaways, pancake festivals, beauty queens, hot dog sales – all the promotions they had tried in the past – would be scrapped. No longer would Food Town tie in special prices with minimum orders of $5 or $10. At a Sunday evening dinner for employees on the Catawba College campus, Ketner laid it out for his troops.

"You're all on the firing line tomorrow," he said. "Tomorrow morning we're reducing prices drastically. You've got to explain to the customer why we cut the stamps. You've got to explain to the customers that they won't see any more weekend features, as such. You're job is to listen to what I'm saying now, and then ask me every question that the customer can ask you tomorrow or the rest of the week. Now the customers are going to be complaining, but show them how much our prices have been reduced."

The immediate concern was about the weekend specials. How could Food Town allow itself to be beaten on those items featured in other stores?

"The answer is, we've got them beat on 3,000 items," Ketner said. "Yes, they will beat us on five or six every weekend."

Food Town officials had decided to call their endeavor "The Big Change." On Monday, January 15, 1968, the company sponsored a breakfast for about 85 salesmen of national manufacturers who would spend the next three days helping Food Town employees lower every price in every store. As they worked, putting in 235 total man-hours, the salesmen wore signs on their backs saying, "I'm busy lowering prices for you."

Ketner imagined that the salesmen resented what Food Town was asking them to do. He could hear in his mind the grumblings of the cereal, dog food, sugar and coffee salesmen: "We're working our tails off for the next two or three days, and he'll have us back next week raising the prices to what they were."

But Wilson Smith remembers that brokers liked The Big Change. "That meant they would get an increase in their products. For instance, a box of soap that normally sold for 98 cents, we were going to sell it for 79 cents. For a guy that was selling us 100 cases, he's going to start selling us 500 cases. So they got paid back real quickly for their labor."

Smith and others were busy changing prices one day when a woman came in and bought a jar of olives. A bit later, she returned to buy two more jars. Smith started a conversation with her.

"Why are you buying so many olives?" he asked.

"Well, someone made a mistake and put the prices wrong," the woman said. "I want to buy them before you change the price."

"No, ma'am," Smith said. "That's our regular everyday price from now on."

Smith had witnessed the excitement Ralph Ketner kept talking about. He also could see how important word-of-mouth advertising was going to be for the concept.

Tommy Eller remembers going over the various charts and details of the pricing strategy at the Julian Road offices in Salisbury. Ketner was adamant, he says, that the first person caught cheating on a price would be fired. Ketner told the top men assembled that they would meet again in six months to see how it was going and then again at the end of 12 months.

The stores set a goal of having all prices changed by the start of business Thursday, January 18. The night before, Food Town took two pages in *The Salisbury Evening Post* to introduce "The Big Change."

"There will be no need to wait for weekend specials," the ad said, "because Food Town's thousands of specials, more than 3,000, will be in effect six days a week. This means that you save money six days a week. In many instances, the price you pay will be at wholesale cost or less."

Dorothy Felts, home economist for East Rowan High School, was pictured holding a can of Stokely peach halves. "It would be impossible not to save money at Food Town with prices like these," she said in the advertisement. For comparison's sake, the ad put Food Town's prices on items under the heading "Our low, low price," and the competitors' under a column asking "Have you been paying this?"

Food Town offered Kellogg's Corn Flakes at 37 cents a box. "Have you been paying 43 cents?" the ad asked. Gainesburgers were 79 cents, not 95 cents; Lipton Tea Bags were $1.09, not $1.25; Clorox bleach, 55 cents, rather than 65 cents; Dial soap, two for 27 cents, not two for 33 cents. The list touched on items from every grocery category.

For some time, Ketner had been working hard to persuade *Salisbury Evening Post* reporter Ned Cline to write a news story about this new pricing strategy. Customers would pay more attention, Ketner believed, if they saw The Big Change being given news space. Cline balked, telling Ketner he was just after some free advertisement for Food Town. At the time, Cline also had other stories on his mind. He was covering a Ku Klux Klan conspiracy trial accusing ten Rowan and Cabarrus countians of depriving various citizens of their civil rights. The Klan trial may have seemed more important to Cline than a new gimmick at a local grocery.

"If I invented a gasoline that would get 20 percent more mileage, effective immediately, God, you'd love it," Ketner argued to Cline. "If I gave you the exclusive, you'd hug my neck. Here, I'm telling you something that's going to save people 10 percent on their grocery bill, and you're just trying to ignore it. I want you to write it as a human interest story. I don't want to pay you anything for writing it. Hell, it's something that The Post should be glad to get."

Years later, Cline recalled the conversations with Ketner: "There was, I felt, a legitimate news story that a local businessman was restructuring how he did business, but what Ralph wanted was a story outlining what a great idea this concept was. And I told him that was an ad, not a story. I just knew ethically I could not write a puff piece, which is basically what he wanted. I told Ralph he would simply just have to buy an ad."

Ketner agreed, but he still wanted Cline to write him ad copy that read like a "human interest" story. Plus, he wanted the page, with five pictures and three stories to be laid out like a regular news page. The only acknowledgement that the whole page was an advertisement would come in agate type, hardly noticeable, at the bottom of the page. The Post's advertising department agreed.

"As I recall," Cline said, "I checked that out with (editor) Jimmy Hurley, and he said, fine, as long as it didn't interfere with my reporting duties. So I met several times with Ralph to go over what he had in mind and to write the ad copy to his satisfaction. His point, of course, was to make it appear to be a news story although he had bought and paid for the ad space. It worked."

Ketner paid Cline for his free-lance effort, besides paying The Post for a full-page advertisement. He offered Cline $300 cash or $300 worth of Food Town stock. "I opted for the money," Cline said, "because I knew the cash would be good but wasn't too sure about the value of Food Town stock."

The advertisement ran the first Sunday after Wednesday's announcement of The Big Change. One of the "stories" detailed the findings of a spot check of competing grocery stores the previous weekend. This survey, Ketner said, showed that a $68.84 order at Food Town would have cost $10.85, $9.03 and $8.87 more at three competitors. In a reproduction of an ad Food Town had run the previous Friday, a comparison of 20 items with other stores showed Food Town shoppers saving $2.74 or 16.41 percent.

One of the stories in the advertisement invited shoppers to an open house the coming Thursday night, January 25. "Once the customer sees what Food Town has done," Ketner was quoted, "she'll be convinced that Food Town has the money-saving values day in and day out."

"Everybody worked hard to make it a success," Tommy Eller says. "Wilson Smith should get a lot of credit for developing the merchandising theme to put this thing across." For the stores, Smith devised little cards for most of the grocery items that said, for example, "Why pay 86 cents? Our price, 74 cents." To this day, Smith believes customers spreading the word to their neighbors about the lower prices at Food Town led to the snowball effect on sales. Within two weeks, Food Town stores noticed an upswing in business. Within a month, any lingering doubts Smith had harbored were gone.

"Advertisement is whatever causes the customer to trade with you," Ketner says. "Low price is the best advertisement in the world."

As a worried shareholder and board member, Archie Rufty called Ketner one day during the first six months of The Big Change. "Ralph," he said, "do you know what you get on Liquid Plumr, half a gallon?" Ketner knew every price. "We get 69 cents," he said.

"Well, do you know what A&P gets, and Winn-Dixie and everybody else?"

"Yeah," Ketner replied. "$1.69."

"Do you mean to be a dollar cheaper than they are?"

"Yeah."

"Don't you think a 50-cent spread would be enough?"

"Would you feel better if I made it 50 cents?"

"Yes, I would."

"Good, I won't do it," Ketner said.

"I thought you agreed with me," Rufty cried.

"No, you agreed with me."

"I haven't agreed with you at all."

"You did, Archie. You're excited about a dollar, but you wouldn't be excited about 50 cents. The whole concept is based on excitement."

By the spring of 1968, Ketner was toying with the idea of a new slogan, something that would aid in getting the message out. "We had a concept to sell," he says, "and it's harder to sell a concept than it is a price."

He kept trying to come up with some catchy combination of letters that would tell people about prices. A friend mentioned that, well, Food Town had the "lowest food prices in North Carolina." Ketner liked the ring and scope of that. So he just borrowed the first letters from the phrase, "Lowest Food Prices in North Carolina," and Food Town's strange rallying cry became "LFPINC." When a person saw it for the first time, he immediately asked what the odd combination of letters stood for. By that time, Food Town had gained what every advertiser wants: attention. Print some LFPINC bumper stickers, Ketner ordered.

"When we changed the concept on prices, it took a little time for it to take off," Tommy Eller says. "But we had a lot of customers now who would come in and ask for those bumper stickers – customers who were sold on the LFPINC concept. I remember a guy who used to trade with us at the Ketner Center, Stanford Holden. He would take them by the handful, like 10 or 15, and give them away. I was in Greensboro one day, and I saw a car that had LFPINC on it. I came back and talked to Stanford Holden and he said, 'Yes, I've got a daughter who lives over there and I made her put one on her car.' We had a lot of those. I couldn't begin to name all the people, and they loved sticking those bumper stickers on their car with LFPINC. The people who were convinced that we were doing what we said we'd do were trying to help us."

Food Town's competitors weren't convinced. They thought the struggling Salisbury chain had implemented another gimmick. Frank Hinds, who at the time was still a Winn-Dixie store manager, says competitors assumed Food Town was cutting specific categories of groceries that moved fast off the shelves but carried high markups on other items to make up the difference. Winn-Dixie stayed with the tried and true weekend specials. It wasn't until years later that Hinds and Winn-Dixie confirmed for themselves that Food Town had more than a gimmick.

Ketner kept a form letter for all the people who wrote to complain that other stores had Food Town beat with their weekend loss leaders. The letter asked shoppers to take their weekly grocery list and make a note beside any of the items on the list offered as weekend specials at other stores. Then visit Food Town, he urged. The shopper would learn that any item not marked as a feature in other stores would cost her less at Food Town. Ketner then encouraged the shopper to drive across town to the competition and buy its loss leaders. It would help the competition go bankrupt, Ketner said, and save Food Town money at the same time, because "anything they run a loss leader on, we're already selling it at cost or below."

"So you do us a favor if you don't buy from us," he concluded. Ketner enjoyed using reverse psychology.

Food Town sales climbed steadily, but Ketner still worried that too many shoppers didn't know what they were missing. In the first six months of The Big Change, alias LFPINC, sales were up 35 percent. Ketner needed one more push. He hired two teachers from Rowan County, Pat Barrow and Viola Dixon. He gave each $100 to buy groceries at other stores in Salisbury – A&P and Winn-Dixie among them. He asked them to compare the prices on the groceries they bought elsewhere with Food Town's, and he ran a full-page advertisement based on their results. Food Town was roughly 16 percent cheaper than the competition.

For one of the first times, Ketner specifically singled out the competition by name. "We called them like they were," he says. It would become a common Food Town approach, answered in kind by its competitors. Ketner hired the two teachers through the three summer months and had them knocking on doors across Rowan County. They conducted consumer surveys on grocery shopping habits. At the end of their questioning, they employed one of two standard exit lines. If the respondent, usually a woman, said she shopped at Food Town, the women might say, "Mrs. Jones, you were kind enough to answer this questionnaire for me. I want you to know you are shopping at the lowest-price store." If the person had named Winn-Dixie or some other competitor as his or her store of choice, the teacher-surveyor would say, "I think I owe it to you to tell you about a place to shop." They also offered two-dollar gift certificates to shop at Food Town. Ketner met with the surveyors every Saturday morning to hear their results.

The increasing sales volume caused a problem at the Save-Rite warehouse. Based on the percentages of stock each party owned, Food Town had been buying 40 percent of the goods; Oren Heffner, 23 percent; and Russell Walker, 37 percent. Save-Rite needed more money to expand the warehouse because of all the increased business Food Town stores were doing. Instead of 40 percent, Food Town represented about 60 percent of the movement of goods in the warehouse. Heffner and Walker said Food Town should pay for the expansion. Ketner agreed, on the condition that

Food Town be given 60 percent of the Save-Rite stock, so he would have controlling interest. They refused, and Ketner declined to buy non-voting stock to build a bigger warehouse from which Walker and Heffner would benefit. They agreed to have a friendly parting of the ways, with Food Town buying out Walker and Heffner's shares in Save-Rite and also purchasing two stores in Mount Airy that had been bought by the partners under the Save-Rite flag.

By the end of 1968, Food Town had more than survived. The 50 percent increase in sales Ketner had hoped for actually turned out to be an 80 percent increase in his book. The increase from 1967 was from $5.8 million to $8.95 million in 1968 – a 54 percent increase. But Ketner figured that 1968's projected sales were only $5 million before the changeover to LFPINC. Hence, his arithmetic said Food Town had an 80 percent increase from $5 million to $8.95 million.

The bellman at the Manger Motel in Charlotte would never know the importance of those boxes he carried to Ralph Ketner's room that November morning. The day seemed long ago to Ketner. By now, he was imagining a new slogan: LFPIUSA.

9. Riding a wave

Lowering prices to increase sales volume hardly stood as a new concept for the grocery industry or, for that matter, any retailer. But somehow the philosophy is rediscovered from generation to generation and it can be highly successful when applied correctly. Sam Walton took the idea and built his Wal-Mart discount empire from the humble beginnings of one store in Rogers, Arkansas.

George H. Hartford and George Gilman revolutionized the tea industry in the late 19th century by realizing they could retail quality teas at low prices on a large scale. Hartford's concept sprang from a Yankee conviction that it made sense to base a retail business on a consumer-oriented philosophy. He followed through to establish the Great Atlantic and Pacific Tea Company, which he left in the capable hands of his sons, John and George.

"We believe it sounder to take a small profit on many sales than a larger profit on a few sales," John Hartford said once in a statement that mirrored Ralph Ketner's philosophy that five fast pennies are better than one slow nickel.

It was John Hartford who established the idea of A&P's Economy Stores in 1912. As an experiment to challenge his own company, Hartford set out to eliminate every unnecessary selling expense such as credit, home delivery, telephone orders, stamps, premiums and all advertising. He aimed for a 2 percent net profit margin – a 12 percent gross margin minus a 10 percent expense rate. He bought $1,000 worth of inventory and opened a small, obscure, unnamed store close to an existing A&P in Jersey City,

New Jersey. Within six months, his no-nonsense, low-price approach ran the traditional A&P store out of business.

"I have always been a volume man," John Hartford used to say, "and it's hard to divert my mind to any other policy." At his death on September 20, 1951, the 31st birthday of Ralph Ketner, the following tribute was paid to Hartford, the A&P mastermind: "He pioneered in foodstuffs just as Henry Ford did in transportation. Their philosophy was blunt and simple, just as most works of genius are simple: 'Sell more for less.' "

William I. Walsh detailed the A&P history in his book, *The Rise and Decline of the Great Atlantic and Pacific Tea Company.* He concluded that "despite the multitude of frills and niceties, price always has been and will continue to be the ingredient which separates the leader from the rest of the pack in the supermarket business."

Americans were very much preoccupied with supermarket prices in the mid- to late-1960s, and Ralph Ketner wasn't alone in believing that cutting prices on all groceries could lead to increased sales volume and better profits.

Resentment against increasing food prices became a rebellion in 1966. In cities across America, women forming "petticoat brigades" protested outside stores and led boycotts of grocers they thought were gouging them on prices. "Prices Must Go Down" screamed the placard of a protester in Levittown, Pennsylvania.

Shoppers had reason to gripe. In January 1967, *Chain Store Age* reported that food prices had risen dramatically in the past 18 months, and that was the perception among the buying public. In a nationwide *Progressive Grocer* survey, a whopping 94 percent of the respondents said their food bills were either "somewhat higher" or "much higher" than a year earlier, and four out of 10 thought the recent boycotts of grocery stores had been justified.

In the same survey, nine out of 10 said they would accept the curtailment of contests, games, sweepstakes, trading stamps and other promotions if it would lead to lower prices. So Ketner and Food Town had touched another nerve.

The industry blamed the higher prices on inflation, the rising cost of doing business, higher wages and the escalation of the Vietnam War. Many chains made price the issue in their advertising against competitors and exploited the rebellion aimed their way. Chatham Food Center in Detroit capitalized on the price unrest in Denver by comparing its prices to the Denver market and warning its shoppers, "Don't visit your sister in Denver. She's probably in a bad mood."

Daitch-Shopwell told customers to clip out a coupon at the bottom of its ad and send it to President Lyndon Johnson, volunteering support of "any realistic program" designed to fight inflation. During the peak of unrest against high prices, Safeway plugged its own labels as offering big savings. Jewel of Chicago launched its "miracle price" campaign, followed shortly by the Independent Grocers Association's establishment of "miracle prices" on 5,000 "newly-reduced" items in its Florida stores. Foodtown of New Jersey took credit for starting it all: "Before anyone else was carrying on and screaming about high prices, we were doing the only thing that really counts – cutting prices."

Lucky Stores of California asked, "Who says food prices are up?" The chain used figures supplied by the National Association of Food Chains to show that food prices had risen less than housing, transportation, medical care and wages.

A group of independents in western Pennsylvania, Foodland Super Markets of Belle Vernon, unleashed their own low-price, low-cost program in early 1964. The "Blitz" pricing program took on the five bigger grocery chains in the Tri-State area of Pennsylvania, Ohio and West Virginia. This concept also called for the elimination of trading stamps and cutting the gross operating margin so that prices were 4 to 5 percent below the competition's. Foodland calculated that it would have to increase sales 30 percent to make up for the price cuts. Regular shelf prices on 90 percent of the groceries were reduced, with more than 50 items offered at cost. Certain staples such as baby foods, butter, detergent, dog food, salad dressing, starch and sugar were offered at below cost.

Lion's Share

As Food Town would do four years later, Foodland called its new pricing program "The Big Change." Ads boasted that "only Foodland features weekly specials that last all week," or "You can't eat games and gimmicks, so why let anybody hang 'em on your food bill?" Foodland featured national brands, and its sales doubled in the first year of "The Big Change."

Meanwhile, the mid-1960s witnessed the dawn of what the industry called "new wave discounting." It meant selling groceries at an average drop of 5 percentage points in gross profit, from the then conventional 21 or 22 percent to a maximum of 17 percent. Prices were reduced across the board, not just on a few hundred leaders. In Nashville, Tennessee, Giant Foods of America unveiled a monstrous 60,000-square-foot store in 1967 that showcased a broad assortment of groceries, across-the-board discounting and an emphasis on specialty shops such as deli, bakery and gourmet food sections.

Other new wave discounters included Lucky Stores, Stop & Shop, Jewel, Food Fair, Shop Rite, Borman Foods, Penn Fruit, National Tea's Big D stores, Marsh Supermarkets and Red Owl. They also added specialty sections for delis, seafood and flowers. The stores were larger by 2,500 to 5,000 square feet. They used price-oriented, high pressure advertising and enjoyed considerable success. Lucky Stores credited new wave discount stores in Southern and Northern California for its 16 percent sales gain in 1966, and Stop & Shop's net earnings rose 40 percent in 1966 thanks to the new structure.

But Food Town found a somewhat different low-price niche in the late 1960s. It capitalized on being efficient, convenient and neighborly. Food Town's smaller stores stayed away from the trend toward specialty sections and the high overhead costs associated with them. Because the company was small, stores remained close to the Salisbury base of operation, and were not only accessible to a growing number of loyal customers, they were easy to reach through distribution and supervision. Those factors – centralized control, basic store designs, convenient locations –

would remain key ingredients throughout the company's growth. And grow it did.

After registering $8.95 million in sales with nine stores in 1968, Food Town chalked up a 71 percent increase in sales to $15.5 million in 1969; and a 46 percent increase to $22.4 million in 1970. By the end of 1973, Food Town had 19 stores and $71.3 million in annual sales.

"So many people come up with a good idea, which was our LFPINC, and start cheating on it," Ralph Ketner says. "The first year, we had an 80 percent increase. It would have been easy for me to say, 'Lord, I've cut too many prices. I needed a 50 percent increase. I had an 80. I need to jack prices up.' But I'm just exactly the opposite. I said, 'The Lord's letting us have an 80 percent increase. He wants us to cut more prices.' "

So the original 3,000 prices that were reduced grew to 4,000 and 5,000. How was Food Town doing in comparison to leader A&P, already in a decline, and the average chain in the Supermarket Institute? A&P had a sales increase of 6 percent between 1972 and 1973; the industry average was 14 percent. Food Town sales went up 42 percent.

A&P had average weekly sales per store in 1973 of $33,974; the industry average, $58,000. Food Town's stores averaged selling $72,239 a week. Food Town showed a net profit on sales of 2.26 percent – way above the industry average of 1.3 percent for grocery chains. A&P's earnings on sales hardly registered.

To understate it, Food Town was on a roll.

"With Winn-Dixie, you had the Davis family," recalls Harold "Hap" Roberts, who joined Food Town as assistant controller in 1972. "The last of the Davis family was dying out, and they sort of became stale in the early '70s. About the same time, A&P was having labor problems. Hell, we were all out there hungry. Ralph Ketner was going out prowling, with a crazy look in his eye, wanting to go for it. That's what built us up."

In 1969, Food Town needed more money to add stores and enlarge the warehouse. Glenn Anderson of Carolina Securities in

Raleigh offered to underwrite $275,000 worth of debentures that paid about 6 percent interest and were convertible to common stock in Food Town, which had a five-year period to call them in. The Food Town board agreed to issue the debentures and, as part of the deal, Anderson became a member of the board. Within a year, sales continued at such a brisk pace that Ketner told his board it would be ridiculous to keep paying the interest on the debentures. Wilson Smith and other members of the board agreed to call them in.

"Now it was risky to call them all," Ketner recalls, "because we didn't have the money to call them all. But my feeling was that the fact we could call them that far ahead of time would say to that person, 'They know something that's really good. We'd better keep them.' And we wanted them to keep them, quite frankly, so we didn't have to pay the money. If they converted to common stock, then you have no interest to pay, and we were paying no dividends, so we had the use of that money free, whereas with the debenture, we were paying 6 percent."

Almost 90 percent of the people who bought the interest-bearing bonds converted to common stock. The conversion to stock actually made sense. By February 1970, Food Town split its stock five for one. Ketner told *The Salisbury Evening Post* the move was "to facilitate a public offering should one later be felt advisable." Original investors who bought 100 shares in 1957 and watched it split four for one in 1963 and five for one in 1970, now had 2,000 shares. By mid-November 1970, the stock offering became a reality as Food Town went public on the over-the-counter market. Food Town hired the Parker/Hunter firm of Pittsburgh, Pennsylvania, to handle the offering.

Ketner favored the public offering to provide money for what he already envisioned would be tremendous future expansion beyond the 12 stores operating in 1970. Parker/Hunter served as underwriter for the offering of 108,575 shares at $12 per share. Food Town put up 51,575 shares for sale. Principal stockholders – by now Ralph Ketner and Archie Rufty were the largest stockholders – offered an additional 57,000. Rufty had accumulated a good portion of his many shares by buying out the stock of Brown Ketner and his family and those of former employee Robert Roseman.

For the public offering, Ketner was selling 25,000 shares; Rufty, 8,950; Wilson Smith, 6,000; Clifford Ray, 6,000; Frances Rufty (as custodian for her children), 3,550; Jim Berrier, 3,000; veteran store manager O.L. Casey, 2,500; and Tommy Eller, 2,000.

Those sales left Ketner with 57,980 shares, plus 12,445 owned by his wife and children; Rufty, 31,330, plus 2,525 owned by his wife, Frances; Smith, 24,500 shares, plus 1,600 owned by his wife and children; Ray, 14,500, plus 500 owned by his wife; Eller, 8,950 shares, plus 250 owned by his wife; Casey, 7,750, plus 1,000 owned by his wife; and Berrier, 7,000, plus 3,250 owned by his wife.

The company's first prospectus revealed that Ralph Ketner, as president, treasurer and director, earned an annual salary of $43,313.

Food Town's stock steadily climbed in value, and Charles Allmon, editor of the Growth Stock Outlook, drew the first real national attention to Food Town with a glowing recommendation. Allmon, who would follow Food Town closely through the years and always be one of its chief promoters, said the little North Carolina company's stock would be a good buy up to $28 a share. The previous week, Food Town stock had sunk to $19.50 a share after a stockbroker's letter went out advising clients of a lawsuit pending against the company. But Allmon's advisory sent the stock price up to at least $34 a share the morning of September 13, 1971. The stock gradually backed off the high asking price later in the day

That night Ralph Ketner was attending a local meeting when Miles Smith Jr., a onetime Food Town board member, walked up to him and said, "I want to shake your hand."

"What for?" Ketner asked.

"I've never shaken hands with a man who has made a million dollars in a day but also lost a half million dollars in the same day."

"I don't know what you're talking about," Ketner said, "but that sounds good, if it's real."

Ketner had not heard of the dramatic spurt in the stock following Allmon's advisory. "To my knowledge," Allmon says, "Growth Stock Outlook was the first investment adviser in the United States to take a careful look at Food Town. Before we recommended the company, I spoke at considerable length with Ralph Ketner. It so happened that my sister had shopped at Food Town on a regular basis and said that the prices were the best anywhere and quality was tops. What more can you ask for?"

The lawsuit that had prompted a dip in the stock a week earlier involved, chiefly, C. Brown Ketner. Once Food Town's biggest stockholder, Brown had sold off his shares at various prices – as high as $25 a share, in fact – so that by September 1968 he owned 7,700 shares. On September 4, 1968, Archie Rufty offered to buy all of Brown Ketner's stock, plus 476 shares from Jeff Ketner, 100 shares from Marsha Ketner Carter and 450 shares from Robert Roseman and his wife. They agreed, receiving $9 a share for the 8,726 total shares – $78,534 in cash.

Rufty's newly acquired stock split five for one in February 1970. Then came the public offering paying $12 a share to some of the principal stockholders, Rufty included. But it was the prospectus issued on the filing with the Securities and Exchange Commission that caught the eye of Brown Ketner. He discovered for the first time that his brother Ralph and Wilson Smith had bought from Rufty some of the stock that he, Roseman and their family members had sold in 1968.

From what the prospectus indicated, Ralph Ketner had used $31,500 and Wilson Smith $4,500 in corporation funds to buy some of the stock from Rufty. Brown Ketner also recalled that on May 5, 1967, Food Town sent a letter to stockholders, over Ralph's signature, that said the "Board of Directors approved the purchase of any Food Town common stock which might become available if at a price of approximately $6 a share." Ralph's letter continued, "Should you know of anyone having an interest in selling at this figure, please suggest they contact me."

While the letter stating a $6 value on the stock had come out about 10 months before the implementation of the successful LFPINC concept, Brown Ketner still smelled a rat. He reached several conclusions, as expressed in the lawsuit that named him and the others who had sold to Rufty in 1968 as plaintiffs against Rufty, Ralph Ketner and Wilson Smith.

Sometime prior to March 5, 1967, the suit claimed, the defendants conspired as company directors to depress the value of shares to a price ceiling of $6 each, then followed up this agreement by sending out the letter to stockholders mentioning the $6 figure.

"The defendants knew," the suit said, "that this would create a financial hardship for the plaintiffs, some of whom had their own stock pledged as loan collateral at a value greatly in excess of $6 per share. The defendants entered into and carried out this conspiracy for the purpose of acquiring the stock of the plaintiffs at a price per share which was grossly less than the true value or fair value."

When Rufty approached Brown Ketner and the others, the suit said, he acted as an "undisclosed agent" for Ralph Ketner and Smith. The plaintiffs also contended that the defendants, as directors of the company, had failed to give them, as stockholders, a true financial picture of Food Town. "Because of the price ceiling," the suit said, " ... and not having information with respect to the true financial condition of the company and being unaware of the plans of the corporation, the plaintiffs ... agreed to sell all of their stock to the defendant Rufty for $9 a share."

The suit added, "If the plaintiffs had been fully informed by the defendants as to the true financial condition of Food Town Stores Inc., and its future plans, they would not have sold their stock." It was the defendants' "fiduciary duty" to make full disclosure, the suit alleged.

The plaintiffs asked that the sale of their stock be set aside and that their shares be returned to them, factoring in the five-for-one split in 1970. Meanwhile, the plaintiffs tendered to the court $92,670.12, representing the money they originally paid to Rufty, plus interest at a rate of 6 percent per year between Sept. 4, 1968, and the commencement of the suit Aug. 31, 1971.

In effect, Brown Ketner and the others were seeking a jury trial to claim 43,630 shares that they believed should rightfully belong to them. If the stock were trading at Charles Allmon's recommended $28 a share, the suit could have cost Rufty, Smith and Ralph Ketner $1,221,640 worth of stock, not counting legal fees.

Wilson Smith remembers Archie Rufty coming to him and Ralph Ketner asking for their help in purchasing Brown Ketner's stock. "Archie bought it, and he had so much he couldn't handle it all, so he offered Ralph some and offered me some. I could only get very little because I didn't have any money. But Archie bought all of it, and then, because Archie bought it, and then Ralph bought it and I bought it, he (Brown) thought we had inside information. That's why he sued us."

The ensuing legal battle lasted about two-and-a-half years behind closed doors, where the parties gathered with their attorneys in tense, awkward meetings. "They finally came to a conclusion it would be a landmark case," Wilson Smith recalls. "In case we won, they felt they would appeal it, and in case they won, we would appeal it, and it would keep going until it got to the Supreme Court. I think somewhere along the line somebody got cold feet and figured they didn't have enough money to keep it going, so they said, 'OK,' and the boys got together and said, 'Let's settle it,' and so it was settled for a lot less than they were suing for."

When asked about it years later in an interview for this book, Brown Ketner laughed and said, "Don't bring it up in my part, all right?" But then he added, "perhaps I should have insisted on taking it to court. It could have meant a million dollars or so. Whatever they did, they did to the best of their abilities – what they thought was advisable. No hard feelings. No grudge." Brown still shops at the company he helped to found in 1957, always did. "That sounds crazy," he said. "But if I had a lot more money I might be able to trade somewhere else. He (brother Ralph) is deserving of all the credit he can get. It's a damn good baseball batter who doesn't strike out once in awhile."

Brown kept going with his cafeteria business, while Food Town met a couple of other obstacles about the same time the lawsuit surfaced. In one instance, the North Carolina Milk Commission accused Food Town of selling milk too cheaply. Ralph Ketner loved being accused of that and already had a full-page advertisement in mind, picturing him being led off to jail in handcuffs. His ad copy would have read, "The Milk Commission feels that we are selling you milk for too little, and they're going to take me to jail about it. If you believe that you should pay more for milk, do nothing. But if you agree with me that I should be able to sell you milk for as little as I want to, then write your representatives in Raleigh and get them off my back."

In September 1971, the milk commission was set to take disciplinary action against four dairies for alleged violations of fair trade regulations. Food Town, which bought most of its dairy products from Bordens, had been selling milk at 99 cents a gallon, 6 cents below the $1.05 price per gallon wholesale price that Bordens had filed with the commission. Meanwhile, Borden's had denied selling milk below its wholesale cost. Food Town was simply taking a loss on milk. Officials with the commission said indications were that other dairies were dropping their established wholesale prices so they could compete through their retailers.

But Ralph Ketner persuaded the milk commission to allow him to sell milk at the price he wanted. "Your law reads that we cannot sell milk below the cost of doing business," he argued. "All right, in your interpretation, we can't sell it for less than 7 percent markup, which implies that 7 per cent is the cost of doing business. If you can find me anybody in the world that can operate for 7 percent, especially on a dairy item that requires refrigeration, I would say your law makes sense. But until you do, you haven't got a law that can stand up in court."

The milk commission backed off and Ketner continued selling milk below cost. In 1971, Food Town also had its first of several confrontations with the Better Business Bureau, which continually challenged Food Town on its slogan of "Lowest Food Prices in North Carolina." The BBB said the claim was unprovable and that Food Town unfairly stacked the deck in its price comparisons with named competitors. By August of 1974, The Piedmont Better Business Bureau said Food Lion should change its LFPINC slogan because it wasn't true. The statement came after a BBB shopping survey in which it purchased 57 items at Food Town and six competing chains. Ted G. Law, president of the BBB in Charlotte, reported that all of the other stores sold some items cheaper than Food Town.

Ketner didn't dispute Law's findings: "Anyone who thinks every item is the lowest hasn't read our ads. We've never made a claim on all 8,000 items. We are saying it's the total package that you save money on." The Food Town president defended the slogan's veracity and added that he was tired of the BBB's "nitpicking." To this day, Ketner believes the action against Food Town was prompted by his company's declining an invitation to join the organization for a $500 fee. "I said, 'My God, for $500, I can lower some more prices.' "

Ketner wrote a sarcastic letter to Law in Charlotte one day. "I said, 'In *The Charlotte Observer* this morning, it says Harris Teeter has "the friendliest store in town." Now I'm sure you checked it out and they do have the friendliest store in town, but what measures the degree of friendliness? Are they 10 percent friendlier than we are, or are they 5 percent friendlier? Obviously, you wouldn't let them say that without being critical of them. Now another one. This fellow said he has the widest gun selection in America. How many guns does he have to select from? And what is the second most? Obviously, you've checked that out.' And I went through 20 different things in the newspaper. And I said,

'Ted, I'm sure you checked all these things out. But if you haven't, and I'm sure you haven't, now that I'm calling these to your attention, you must do it because you can't let these people go in your hometown. I'm over here in Salisbury. I'm not bothering anybody in Charlotte.'"

Despite the lawsuit, milk commission and BBB, Food Town's growth continued and the original investors began to realize that maybe they had something. By the time the stock split two-for-one April 25, 1972, an investor with 100 original shares in 1957 had 4,000 shares. If the stock traded for $10 a share in 1972 – it usually traded much higher than that – the $1,000 original investment was worth $40,000. The company had a secondary offering of 80,000 shares in the fall of 1972.

Locals who received regular updates on the company's growth in *The Salisbury Evening Post* viewed the company's stock as a good place to make some quick cash. In the early 1970s, Jim Woodson, a Salisbury attorney, longed to have a riding lawn mower to cover his two-acre backyard. He bought a couple hundred dollars' worth of Food Town stock, made about $3,000 by selling it soon after and put the proceeds toward the purchase of his mower. Others decided to ride with the stock and see how far it could go. They weren't getting rich on dividends. The way Food Town was growing, Ralph Ketner saw no justification for paying a dividend. That money had to be plowed back into the company for growth. At the annual meetings, shareholders received coffee and doughnuts instead.

Collecting dust, but hardly forgotten by Food Town officials, the Bi-Lo stock the company had received in 1966 when it sold the mountain stores to Frank Outlaw had grown from 40,000 shares and an initial value between $90,000 and $100,000 to 72,000 shares worth $1.7 million by 1971. Food Town wasn't going to cash in yet on its competitor.

By the end of 1973, Food Lion had an average of 865,000 shares outstanding with a total of 1,750 stockholders spread across 36 states and one foreign country. The biggest portion of those investors, of course, remained in Salisbury and Rowan County.

Food Town paid $150,000 for 76 acres off Harrison Road in Salisbury in April 1972 and immediately announced plans to construct a 130,000-square-foot warehouse. By December 1973, the warehouse was in operation, and Food Town executives readied to move into new offices beside the warehouse in early 1974. The Julian Road warehouse was converted to a distribution center for frozen foods, dairy products and produce, as 66,000 of the building's 84,000 square feet were put under refrigeration. By April 1974, the company had signed contracts to double the size of the Harrison Road warehouse.

When the warehouse was first under construction, Ketner noticed one day that about 25 rolls of steel mesh were sitting out front that should have been at the bottom of the concrete floor that already had been poured. He also knew from the invoices on his desk that Food Town had been billed for the mesh. On passing by the site the next morning, Ketner noted that the steel mesh was gone.

Food Town still owed a final payment of approximately $20,000 for the work, but he told the contractor that he wouldn't pay because the work cheated on specifications and left out the steel mesh. The contractor denied it, so Ketner proposed that each man take a lie detector test and, if he were proven wrong, Food Town would pay the contractor double – $40,000. On principle, the contractor said, he would have to refuse. So Ketner refused to pay. Later, Food Town had to replace the concrete floors. "If you go out there now," Ketner says, "you can see the different colors where we replaced the floors. He messed up."

Running the Save-Rite warehouse on Harrison Road was Tom E. Smith, the former Food Town bagger and store manager who chose a job with Del Monte after graduating from Catawba College in 1964. In six and a half years with Del Monte, Smith had steadily received promotions to become a supervisor and recruiter. He was in line for another promotion – one that would take him to

114

New York – when he received a call in the late summer of 1970 from Ralph Ketner.

Ketner had been going through buyer after buyer. No one satisfied him. They made mistakes that Ketner just could not tolerate. He was at his wit's end when his wife, Ruth, finally mentioned Tom Smith's name. "He's exactly the man," Ketner thought to himself.

Because of Smith's various transfers since leaving Food Town, Ketner had lost contact with him, but he had heard that Smith was working back in North Carolina. Charlotte, if he remembered correctly. He called a Tom Smith in Charlotte and reached an employee of Libby Foods who happened to know both Ketner and the other Tom Smith.

"Well, do you know where he is?" Ketner asked.

"Yes," said the wrong Smith. "He recently got transferred up here, and we had this agreement from years ago that since we've both got the same name, and I work for Libby and he works for Del Monte, we agreed to keep each other informed where the other one is so we can pass on mail that we get by mistake. Here's his telephone number."

The right Tom Smith told Ketner he had no interest in joining Food Town.

"You owe it to yourself to talk to me," Ketner said. "If you want to make more money than you've ever made in your life, come with me. You won't make it right away, but you will make it."

Smith said he would be in Salisbury for his weekend duty with the 991st Transportation Co. of the U.S. Army Reserves. He had to report by 8 a.m. Sunday. He could meet Ketner at the Holiday Inn in Salisbury for breakfast between 6:30 and 7 a.m. Ketner agreed, and Smith showed up in his fatigues.

"Now I would be hiring you as a buyer for Save-Rite," Ketner told Smith. "I want you as a buyer, but I'm also hiring you as the next president of Food Town. That's who I'm looking for. That's the capabilities you must have or else don't come."

"Well, how long does a buyer last with you?" Smith asked, having a notion that it wasn't long.

"The longest anyone has ever lasted is three weeks," Ketner said. "The average is about one week. With me, '98' is failing. If you're going to make two percent errors in business, you can't make it."

Smith seemed unfazed. "How will we get along personality wise?" he asked.

"We'll love each other or one of us will leave, and it sure won't be me," Ketner answered.

To sweeten the offer, Ketner told Smith he would give him a stock option. To that point, no one in the company had had a stock option, not even Ketner. The president said he'd give Smith a stock option for 5,000 shares if he stayed five years. "I knew if he stayed five years, hell, he's my man," Ketner recalled later. Smith left the breakfast meeting saying he would think it over. He was with a strong company in Del Monte and was rising fast through the ranks. One thing in Food Town's favor: Smith didn't fancy moving to New York.

"As I thought," Smith said years later, "I really realized that where I preferred to be in the grocery business was in the retailing end of it. I had been selling and, of course, I was tied in with the manufacturing end of it. But I had just learned to like the retail business that much when I was with Food Town. I felt that I could achieve more with Food Town, more than I possibly could with Del Monte."

Some months later Ketner was at a food dealers' convention and was seated with Smith's former boss at Del Monte when he overheard a conversation at an adjoining table. "That Tom Smith is a real son of a bitch," the unknown man said.

"Do you think he could be talking about our Tom Smith?" Ketner asked the Del Monte official.

Ketner approached the man doing the talking, introduced himself and asked him if he had been talking about Food Town's Tom Smith. "Yes, and he's the rudest man I've ever run into," the man, a corporate vice president, said. He went on to explain a disagreement that he had had with Smith.

"But was he right?" Ketner wanted to know.

"Yes, he was," the vice president said.

Ketner was grinning by this time. "Well, I'll go back and talk with him, but it won't be about what you think. I've told Tom never to talk to subordinates. Always deal with the president of a company."

"The president of our company is afraid to talk to him," the VP said.

Ketner knew he had his man, and Tom Smith had his own new obsession. By April 1973, Smith became a member of the Food Town board of directors. He was soon to be named president of Save-Rite.

Food Town had a score of stores in North Carolina cities and towns by 1974 when suitors came calling. They were mysterious, worldly and experienced. They spoke funny, too.

10. 'It all depends'

As Ralph Ketner sorted through his stack of mail early one morning in the fall of 1974, a letter with a Boston return address caught his eye. A firm specializing in mergers and acquisitions, Robert A. Weaver Jr. and Associates, had written to ask a simple question of the Food Town president: "Would you be interested in selling part interest in your company to another?"

And Ralph Ketner had a simple response: "It all depends." He scribbled that sentence on the bottom of the same letter, signed his name and drew an arrow to the top of the page – a direction understood by his secretary that she was not supposed to waste time typing an answer, just copy the letter and send it back to Boston, keeping the other copy for Food Town.

On receiving Ketner's response, a representative from the Weaver firm called Ketner and said, "We'd like to talk." He promptly visited Salisbury to meet Ketner.

The country, still reeling from the bad vibrations of the Watergate conspiracy scandal and in the midst of a recession, had seen the stock market steadily decline. Food Town's stock had sunk to $13 a share. Ketner said Food Town would be interested in an offer that paid $26 a share – double the price. He still had no idea what other company was interested in Food Town or where it was from.

The man from Weaver and Associates returned about a week later and said the company he was representing had an interest at $25-1/2 to $26 a share.

"I have no interest," Ketner said.

"I thought you did," the startled man from Boston replied. "No, I never mentioned 25-1/2. I mentioned that at 26 I have an interest. If you mention over 26, I think you're crazy, and if you mention less than 26, I have no interest."

"OK," said the Weaver representative, "we have an interest at 26."

The Weaver firm began assembling information as to what its client would require as part of a deal. By now, Ketner had learned only that it was a Belgian company. On a Friday, Ketner received a letter from Boston listing 31 items that the Weaver client sought agreement on: weighty matters such as equal board representation, the paying out of dividends, the amount of stock the firm would purchase and the like. Meanwhile, a meeting had been set for the following Monday in New York. Ketner immediately called Boston.

"These are 31 things we're in disagreement on," Ketner told the Weaver go-between. "You listed 31. I disagree with all 31."

"Well, they're already on their way over," the Boston man said.

"That's their problem, not mine. I'm in Salisbury, and I'm staying here."

"Wouldn't you like to talk to them?"

"No," Ketner said. "I forbid the company to have the expense of me and Tam Shuford (the company attorney) going to New York."

The Weaver representative talked Ketner into a meeting with the Belgians in Charlotte.

"It's not going to change anything," Ketner warned. "All 31 points have to be conceded or just don't waste their time."

Flying across the Atlantic Ocean were Guy Beckers, president of Establissement Delhaize Freres et Cie, operator of Belgium's second largest supermarket chain; Gui de Vaucleroy, a member of the company's executive committee; and Jacques LeClercq, the company executive whose idea it was to invest in America.

Delhaize's growth in Belgium had been stifled by government

regulations aimed at protecting the small shopkeepers, the independents that tourists, Americans among them, find so charming. Small proprietors accounted for distributing more than 50 percent of the food in Belgium because the government restricted the number of food stores per 1,000 people and set the hours on grocery stores – from 8 a.m. to 8 p.m. Monday through Saturday, closed Sunday. In some years, Delhaize would be prohibited from opening any new supermarkets.

While these laws, prevalent throughout Europe, were preserving ageless traditions, such as the quaintness of buying foodstuffs from local shopkeepers, butchers and fishmongers, the supermarket chains viewed them as protectionist measures. They had to look elsewhere to invest, grow and reward their stockholders.

In 1972, Delhaize began looking at and visiting other countries in Europe. By 1973, company officials turned their attention to the United States, which they believed offered a safe place for investment in a market-driven economy. They chose Weaver and Associates to help with their search because the company also had an office in Belgium. Weaver's marching orders: Seek out a supermarket chain of a smaller size than Delhaize. First, the Boston firm presented Delhaize with projected U.S. growth areas of the mid- to late-1970s: the Southeast, the Southwest, California and the Northwest. The West Coast states were eliminated because travel would have been too expensive between Belgium and any interests there. So Weaver narrowed its search to an area between Washington and New Orleans. Weaver presented Delhaize with a list of 10 companies, from which two were selected. One was Food Town. LeClercq said years later that the other chains were much too large or only wanted to sell a category of shares.

From Food Town's point of view, the offer from a foreign company to buy a considerable portion of stock loomed primarily as a benefit to the original investors. Until then, any wealth they had derived from Food Town was wealth only on paper, not hard cash. Here was a possible chance for the many faithful investors to cash in. Through the company's own sale of some stock, Food

Town also could receive an infusion of cash to help its continued growth, and Ketner was sure LFPINC would foster that growth.

In Charlotte, Ketner and Wilson Smith met the Belgians for the first time. Ketner bluntly told them Food Town could not agree to any of the 31 points, but he gave in to their invitation to meet again in New York the next day. Ketner flew to New York with Tam Shuford and the two parties resumed their negotiations – Ketner considered the discussion more like an argument. They met in the uptown New York law office of White and Case. Attorneys Gwynne Wales and Robert Clare assisted the Belgians, who kept insisting on equal board representation should they buy a large stake in the company

Ketner said they could have one less director than Food Town. If the Belgians had three directors, Food Town would have four. If the Belgians had 21 directors, Food Town would have 22. The Belgian negotiators finally asked to be excused. They said they would have to call Belgium.

"They went into a restroom and shut the door – I'm sure they didn't call anybody," Ketner said many years later. "Hell, they had the authority."

Beckers, LeClercq and de Vaucleroy returned and said they would agree to Ketner's proposal on board representation. Food Town would have one more than the Belgians. A big argument on dividends soon followed. Ketner said Food Town would not pay any dividends. The Belgians said the company would have to pay them. It seemed to Ketner that the negotiations had hit a brick wall. The Belgians said they could not concede this point.

"I'm sure you did the same thing I did when you came here," Ketner said, receiving quizzical looks from the parties on the other side of the table. "I bought a return ticket. I can get back home, and I'm sure you all can. No hard feelings. We just misunderstand each other."

Deep down, Ketner wanted the deal to go through because the Belgians were going to buy a third of his considerable chunk of stock, and he was going to recommend that all shareholders, if they wanted to, follow his lead. But the Belgians had been told by their board that the American investment company must agree to pay a dividend.

"I'll tell you what I'll do," Ketner said. "If Mr. Shuford says it's OK, I'll agree to *think about* paying the dividend. I can tell you now, I'm not going to do it. But if it would make you look better and feel better, I will agree to sign an agreement that I'll think about it each year."

The Belgians agreed. "The negotiations lasted for several days and could be qualified as tough," LeClercq recalls. "It is hard to say if the deal came close to falling through. We never had that feeling. To give you an example of how stressed we all were – one evening, probably 10 or 11 p.m., we were having a late dinner, all together. I was serving the wine, and it took some time before somebody realized that I was pouring it next to the glass. Mr. Ketner even started to speak what he thought was French but, in fact, was Italian."

Ketner sheepishly acknowledges that the Belgians, who spoke perfect English, had to correct him in New York when, while complimenting his adversaries on their English, Ketner said that the only French he knew was, "Buon giorno." One of the Belgians politely told him "Buon giorno" meant "Good day" in Italian.

LeClercq adds: "All of us who negotiated with Mr. Ketner were familiar with the United States' way of doing business, as most members of the Delhaize executive committee had frequently traveled to the United States and had good connections with many U.S. retailers." And the Belgian executives never viewed Ketner's reception to their offer as cold. Few presidents of U.S. companies at that time had a positive attitude about foreigners making major investments in their firms.

Late in the evening, Ketner and the Belgians told their attorneys to hash out an agreement. Ketner went to bed that night not knowing whether a package could be worked out. Indeed, Shuford and the other attorneys stayed up all night. The signing of the agreement took place at a Charlotte Holiday Inn a day after the talks finished. "We had received a mandate from our board to acquire 51 percent (of the stock) with the money available to us," LeClercq says. "We only succeeded in obtaining 34 percent, which, of course, we had to explain later in Brussels."

The Salisbury Evening Post reported the agreement October 24, 1974. Its terms: 1) Delhaize would purchase 50,000 shares of stock from Food Town Stores Inc. at $26 a share, for a total of $1.3 million; 2) Delhaize would purchase 68,000 shares from the five directors of Food Town stores at $26 a share, for a total of $1,768,000. (This represented 37 per cent of the holdings of each director.); 3) Delhaize would purchase up to 198,000 shares of the common stock at $26 a share in cash, for a total of $5,148,000.

In all, Delhaize's investment came to $8,216,000, for essentially 34.5 percent of the company.

By year's end Food Town had 22 grocery stores, generally in the Piedmont region of North Carolina but also, for the first time, in South Carolina. Food Town had just less than $92.5 million in annual sales. The company employed 1,250 people on a payroll of $6.5 million. Stores ranged in size from 10,000 square feet to 32,000 square feet, and they were served by the Salisbury warehouses on Julian and Harrison roads.

Officers and directors of Food Town at the end of 1974 were Ralph Ketner, president and treasurer; Wilson Smith, vice president; James Berrier, secretary; Tommy Eller, assistant secretary; and Clifford Ray and Tom Smith, directors.

Shareholders, such as railroader William Alsobrooks, who had long since moved to Asheville, had seen their 100 original shares grow to 4,000 by 1974. Those who wanted to cash in on a third of their tendered stock could realize a return as high as $315,000.

The Belgians could never have anticipated locking horns with the likes of Ralph Ketner. They had failed in three major points of their mission: They had not acquired 51 per cent of the U.S. company's stock, that company was not going to be paying dividends to them and they did not have equal board representation.

Lion's Share

But the Belgians had a big foot in the door at Food Town. Ralph Ketner considered himself smart enough to realize that the Belgians would eventually try to purchase controlling interest, but he was taken aback two years later when a caller told him Delhaize was buying up Food Town shares on the open market. He called his Belgian associates to find out the reason.

Belgian law requires that a company have controlling interest in order to consolidate profits. That is, Delhaize ownership of just more than 50 per cent of the voting stock in Food Town would allow it to combine the Food Town figures with Delhaize. Thus, the Belgian numbers would show growth, as would its stock. If Delhaize owned 50-plus per cent of Food Town's voting stock, then it could include 50-plus per cent of Food Town's earnings in the Delhaize earnings. If it owned 49 per cent – or, in its case, 34.5 percent – then Delhaize reaped no reward for its shareholders through the Food Town association. One way or the other, it was important to Delhaize to pick up some of the Food Town earnings.

Ketner agreed to meet with the Belgians again in New York to discuss how they might obtain their additional 17 per cent. The stock had split again in 1976 – this time, three for one. Ketner kept asking that the Belgians pay $25 a share which, in fact, would have been $75 a share compared to the $26 a share Delhaize had paid in 1974. Again, Ketner was playing hard to get. An attorney for White and Case, working for the Belgians, finally spoke up.

"Mr. Ketner, I don't believe you understand," he said. "They don't need your approval to do this."

"I understand that," Ketner answered. "They understand that. The thing you probably don't understand is that they don't want to make me mad. And if they did it any other way, it's not going to make me mad, it's going to make me mad as hell. And I don't think they want to do that."

Ketner was right. On October 15, 1976, the two parties announced that Delhaize had agreed to pay $25 a share to any shareholder wishing to sell his or her Food Town stock. To attain its desired percentage, Delhaize would purchase up to 391,000 shares, to add to its 1,027,000 shares. The open market price at the time was about $20 a share. The Belgians also would purchase 50,000 shares of stock from Food Town, putting the total Delhaize investment in 1976 at an additional $11,025,000. Ralph Ketner decided to hang on to his own stock this time.

The big and bold *Salisbury Evening Post* headline announcing the arrangement seemed to carry a new concern with its kicker that said, "Could Gain Controlling Interest." The Belgians suddenly assumed the persona of carpetbaggers, raiding North Carolina to take over a home-grown company. Ketner moved quickly to quash any perception that the foreigners were taking over management of the company, which had grown by then to 42 supermarkets and $173 million in annual sales, almost double the numbers from 1974. The 100 shares purchased in 1957 had grown to 12,000 by the end of 1976.

Ketner told the newspaper: "There will be absolutely no change in management, as there has been no change during the past two years during which Delhaize has owned 34 percent or more of Food Town stock."

Ketner felt confident in his assurances because of the voting agreement the two parties had signed. The agreement said that it would take 80 percent of the board to approve changes at Food Town and that at least 50 percent of the board would be Food Town people. "So that gave us in writing that they didn't want to be over here running this company," Tom Smith said years later. "They wanted us to run it. They've helped a lot by sticking with their agreement."

By mid-November 1976, Delhaize had successfully purchased the additional stock it needed to gain controlling interest in the company.

Delhaize actually started in the grocery business 90 years before the founding of Food Town and, like its American counterpart, brothers were involved in the beginning. Jules and Auguste Delhaize opened several small stores and a supply house in 1867. The brothers were later joined by other brothers and a brother-in-law, and the company became one of the first in Belgium to sell groceries at fixed costs, rather than the prevalent bargaining of their day.

By 1883, the Delhaizes were the first to organize their stores as a chain. The company also built its first warehouse in Brussels and began manufacturing some foods. All of the manufacturing plants had closed by the end of the Second World War except for the coffee roasting division and wine-bottling warehouse. By 1950, the company operated 400 small groceries and sold groceries wholesale to 1,667 outlets.

In 1957, the same year Food Town opened its first store, Delhaize opened its first true supermarket. The company became a publicly held concern in 1962. The Delhaize stores became recognizable throughout Belgium for their lion in the company logo, a symbol later adopted by their American sister.

The protectionist measures passed by the Belgian government in the 1970s threatened the survival of supermarket chains. "The mom and pop groceries and the unions said to the politicians, 'Protect us, or we die,' " said chief executive and fifth generation Delhaize family member Philippe Stroobant in a 1990 interview with *The Charlotte Observer*. "We, like many big companies in Belgium, made the mistake of not taking them seriously."

While the United States has one 20,000-square-foot grocery store for every 5,000 residents, Belgium has one 8,000-square-foot store for every 10,000 people. In 1976, Delhaize had 87 supermarkets. By 1990, 14 years later, the number in Belgium had only increased to 106, a figure the company had been holding at for five years because of government restrictions. Delhaize had to turn to America for growth.

Delhaize wasn't the only foreign company that looked to invest in U.S. supermarkets. In 1977, Ahold NV of the Netherlands bought Bi-Lo, Frank Outlaw's old company. By 1981, the West German Tengelmann Group had bought controlling interest in the declining Great Atlantic & Pacific Tea Co. Welsh grocer Albert Gubay audaciously announced in 1979 plans to build 50 stores in the Carolinas under the name of 3 Guys Ltd. He then set about the task by placing his headquarters and warehouse in Salisbury, Food Town's backyard.

Delhaize has other interests in Belgium, the Netherlands, Portugal and the United States. In Belgium, Delhaize operates 51 "Dial" discount stores, 50 "Di" drugstores and supplies approximately 150 affiliate stores. The company has about 25 supermarkets and seven smaller food stores in Portugal, operating under the name Pingo Doce. But it was Delhaize's other U.S. interests that caused Food Lion's management some concern in 1979.

According to minutes from a July 4, 1979, Food Town board meeting, Ketner demanded that Guy Beckers inform the directors of Delhaize's rumored intentions to buy another grocery chain in the Southeast. Beckers declined. He said it was inappropriate for the matter to be discussed because it might violate rules of the Securities and Exchange Commission. The minutes continue: "The Chairman (Ketner) stated that he felt a responsibility to bring before the board any matter which he felt could adversely affect the company." Food Town attorney Tom Caddell agreed with Ketner's position.

"With Mr. Beckers approval," the minutes added, "the Chairman then stated that he had been advised by Mr. Beckers that Delhaize was negotiating for the acquisition of a retail food chain, Alterman Foods, which is located in Atlanta, Georgia. After discussion, Messrs. Ketner, T. (Tom) Smith, W. (Wilson) Smith and Caddell stated that they were strongly opposed to the acquisition of Alterman by Delhaize or by the Company."

Beckers told the board that discussions were in the preliminary stage and the matter should be kept confidential. But four days later, Ketner sent out a memo to Food Town's management, from store managers on up. "Delhaize has signed an agreement of intent to purchase Alderman (sic) Supermarkets of Atlanta, Georgia," the memo said. "We see nothing about this transaction that will affect Food Town but wanted you to be aware of this transaction in the event some people questioned you."

Lion's Share

The deal in Atlanta was particularly attractive to Alterman family members who owned 51 percent of the company's stock. Alterman operated 93 supermarkets, mostly under the names of Food Giant and Big Apple, in Georgia and Alabama. By 1979, Food Town had stores in North Carolina, South Carolina and Virginia, so the territories did not overlap with Alterman. Max Alterman, executive vice president, said his management team would continue to oversee the day-to-day operations of the supermarkets, even though Delhaize would own the company.

"The thing that bothered me," said a former executive of Food Town, "is that they (the Belgians) didn't discuss any of it with us. They just told us they were doing it." Delhaize had bought into a company that was unionized "so that effectively locked us out of the Atlanta market," the executive added. "We always had a fear of unions."

The Food Giant venture did not go well for the Belgians, to say the least, and they disposed of the company in 1986. "We figured when they bought it, maybe it wasn't the best thing for them to do, and we told them," Tom Smith says. "We said, 'Now don't ask us to send any people down, because we're growing in this company and have a full slate here. So don't ask us.' They ran into trouble and never asked us to help them at all, and I think that really demonstrated how honorable they were."

At first glance, the Belgians thought they couldn't go wrong with their Food Giant acquisition in Atlanta. The chain had a 25 percent market share, a percentage equal to Big Star's. The two chains dominated Atlanta. But Delhaize failed to realize that the Food Giant stores were in bad locations. Atlanta's growth was to the north and outside the perimeter highway circling the city. Food Giants were inside the perimeter, and the chain had few stores in northern Atlanta. The country also faced a terrible recession in the early 1980s. Food consumption was down. It was a terrible time to build. Meanwhile, Kroger had decided to make a run at being No.1 in the Atlanta market, and the Cincinnati-based company succeeded by investing in the good locations where all the growth was happening. Kroger's market share eventually grew to a whopping 30 percent.

Delhaize also had management problems with Food Giant that they had never experienced with Food Town. "We wanted to leave Food Giant management there, as we had done at Food Town," Guy Beckers told *Supermarket News* reporter David Merrefield in 1987, "but that wouldn't work: The Alterman family was retiring. We also found that accounting procedures at Food Giant were very bad. There was no accounting plan and no budget control. For us, it is a 'must' to have budget control."

Delhaize installed its own management but could never catch up. Delhaize sold its Food Giant warehouse and supermarkets in Atlanta to Super Valu Stores in Minneapolis, Minnesota. But the Belgians also established Super Discount Markets, which operates Cub superstores in Atlanta. Delhaize owns 80 percent of the Cub stores; Super Valu, 20 percent.

By the end of the 1980s, Delhaize the Lion America, Inc., a holding company and wholly-owned subsidiary of the Belgium parent, was operating seven Cub Foods in the Atlanta market. LeClercq serves as president of Delhaize The Lion America, which maintains an Atlanta office.

Not everyone has been enamored with the Belgian influence on the company that began as Food Town in 1957. Delhaize benefited from good timing in 1974 when it first approached Ketner, who had seen his company's stock drop from as high as $36 a share to $12.25 a share. One former executive theorizes that the Belgians looked like a knight on a white horse coming to the rescue during those recessionary times. The same executive says he was shocked when the Belgians gained controlling interest of the company stock and then bought a unionized company that could have some day been Food Town's competitor.

"I don't know why we ever got the Belgians involved," says the former company official, who asked for anonymity. "It was my personal opinion that we had the machinery in place to go with it. I think it was good in the sense that it freed Ketner up a little bit

129

and we could grow faster. I think Ketner was really concerned about our growth and the fact that if we grew too fast and things didn't go right, he would be blamed for it. The Belgians came in and took over some substantial ownership, and I think he had an out there. He said to himself, 'If it doesn't work out, they know it wasn't solely me.' "

The United Food and Commercial Workers union takes every opportunity to play up the fact that the non-union Salisbury grocery chain is "foreign-owned." Union newspaper advertisements have attacked the company with headlines saying, "Parlez-vous unemployment?" – suggesting that low wages at the company drive other stores out of business. But the grocery chain itself functions with the Belgians well in the background. Indeed, a casual observer would have no idea foreigners control the stock.

Tom Smith says Delhaize board members have offered an outside perspective that has benefited the company. "We've never disagreed on anything," Smith says. "They've never said, 'We want you to do this,' but they do look and say, 'Have you thought of this?' They've honored everything we've ever requested."

The voting agreement, which is periodically renewed, has left the day-to-day management in American hands. Smith describes the relationship with Delhaize as smooth and positive. The Belgian members of the board visit Salisbury about five times a year.

Tom Smith wrote his views on foreign ownership for the *Supermarket News* on May 10, 1988: "A mistake is for a foreign interest to come in and try to implement things here that they have had experience with there. When Delhaize took interest in the company in 1976, they were looking at us as an investment. And we provided them with a good investment.

"Delhaize chose to leave management up to the company. They have not tried to force things on us that worked in Belgium. They have depended on the American management. There are differences – in the products, the purchase systems, the style of management, the way they deal with people and the approaches they use, even in the way they deal with their employees."

Not surprisingly, the United Food and Commercial Workers union likes to drive home the fact that the majority of Delhaize workers in Belgium are unionized, represented by the Federation of Belgian Retail Employees. At Delhaize supermarkets, customers bag their own groceries, reflecting that much less emphasis overall is placed on customer service. Items on the Belgian shelves also have to be labeled in two languages: French and Flemish. The differences in operations are pronounced.

In simple language, Delhaize has made a killing on Food Lion stock. Earnings consolidated from Food Lion account for 50 to 75 percent of Delhaize's annual earnings, according to fluctuations in value between the Belgian franc and U.S. dollar.

"We believe that we have set our goals together and have agreed on our means to achieve them," says LeClercq, a member of the board since the Belgians became involved. "The influence of Delhaize could be characterized as a consensus between two partners ... a good marriage. The association has meant to our shareholders a serious improvement in their stock and an improvement of the dividends, although it is only lately that the dividend policy was slightly modified."

LeClercq says he visits more than 120 stores a year throughout the Southeast.

"The first 15 years of voting," Ralph Ketner says, "they had no authority or input. Each time we had another voting agreement, certain points were conceded – increase the dividend, do this or that. As far as actual management of the company, determining the direction and so forth, they are made aware. There's never been a time where they've disagreed. So, as I say, they've not prohibited us from doing what we thought was in the best interest of the company."

Once the Belgians suggested that Ketner's top executives take French courses at Catawba College in Salisbury, so they could converse in French with Delhaize people.

"Let me explain to you," Ketner answered, "that when my top people know 100 percent of everything there is to know about the grocery industry, then and only then will I consider letting them spend time learning to speak French. And I can assure you now that time will never come."

Ketner didn't even *think about* that one.

11. The go-go years

People who worked for Food Town in the 1970s learned quickly about life in the fast lane. Count Harold "Hap" Roberts among them.

A business graduate of Catawba College, Roberts had worked in his spare time during school for the Salisbury accounting firm of Sherrill and Smith. Jim Berrier, the corporate secretary and office manager for Food Town, recommended him for the job of assistant controller. Food Town didn't have a controller, but "assistant controller" seemed better suited to the station in life of the 21-year-old, fresh-faced Roberts.

Soon after his joining the company in August 1972, Food Town had its secondary stock offering in October. Ralph Ketner was supposed to assemble some paperwork and attend a meeting one day with the underwriters in Pittsburgh. But he had another commitment.

"Mr. Ketner wants to see you," secretary Lawanda Parchment told Roberts, who had learned already not to relish the invitation.

"OK, this is what we got to do," Ketner told Roberts when he got to the president's office that morning. "You're supposed to be in Pittsburgh this afternoon to deliver some documents. The documents need to be signed by Bill Sherrill of Sherrill and Smith. Then they need to be taken over to the CPA firm in Asheboro. They need to be signed. Then they need to be taken to Washburn Press in Charlotte. And so, you'll get a final brief from Washburn Press, get on a 4 o'clock plane, and they'll wait for you at Parker/ Hunter. You haven't got time to go home and pack or do anything.

Just make a couple of calls and tell them you won't be home tonight. If you are, it'll be late."

Roberts was off. He easily gathered the signatures of Bill Sherrill in Salisbury, but he ran into problems in Asheboro, about an hour's drive away. The Asheboro accountant's father had become ill and was in the local hospital. He refused to see Roberts, who made a desperate call to Ketner.

"Oh, my God, plead with him like a Dutch uncle," Ketner said. But the accountant refused to see Roberts or the papers. He wanted to stay with his sick father. Roberts called back, and Ketner was able to reschedule the Pittsburgh meeting for 3 o'clock the next afternoon.

"You've got to have the documents signed," he ordered. "You've got to have everything ready."

Roberts checked into an Asheboro motel, but continued his efforts to talk with the accountant. "I gave an orderly in the hospital $10 to ask him if he would come and see me," Roberts recalls. "That made him mad. So I just waited, and he said, 'I'll be at my office at 9 o'clock in the morning.' " Roberts was able to talk him into an 8 a.m. meeting. He went to a nearby drugstore for a toothbrush and toothpaste and spent the night in Asheboro. The next morning, he put on the same clothes from the day before and rushed to the Asheboro office for the signatures. Finally, success.

Roberts started on his two-hour drive toward Charlotte. As his Datsun 240-Z hurtled down a country backroad at about 75 mph, he realized that he had to go to the bathroom. Fearing he would lose precious minutes by stopping, Roberts reached for a paper cup on the floorboard. He used it as a portable urinal and slowed the car enough to dump the contents out the window. He kept the cup, thinking he might need it again. Roberts made it to Washburn Press and his flight out of Charlotte. In Pittsburgh, he met the men from Parker/Hunter, handed over the documents and, dragging from nervous exhaustion, turned an about-face for the trip home.

134

"And that," Roberts says of those hectic days with Food Town, "was par for the course."

Through a combination of buying existing stores from other chains and leasing new locations from developers, Food Town crept steadily across North Carolina and into South Carolina, Virginia and Georgia. Sales increased from $130 million in 1975 to $543 million in 1980, as the number of stores went from 30 to 106. Earnings climbed steadily to $15.2 million by the end of 1980. Partly to appease the Belgians, Food Town also had begun paying a dividend, even though it was only pennies per share.

Dividends of another sort came the way of Food Town stockholders in 1977 and, ironically, they made money off a Food Town competitor. The company finally cashed in on the Bi-Lo stock it had held since 1966. Food Town distributed its 94,500 shares of Bi-Lo stock as a dividend. Shareholders received .0335 of one share of Bi-Lo for each share of stock they owned in Food Town. Receiving the Bi-Lo stock was welcomed at the time because Ahold NV of the Netherlands had announced its plans to buy Bi-Lo for $35 a share. On paper, Food Town's dividend payment of Bi-Lo stock was worth more than $3.3 million.

Bi-Lo, based in Mauldin, South Carolina, had more than 90 supermarkets in the Carolinas and Georgia. As expected, Ahold NV bought the company and purchased the stock at a high price. Bill Alsobrooks, the railroader in Asheville, called his friend Wilson Smith about a year and a half after the call for Bi-Lo stock.

"I've still got my Bi-Lo stock," Alsobrooks said.

"You can't have," Smith said, "They called it all in."

"I don't want to sell it to them," said Alsobrooks. To this point, he had not touched his original Food Town investment.

"Bill," Wilson Smith said, "it's not a question of whether you want to or not. You've got to. Man, this thing was supposed to be done a year ago." Alsobrooks eventually took care of the matter.

Food Town stock rose as high as $39.75 a share on the over-the-counter market in March 1979. By then, an original investment in 100 shares at $1,000 was worth $477,000. Two months later, the stock would split again, three-for-one. A person who bought 100 shares in 1957 now had 36,000 shares.

The growing North Carolina company, quietly tucked away from scrutiny by virtue of its one hour's driving distance from Charlotte, Winston-Salem and Greensboro, could no longer stay a secret from the business press. *The South Magazine,* a regional business publication covering 10 states, listed Food Town among its 1979 Top Growth Companies. Ralph Ketner smiled from the magazine's cover in June 1979. Some of Food Town's growing Southern counterparts were Shoney's of Nashville, Tennessee, Nucor Corp. of Charlotte, Lowe's Food Stores of North Wilkesboro, North Carolina, the Bruno's grocery chain of Birmingham, Alabama, and Genuine Parts Co. of Atlanta. Ketner estimated his personal wealth at the time between $7 million and $8 million.

Forbes magazine took notice with a two-page article February 16, 1981. "Look at the track record of the company Ralph W. Ketner runs out of Salisbury, N.C.," the article began, "and guess what business he's in. For the past decade, return on equity has averaged 30 percent and earnings per share have been compounding at a 41 percent annual pace. Oil? Semiconductors? Neither. Groceries. His chain of 108 Food Town Stores did $544 million worth of business last year in the Carolinas and Virginia netting close to 3% after tax. Almost unheard of in an industry where the average is .75%. In return on total capital, Food Town, at 28 percent, is far and away in first place among the larger supermarket operators."

The title of the *Forbes* story: "What's a LFPINC?"

By 1982, *Forbes* had dubbed Food Town as "the fastest-growing food chain in America."

While Food Town ranked 31st in sales among grocery chains in the United States at the end of 1981, it beat all other chains in return on equity, 24.82 percent; return on assets, 13.86 percent; and net profit margin, 2.9 percent. Food Town also had the lowest long-term debt at .58 percent. The Top 10 supermarket chains in

1981, based on sales were Safeway, Kroger, Lucky Stores, American Stores, Winn-Dixie, Jewel, Albertson's, Supermarkets General, Dillon and Publix. For comparison's sake: Safeway registered 1981 sales of $16.8 billion; Winn-Dixie, $6.2 billion. Food Town was way down the totem pole at $666.8 million. But its explosion was yet to come.

In his capacity as assistant controller, then controller, Hap Roberts headed up the buying of stores. "Mr. Ketner," he recalls, "would talk to the owners of the stores and work out a deal. He said, 'OK, we're buying the equipment for this amount. We're buying the inventory at retail less this percent.' That's all I would have to work with."

As part of their regular routine, Roberts, his assistant Gary Morgan and others would work their full week through Saturday afternoon, then head out to investigate whatever family-owned or chain-owned supermarket Food Town might be buying. They made their first inspection undercover, so to speak.

"We would walk the store late Saturday, see if the material was dated, see if the personnel at the store were doing anything odd like changing prices or taking new calculators out of the store and bringing in crank adding machines. One time they did that to me. And these were just things I learned over the years. You just sort of perfected it. We caught quite a few.

"All in all, during my time, we bought six stores from Oren Heffner, seven stores up in Tidewater, Virginia, we bought a store in Buena Vista, Virginia. We probably bought six Harris Teeter stores. We bought four or five Food Worlds. We bought four or five Lowe's Food Stores. We bought another 10 stores, you know, just scattered around, like two Giant Genie stores in Charlotte, a store in Eden from a private family. We bought a couple old A&P's that had closed down. We just let them close down, and we went into them. No. 64 in Statesville was an old A&P."

Old and new stores joined Food Town in communities of all sizes. The LFPINC battle cry sounded in places such as Greensboro, Raleigh, Cary, Belmont, Laurinburg, Wadesboro and Yadkinville

Lion's Share

in North Carolina; Columbia, Gaffney, Lancaster, Union, Florence and Fort Mill in South Carolina; Danville, Norfolk, Virginia Beach, Portsmouth, Blacksburg, Dublin, Wytheville and Tazewell in Virginia; and, by 1981, Augusta, Georgia – the home of three former Harris Teeters.

In most cases, Food Town turned around sagging operations.

"One of the best stores we bought was Number 30 in Cary that we bought from Kroger," Roberts says. "They must have had somebody sitting at a desk looking at printouts in Cincinnati, Ohio, who said that store's not making money. We bought it and within two months, it became our number one store."

Ralph Ketner remembers that one owner didn't like the experience of being bought out by Food Town.

"Please, for God's sake, don't ever do this to me again," Charles Stroupe of Belmont told Ketner when he and his brother Harold sold their successful Stroupe's Supermarket in 1971.

"What do you mean?" Ketner asked.

"Can you imagine," Stroupe said, "what an embarrassment it is for me to be here the day after you change all these prices? You've got dog food at $1.08, you've got Liquid Plumr at one dollar a bottle. Now all the customers say, 'Charlie, you've been cheating us for years.' "

Oren Heffner, the old partner in Save-Rite, sold his six grocery stores – Heffner's Land of Food – to Food Town in 1981. The Mocksville businessman had been in operation since the late 1940s. Food Town made a big push into Virginia in 1981 by purchasing Valu Fair Supermarkets, a seven-store chain in the Tidewater area. One of the more interesting attempts at a buyout, or merger, came in 1976.

Some 17 years after Ketner and J.C. Faw had locked horns in trying to purchase Tal Pearson's store in North Wilkesboro, the two men announced plans for Food Town and Lowe's Food Stores to merge. In January 1976, Food Town had 30 stores and Lowe's had 37, mostly in the northwestern region of North Carolina, plus two each in South Carolina and Virginia. The proposal had the

Ralph Ketner, left, his brother Brown, center, and Wilson Smith, right, asked family, friends and casual acquaintances to invest in the first Food Town store in 1957. Some investors bought as few as five shares for $50; others as many as 100 shares for $1,000. *Photos courtesy of The Salisbury Post.*

Food Town No. 1 at Ketner Center in Salisbury. "It's big," an advertisement in 1957 began. "It's beautiful. It's bountiful. Salisbury's newest, largest and most modern food store. More than 100 years experience behind the management of Food Town Stores." *Photo courtesy of The Salisbury Post.*

Glenn Ketner Sr. had his grocery chain on the move in the mid-fifties, but few foresaw the dramatic change that came in 1956. Ketner's would merge with the Milner Piggly-Wiggly stores and the chain would become the largest owned by residents of North Carolina. Within weeks of the merger, Winn-Dixie bought all 24 stores and hired Glenn Ketner to head the North Carolina division. *Photo of Glenn Ketner courtesy of The Salisbury Post. Photo of Ketner's Supermarket courtesy of Glenn Ketner Sr.*

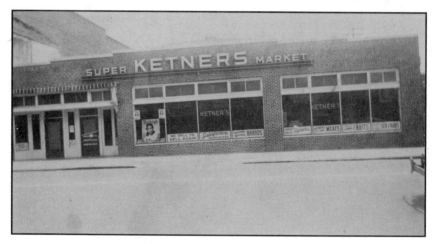

At Food Town's second annual Christmas party at Chanticleer Restaurant in Salisbury were, from left, Wilson Smith, Ralph Ketner, Charles Wilson, Tommy Eller, Brown Ketner, Junior Pope, Bob Roseman, O.L. Casey and Clifford Ray. *Photo courtesy of Food Lion.*

Food Town's Wilson Smith, left, Ralph Ketner, center, and Brown Ketner pose with beauty queens prior to Salisbury's Holiday Caravan Christmas Parade. *Photo courtesy of The Salisbury Post.*

Paging through a trade publication, Ralph Ketner stopped at a first-person article written by Robert Stragand, a small grocery operator in Dayton, Ohio. "This fellow has got what I've been looking for," Ketner said out loud. "I'm going to Ohio." There he got the idea for LFPINC. *Photo courtesy of The Salisbury Post.*

Ralph Ketner films a television commercial. "God, I hated them," he said of the taping sessions. "I'd rather work a week than do one." *Photo courtesy of Food Lion.*

Food Lion chairman and president Tom Smith guards what private moments he does have on his 52-acre spread in Rowan County. He walks his dog, left, and relaxes by a stone fireplace, below. *Photos courtesy of The Salisbury Post.*

Food Lion's philosophy: Buy more for less and buy it all out of one location. Corporate headquarters on Harrison Road in Salisbury, right, and the building as it's dwarfed by huge warehouse in aerial photo, below. *Photos courtesy of The Salisbury Post.*

Food Lion erected a marker outside its Store No. 1 at Ketner Center in 1990. Attending the ceremony were, from left, Vince Watkins, vice president of special projects; Glenn Ketner Jr., Ralph Ketner, Brown Ketner, Tom Smith and Wilson Smith. *Photo courtesy of The Salisbury Post.*

Dalhaize grocery store in Belgium carries the familiar lion logo. Ralph Ketner asked for permission to use the Delhaize lion on his grocery store's private brand, and when Food Town needed a new name Ketner had another money-saving idea: Food Lion. It would require just two new letters. *Photo courtesy of The Salisbury Post.*

New store design for Food Lion: Simple letters with the Delhaize lion. This store on Statesville Boulevard in Salisbury opened in 1987. *Photo courtesy of The Salisbury Post.*

Lowe's stores merging into Food Town in exchange for 201,258 shares of Food Town stock to be paid to Lowe's shareholders. In effect, Food Town would be more than doubling its size. Lowe's, despite having seven more stores than Food Town, had annual sales of $76 million – $16 million less than Food Town.

If the merger went through, Faw would become the single largest individual stockholder (not counting the Belgians) in Food Town. He owned or controlled 65.7 percent of Lowe's stock.

While Food Town and Lowe's proceeded with their plans, the Federal Trade Commission scrutinized the deal. By August 1976, three days before shareholders of the two companies were expected to approve the merger, the FTC asked for a temporary restraining order to block the move, saying it would "tend to create a monopoly." Federal Judge Hiram A. Ward ruled against the temporary restraining order and gave the FTC two days to appeal, which it did. The FTC complaint said the merger would "substantially reduce competition," especially in Winston-Salem, Mount Airy, Jonesville, Kannapolis, Lexington and Statesville – all North Carolina trading areas.

The FTC called the two companies "among the most successful and aggressive competitors in west central North Carolina."

Five attorneys from the FTC argued against the merger at the hearing before Judge Ward in Winston-Salem. Ward didn't buy the FTC's contention that the merger would result in higher prices.

The Salisbury Evening Post's opinion page took issue with the FTC's fears of a monopoly.

"Perhaps the FTC should step in when the shoppers complain that they are being exploited by a near-monopolistic situation," an August 11, 1976, editorial concluded. "But so far, we haven't heard the shoppers claim that. In fact, it is because of Food Town's success in convincing its customers that it offers unusually low prices, that it has gained the major share of its food business. Seems to us that this just proves that the good ol' American capitalistic system is working perfectly."

Food Town and Lowe's shareholders unanimously approved

the merger August 10, but the FTC kept up its pressure. Within nine days after the shareholders' approval, the companies issued a joint statement that they were withdrawing from their merger agreement. The terse statement cited the "uncertainty caused by attempts by the Federal Trade Commission to enjoin the merger."

By that date, August 19, 1976, each of the chains was operating 40 stores.

Ralph Ketner recalled his conversation with J.C. Faw a couple of days after the hearing with Judge Ward: "He said, 'It looks like it will be a knock-down, dragged-out affair to ever get approval. Why don't we just call it off?' I said, 'Well, that suits me OK.' So it's the best thing to ever happen for us, because he would have owned so much of the stock in putting the two together, that probably he would have had too much influence in the decisions."

Food Town also had become frustrated with the FTC. The night before Gary Morgan and Hap Roberts were supposed to leave Salisbury for a month's stay in North Wilkesboro at the Lowe's offices, the FTC informed the companies it was inclined to oppose the merger.

"So that just put us in limbo," Roberts says. "We went through some legal maneuvering trying to get approval for the merger, but the FTC would write Ketner and ask for information. Ketner would write me a note and say send them this and this, financial data, all this sort of stuff. We were running up legal bills. So eventually we just made the decision that we would not fight it any more."

The FTC sent one last letter asking Food Town for 10 more lengthy pieces of information. Because the decision already had been made to drop the merger, Food Town could have ignored the request, but Roberts already had spent time gathering about seven things on the list. He figured he may as well complete the job. He walked into Ketner's office one day when Ketner and Tom Smith were going over some figures.

"They're wanting blueprints of the typical Food Town store," Roberts said of the FTC's latest request.

"Oh, gosh, I can't believe it," said Ketner, worn out from all the bureaucratic requests.

Tom Smith laughed and said, "You know, my dad is in the engineering department at Cannon Mills. He's got some old blueprints of mill additions. We ought to just send some of those up there."

"Well, I don't care," Ketner said. "Don't even send anything. We're not going to do it anyway."

As they were leaving the office, Roberts said to Smith, "Why don't you see if you can find some of those blueprints for a mill addition at Cannon Mills. I'd just like to have a little devilment here and see what the hell happens."

The next day Tom Smith brought to the office a blueprint of an expansion at the Kannapolis towel manufacturer's No. 1 plant. Roberts crammed it into the big box of other material being mailed to the FTC and sent it off to Washington. He didn't hear a word from the commission until a couple of weeks later when his FTC contact called, apologizing, because he had forgotten to ask for one more thing in his previous letter.

"Oh, is that right?" Roberts said, "Tell me what it is and I'll fire it off to you." That bit of business taken care of, Roberts continued, "Well, tell me, how was everything I sent up to you?"

"Oh, everything was great, everything was just perfect, just exactly what I asked for," the bureaucrat said.

Roberts says that was the day he became a Republican.

Ralph Ketner continued to fine-tune his LFPINC concept. (The slogan expanded on billboards and in television commercials to LFPINC/SC/VA.) In 1977, as sales continued rising, Ketner looked for somewhere else to cut prices and keep the excitement going. He decided on health and beauty aids, which were accounting for $5 million in sales through rack jobbers. Ketner knew he could cut prices and sell more of the items if he were able to warehouse them.

Again, when the company went through a middle man, it was paying for his inefficiencies and profit margin. While Tom Smith figured out a way to efficiently warehouse the health and beauty aids, Ketner sliced prices on them by 15 percent. It was a risk. By cutting 15 per cent, Ketner had sliced $750,000 off Food Town's profits with a stroke of his pen. But Food Town soon experienced a 27 per cent increase in sales and a 19 per cent increase in earnings on health and beauty aids.

"That's the type of gamble I like to take," Ketner says. Sales increased 37 per cent, and earnings went up a healthy 64 per cent in 1978. Ketner believes the warehousing of health and beauty aids had a lot to do with the improvements.

Food Town also made changes in the staffing of stores. At the time, produce did about 6 per cent of a store's business; groceries, 74 percent; and meats, 20 per cent. But the produce managers and supervisors received equal pay and benefits, as compared to other departments, even though they represented only 6 per cent of the business. That fact bothered the thrifty Ketner. He transferred the frozen food and dairy sections out of grocery and made them produce's responsibility, so that produce now accounted for 20 percent of the sales; meat, 20 per cent; and grocery, 60 per cent.

Ralph Ketner once tinkered with lowering a shopper's food bill by paying a portion of her sales tax. On July 1, 1980, Food Town began paying 1 percent of the 4 percent sales tax levied in most communities. In North Carolina, the state charged 3 percent sales tax, and most local governments levied an additional 1 percent. What would paying the 1 percent cost the company? Food Town's 99 stores were doing $10 million a week in business and one percent of that would be $100,000. Fifty-two times $100,000 meant Food Town would have to take $5.2 million right off its bottom line. Simple, Ketner figured.

"But I've already done a hell of a lot of research in my mind – and pencil work," he recalled years later, "If we had a 10 percent increase in sales, we would break even. The 10 percent would get the one percent back. So I would rather do $110 volume and make exactly the same thing than I would $100, because I'm stronger. I've got something the competition doesn't have."

Sales tax was a natural to cause buyer excitement. Everybody paid it. In effect, Ketner had reduced a price on something all customers bought, even if it was a tax. He had no idea the states involved would care who paid the tax, as long at they were reimbursed.

The next day, N.C. Attorney General Rufus Edmisten said Food Town could continue with the discount plan as long as it did not advertise the fact. State law prohibited retailers from advertising that they would pay sales tax on a customer's bill. The law even puzzled Edmisten, who had to administer it: "I have people checking to find out what the Legislature's purpose was in passing the law," he said. "I don't really understand it. The state will get its money."

Advertisements about the tax discount continued in South Carolina, where there were no restrictions. Virginia was another story. Officials there acted swiftly to quash Food Town's gimmick.

The prohibition on advertising in North Carolina hurt the promotion. Food Town employees wore "3%" badges and stuck "3%" bumper stickers on their cars. Signs had been placed everywhere in the stores before the attorney general's ruling. The question became, what constituted advertising and what did not? Elizabeth Wilson, then head of the company's advertising, finally sent out a directive August 21, 1980, to store managers in North Carolina. The 3 percent promotion would be discontinued as of the close of business August 23.

Food Town still gained important public relations mileage out of the sales-tax ploy. Like Ketner's battle with the milk commission, it seemed to consumers that Food Town was doing everything in its power to lower food bills over the government's objections.

"To me, excitement – that's what the whole damn thing's about," Ketner says. "When Carter was president, rice and grits. Everybody called him 'Rice and Grits,' so I cut the price of rice and grits to cost or below. Smoking tobacco: cost or below. Everything – Prince Albert, everything you buy – and if you save, you thank the Lord for Food Town: 'I saved 25 cents on my can of tobacco.' "

Ketner once was sitting around a dinner table with others at a food dealers' convention when a competitor challenged him on the LFPINC slogan.

"Ralph," he said, "this thing about you having low prices. I'm getting sort of tired of hearing that. Everybody's got about the same prices."

"I'll buy that," Ketner said. "Everybody except Food Town."

"Oh, my prices are as low as yours," the competitor said.

"Bob," Ketner replied, "I'll tell you what we'll do. You hire a CPA and let him check 5,000 items at your store and the same 5,000 at my store, and the one that has the lowest total takes the other one's store lock, stock and barrel.

"Oh, hell, I won't do that," the man said.

"You just proved my point," Ketner replied, to the smiles of the others around the table.

With Food Town's ever-increasing volume, the Salisbury warehouses on Harrison and Julian roads kept expanding. The Harrison Road grocery warehouse grew from 405,000 square feet in 1976 to 900,000 square feet in 1980. The Julian Road facility had an additional 500,000 square feet, mostly under refrigeration. The weekly warehouse inventory of 10 million pounds had a complete turnover every three to four weeks by 1979. With the help of IBM computers recording orders from stores, warehouse employees were able to load a truck with a store's request 19 minutes after receiving it.

Because it was running out of land in Salisbury and looking to put a distribution center closer to its expanding market, Food Town bought property in Petersburg, Virginia, in 1981 and by early 1983 had constructed a 287,000-square-foot warehouse serving 35 stores in Virginia and the eastern sections of North Carolina. When Food Town added 137,000 square feet in its last expansion to the Salisbury warehouse in 1983, it had placed more than a million square feet under one roof at the Harrison Road site.

Food manufacturers began recognizing Food Town for its large-volume orders and merchandising. National Biscuit Company honored the company for having the world's largest Nabisco display in 1976. One of the company's Charlotte stores featured more than $18,000 worth of Nabisco products in a display. Ralston Purina Co. presented Food Town with an award for being a million-dollar customer the same year. Tom Smith's old company, Del Monte, recognized Food Town as its 1977 "Retailer of the Year" because the chain's stores averaged sales of 8,100 cases of Del Monte foods a year – a 300 percent increase within a five-year period. Food Town ranked second in the nation in the movement of Del Monte products per store.

General Foods gave Food Town its "$10 Million Purchases" award in 1979. American Home Foods, distributors of Chef Boyardee and Luck's Foods, characterized Food Town as one of its "national leaders" because of the company's $3 million sales of American Home Foods products in 1979.

One October morning in 1976, Borden's Elsie the Cow made a promotional visit to Food Town's headquarters in Salisbury. Brian Young, a student at the University of Ohio, led the gentle, dew-eyed Jersey with a necklace of daisies and a red blanket on her back right into Ralph Ketner's office. Meanwhile, her calf, Beauregard, frolicked down the corporate halls, sniffing trash cans along the way. They caused quite a commotion. Salisbury Mayor Jim Summers was on hand to present Elsie with a key to the city. Before Elsie got out of the building, she did what one might expect any cow to do – right on the office's blue carpet. It could have been worse. She was pregnant.

Both Food Town's people and stores were getting older in the 1970s. At the store level, remodelings, expansions or closings of older stores already were taking place. The first store at Salisbury's Ketner Center flourished as one of the chain's best locations. In 1977, it was enlarged by 11,000 square feet to approximately 27,000 square feet.

Men such as Wilson Smith, Ralph Ketner, Clifford Ray,

Tommy Eller and Jim Berrier were into their 50s, some even their 60s as the decade closed. As Food Town officials thought bigger in the 1970s, they also laid the framework in management that would be able to deal with the future growth. Tom Smith, whom Ketner continued to groom for the presidency, became a central figure to those plans. "You have to understand," Tom Smith says, "that in the early 1970s, Wilson Smith did store operations; I did warehousing; and Mr. Ketner, of course, was president of the company. And that was a sufficient setup for then. But with the plans we had, and our wants and desires, that was not a setup that would work long range. It would have been disastrous."

Food Town began hiring men as buyers, managers, supervisors and directors – positions that with a bigger company would be equal to vice presidencies. The company hired James H. Goodwin Jr. as a grocery buyer to help Smith in 1972; A. Edward Benner Jr., data processing manager, 1973; Allyn Adams, director of meat operations, 1975; Kenneth Harris, perishable supervisor, 1976; Eugene McKinley, director of personnel, 1977; Vincent G. Watkins, director of organizational development, 1977; Robert R. McAuliffe Jr., director of real estate, 1978; Spencer D. Storie, store engineer, 1978; George Seger, loss prevention manager, 1978; Edward H. Jones, warehouse manager, 1979; and Thomas R. Crabtree, director of advertising, 1980.

"To me, that was a real interesting period," says Tom Smith, who became Food Town's executive vice president and president of Save-Rite in the 1970s. "That was the time we were setting the structure for the company, and we spent a lot of time deciding what that structure should be. We spent a lot of time finding the right people, realizing that the type of people that we wanted to come with Food Town would have to be people that would be ambitious. It was still a very small company. It was a company that they would have to visualize what it could be.

"They would have to be ambitious, they would have to be hard-working, because of the amount of work it takes to grow a company like we wanted. And we knew they would have to be the type of people that could work as a team because, in a growth company, it is mandatory. So we went to a lot of extremes recruiting these people, really looking, basically, across the United States, using an industrial psychologist to help us. We were looking for what we called the Food Town personality in these people."

Back in 1970, Ralph Ketner had found the Food Town personality in Tom Smith. He followed through on his promise and handed over the company presidency to the 39-year-old Smith in 1981. Ketner remained chairman and chief executive officer.

For all of its growth, Food Town still remained Salisbury and Rowan County's little secret. In 1982, Food Town had 2,468 stockholders of which 1,203 lived in Rowan County, North Carolina. Almost half. And nearly 1,000 of those Rowan Countians had Salisbury addresses. Rowan Countians owned 25 percent of the stock, which by the end of 1982 (the year included a three-for-one stock split) had created 31 Rowan County millionaires, mostly all of whom were people Ralph Ketner, Brown Ketner and Wilson Smith had spoken to back in 1957.

As the country worked itself free from a bad recession in the early 1980s, nothing seemed to be standing in the way of Food Town. Except its name.

12. The name game

As Food Town marched northward toward Richmond, Virginia, in 1982, Gordon Edwards may have felt like Jefferson Davis threatened by advancing Union troops. Food Town's plans for a warehouse in Petersburg already had been announced. Cable television viewers in the Richmond area were picking up the Food Town commercials aimed farther east at Portsmouth shoppers. Everyone knew the fast-growing North Carolina company considered the whole of Virginia wide open for its low-price concept.

Edwards' small, three-store chain in Mechanicsville – a community close to Richmond – stood to lose if Food Town entered his market. But Edwards thought he had a trump card. His company's name was "Edwards' Foodtown." Sure, it was a tad different, but Edwards claimed in a lawsuit that the North Carolina company heading his way already had caused confusion with customers and vendors. He laid claim to the "Foodtown," or "Food Town," name and said the North Carolina firm should be prohibited from using it in his region.

Food Town officials began negotiating with Edwards, who, from their point of view, had started emphasizing only lately the "Foodtown" portion of his name. Before the "Edwards" part of the company handle had been given much more attention. Food Town's Ralph Ketner wasn't really concerned because he had run into no other obstacles in the rest of Virginia. The court eventually ruled Food Town stores could not be placed within three miles of any of Edwards' three stores.

But the name really became a problem as Food Town looked

to grow into Tennessee. Roughly 100 "Food Town" stores, individually owned but often advertising together, operated in Tennessee. The North Carolina version of Food Town was unable to register its corporate name in the Volunteer State because of all the other Food Towns. It became apparent that Food Town would have to change its name, if it wanted to grow westward.

One fall day in 1982, Ketner was driving with his wife, Anne, (he had divorced and remarried), when he snapped his fingers.

"What's wrong?" his wife asked.

"I just happened to think of a new name for Food Town."

"I didn't know you were going to change it," she said.

Food Town officials had not decided for sure to change the name. But what Ketner had figured out during his drive would be the most efficient and logical approach if they did.

With its growth, the chain had begun selling private label merchandise: nothing on the scale of Winn-Dixie, whose private labels such as Dixie Darling and Thrifty Maid accounted for 20 percent of sales, but a smattering of Food Town products nonetheless. As a means to allow shoppers to identify the private label quickly, Ketner had asked the Delhaize partners from Belgium if he could use their lion logo on the packaging. They agreed, and the stylized lion symbol was incorporated into the private labels and some stores' signs – an effective separation between the words "Food" and "Town."

"Our logo is the lion," Ketner told his wife, "and if we change our name from 'Food Town' to 'Food Lion,' in these big canopy signs, all we'll have to buy are two letters: the 'L' and the 'I.' We can move over the 'O' and the 'N' from 'Town,' and we can change our whole name by buying just two letters."

The idea sounded sweeter to Ketner when he learned from Joe Gainer of the Ever-Glo Sign Co. in Salisbury that buying just two new letters instead of, say, four would save the company a half-million dollars. Thinking back over his experience in the grocery business, Ketner rationalized that shoppers really didn't care what a grocery store called itself. He had been associated with names such as "Cash and Carry," "Save-Rite," "Ketner's" and "Winn-Dixie."

"It's what's inside," Ketner reasoned.

On the 25th anniversary of the opening of the first Food Town store, December 12, 1982, Ketner shocked employees at their annual Christmas banquet with the news that the company's name would change to "Food Lion" at the beginning of 1983.

"Food Lion?" said a December 15, 1982, editorial in *The Salisbury Evening Post*. "One can hear the question echoing all over Rowan County. Change is a little hard to swallow, particularly when it involves breaking a 25-year-old habit. But this change comes in the name of progress, and that makes it good news. Such transitions have been made successfully before. Remember Esso?"

Tom Smith placed Vince Watkins in charge of making a list of all the things whose labeling would have to change to the new name. The director of organizational development ended up with 98 items – from grocery bags, welcome mats and shopping carts to stationery, telephone books and in-store Muzak. Food Lion's fleet of trucks would require new stenciling for different decals. The company set March 31, 1983, as a goal for converting all the store signs at approximately 190 locations. In a brief publicity shot for the local newspaper, president Tom Smith climbed to the roof of the overhang at Store No. 1 in Salisbury December 30, 1982, to watch the installation of two new letters and the shift of two others to create the name "Food Lion." Because of weathering to the existing letters, the clean new letters seemed to call even more attention to the name change.

As it had with the LFPINC and sales-tax promotions, Food Lion resorted to bumper stickers as part of its advertising to make shoppers aware of the change. Prizes ranging from $5 to $1,000 were given away in drawings for people who had bumper stickers on their cars. The words "Food Town" were printed in dark blue ink on a yellow background. A bold red line marked through the word "Town," and "Lion" was written in red beside it. Effective, except that red dye fades more quickly in packaging than other colors. As the bumper stickers were exposed to the hot Southern sun and evening thunderstorms that year, the red mark through "Town" and all of the word "Lion" disappeared, leaving many a car traveling the highways with "Food Town" bumper stickers.

For the Salisburians who had spent the past quarter century shopping at Food Town and talking about its growth, calling the company "Food Lion" didn't come easily. Even some folks in the industry became confused by the name change. *Progressive Grocer* said in its February 1983 issue that the name had changed to "Red Lion."

Food Lion committed to a two-month advertising campaign under the slogan "because our prices are something to roar about." Ralph Ketner, who for years had been doing Food Town's advertising on television, entered a studio to do a spot with a thick-maned lion – a real one. "Food Town is changing its name – that's all we're changing though," he said, looking over his shoulder at the lion behind him. He explained the change, and concluded by telling viewers that "lowering your food bill is really something to roar about." The commercial ended with the Food Lion logo shaking from the vibration of the lion's roar.

"The only thing we're changing is our name" served as another theme for the transition.

The name change had the desired effect. It allowed Food Lion to push into Tennessee, first with stores in Johnson City. In all, 1983 was a significant year for the company. For the first time, sales reached the $1 billion mark. By year's end, Food Lion had 226 stores in five states: North Carolina, South Carolina, Virginia, Georgia and Tennessee. It was in 1983 that the company also divided its stock into two classes – voting and non-voting. Ralph Ketner recommended the move to help the Belgians.

"They explained," Ketner says, "that they paid less dividends than anybody on the Belgian stock exchange, and they paid less because they had no money. Our company was growing like mad, but unless we started paying a dividend, they wouldn't have any money to provide a dividend of any consequence. We didn't want to pay that much dividend. We had started paying a slight one as consideration to them and our stockholders. I said, 'Well, why don't we split the stock to voting and non-voting, because you must keep the 50 percent voting, but if you have some non-voting stock, then you can sell all or part of it.' So they did. I think they sold $30 million worth of the non-voting back and that gave them enough money. And now we're paying out approximately one-third of our earnings in dividends. So that gives them enough cash so they can operate."

For Food Lion shareholders, it meant another split. The biggest confusion came with future investors, wondering if they should buy Food Lion A or Food Lion B. It really didn't matter, since the Belgians controlled the majority of voting stock.

Each share of common stock outstanding was redesignated as one share of Class B (voting) stock, and a like number of certificates for shares of Class A common stock were distributed to shareholders October 5, 1983.

So after the conversion to two classes of stock, an original investor with 100 shares in 1957 now had 216,000 shares total – half in Class A and half in Class B. A big three-for-one split occurred in June 1986, as those 216,000 shares became 648,000. Ketner announced the split at the annual May shareholders meeting and proudly proclaimed that an original $1,000 invested in the company in 1957 was worth $7 million. Speculation about the pending stock split drew a big crowd to that 1986 annual meeting, as 86 percent of the company's by then 22.6 million shares were represented either in person or by proxy.

Over time, the separate Save-Rite subsidiary was dissolved and absorbed into Food Lion. The company's LFPINC slogan also became outmoded since Food Lion had expanded into several other states. Maybe it was for the best. Competitors and the Better Business Bureau had continually challenged the slogan's "lowest" claim. In May 1981, Ted Law's Charlotte Better Business Bureau chose 37 items at random from Food Town, Kroger and a new grocery chain in the area, 3 Guys. (When 3 Guys first came to the region, its owner, Albert Gubay, filed a suit against Food Town's claim of having the lowest prices in North Carolina.) All three – Food Town, Kroger and 3 Guys – were claiming in advertisements that they had the lowest prices. The BBB reported that a consumer would have paid $38.53 for the 37 items at 3 Guys, $40.73 at Kroger and $42.06 at Food Town. Law sent the results to assistant attorney general Allen Hirsch and asked him to consider legal action against the higher-priced grocers.

"We are not trying to show a consumer where one might get the best deal or save the most money," Law told reporters. "Our sampling did not include specials, 'no-brand' items or private labels. But it is obvious that if three firms are claiming the 'lowest price,' one must be correct and the other two incorrect."

Ketner shrugged off the BBB survey as meaningless: "Anybody who would try to come to a conclusion on 37 items when normally a supermarket carries 8,000 is just unbelievable," he said. No legal action was taken against the grocers.

The Food Lion slogan eventually changed to "6,800 lower prices," but the Virginia attorney general's office ordered Food Lion to change the word "lower" to "low." The Retail Merchants Association of Virginia and Kroger had complained to the state that the Food Lion advertisements for "lower" prices were misleading. The agreement with the attorney general stood as an out-of-court settlement of a three-count complaint filed in Campbell County Circuit Court in Virginia. The complaint accused Food Lion of violating two counts of Virginia's consumer-protection act and a code relating to false advertising.

Kroger's Edwin Sieveking, vice president of the division based in Salem, Virginia, told *Supermarket News* in May 1983 that Food Lion's change to the word "low" was an admission by the company that it did not have 6,800 "lowest" retail prices in Virginia. He added, "We know of no way any concern can substantiate having all their 6,800 items priced the lowest at all times in every store they operate."

Big Star Stores Inc. vowed to match Food Lion's prices as part of its advertising campaign in 1983. And several grocery stores – not Food Lion – tried to compete by offering double redemption values on coupons. Food Lion continued to thrive and appreciated the attention paid to its prices by Big Star.

Frank Hinds, the store manager for Winn-Dixie in Salisbury, had tired of the retailing pressures by 1978 and joined Winn-Dixie's auditing department. In 1983, he was with inventory crews in Tennessee when the word came from headquarters to do a complete price check of Food Lion stores in the area – everything but meat and produce. Hinds was part of two five-man crews.

"At Winn-Dixie," Hinds recalls, "you can come and write down all the prices you want. You can check prices. We're happy to have you. But with Food Lion, you get thrown out on your darn ear."

So the crews had to be discreet, scattering from one store to another so they would not arouse suspicion. It was difficult. Hinds remembers one close call during the price checks: "An assistant manager – apparently he was new on the job and the manager wasn't there – he came over and asked a member of our crew what he was doing. He saw the man had a little dictaphone and paper. He said, 'Well, we're with an independent survey group, making a survey,' and the guy said, 'Well, how do we look?' And our man said, 'You look darn good. I believe we're going to recommend your store.' But some of them were told to get out of the stores. Like I said, we had to be real careful."

Hinds and the rest of the inventory crew were astounded at the differences in price between Food Lion and Winn-Dixie. Food Lion definitely had lower prices. "It was not just one or two items, Hinds says. "It was all the way across the board." Hinds believes it was that price check and others that led to Winn-Dixie's decision to lower prices in some divisions. Indeed, Winn-Dixie unveiled its "10,000 Low Prices" concept in early 1985. First, the Raleigh division closed its 105 stores for one day in January and reopened with lower prices. The Florida chain also closed its 112 stores in the Charlotte division for a day in April and reopened to the "everyday low price" strategy. Winn-Dixie billed itself as "the new place for low prices" and invited shoppers to compare its list of 10,000 low prices (available in tabloid form at the store) with those offered at Food Lion. "That's 10,000 low prices even Food Lion can't beat," the advertisements said.

Why did Winn-Dixie single out Food Lion? "The basic thing is that we operate against Food Lion in more places than anybody else, or they operate against us," Bruce Baxter, Winn-Dixie's advertising director, told *The Salisbury Post* in April 1985. "What our surveys showed was that though we were known for having the best produce and meats, they were perceived as having the best pricing."

Other stores in the Charlotte area set out to prove themselves the low-price leader in Food Lion territory. Bi-Lo's new slogan became "The First Place for Low Prices." Kroger ran a full-page advertisement in *The Charlotte Observer* proclaiming the "lowest prices in Charlotte." Ralph Ketner salivated at this latest version of a price war. A television reporter asked for his comment.

'Well, up until now, the only place I've read about miracles has been in the Bible," Ketner said. "Now I'm seeing one."

"What do you mean?" asked the reporter.

"For competitors to run a full-page ad saying, 'Look, we've been cheating and overcharging you for years, but because of Food Lion we're going to do better, and we're going to reduce prices, not for your benefit, but because they've forced us to.' That's a miracle. It's unbelievable people would come out and admit they're cheating and overcharging people."

Winn-Dixie's introduction of 10,000 low prices led to Food Lion's abandonment of its own numbers game, which ran up to 6,800 low prices and kept expanding. "It got to be so ridiculous," Tom Smith recalls. "We were just changing, changing, changing. And then we made the mistake of putting the decal on the trucks, and it quickly became outdated, so we got that off as far as the number goes."

Lion's Share

Food Lion's new slogan became "Extra Low Prices."
One of the last things Ketner passed on to Tom Smith was the formula for setting prices. It was like a secret family recipe. "The basics are still there," Smith says. "The buying in today's market is much more complicated. The pricing is more involved because there are a lot more allowances, deals and promotions than there were in those days. However, the formulas for markup are still there. That's still the basic pricing policy."

Food Lion roared through the mid-1980s. The company's biggest purchase occurred in the latter part of 1984 when it acquired 25 Giant Food Market stores. The Kingsport, Tennessee, firm also sold Food Lion 23 convenience stores in the deal. Food Lion sold the convenience stores and closed three of the newly acquired Giants because they were close to Food Lions.

In 1980, Food Lion had 5,000 full-time and part-time employees. By the end of 1986, the company employed 20,871 people in 475 stores and three distribution centers in six states. The company had entered Maryland in 1984 with a store in Ocean City, and opened a 445,692-square-foot distribution center in Elloree, South Carolina, in June 1985. A fourth distribution center would open in Dunn, North Carolina, in 1987, and plans were underway by 1986 to enter Winn-Dixie's backyard in Florida and build a new distribution center in Clinton, Tennessee. Food Lion recorded sales in 1986 of more than $2.4 billion and earnings of $61.8 million. Tom Smith also added chief executive officer to his duties heading into 1986, as Ralph Ketner kept the title of chairman of the board.

Construction workers put the finishing touches on a new two-floor addition to Food Lion's headquarters in Salisbury in 1986. The austere offices remained basic meat and potatoes – built for haste, not waste. They also had been built to support additional stories in the future. The construction crews had a feeling they would be back soon.

13. Food fight

Albert Gubay knew exactly how he wanted to get his new grocery warehouse concept off the ground in America: Challenge the best operation in a region, beat it over the head with low prices and take control of 30 percent of the food market. No problem.

Welshman Gubay was a short, effervescent man whose curly hair gave him the appearance of Harpo Marx. But he had the confidence of a snake handler. His Kwik Save supermarkets became the most profitable retailing operation in the United Kingdom in the late 1960s and early 1970s. In 1972, he founded 3 Guys Ltd. (he had two silent English partners) in New Zealand. Again, his discount grocery stores captured a lion's share of the market. He next invaded Ireland, where he enjoyed more success and eventually was bought out by a competitor, Tesco, one of the United Kingdom's biggest food retailers.

With an estimated $30 million in his pocket from the sale of his Irish stores, Gubay looked longingly across the Atlantic Ocean toward the United States. He had become a millionaire on two continents, he boasted, why not make it three?

The lovely dogwoods of Charlotte, North Carolina, had left an impression with Gubay during a springtime visit to the United States in 1975. He remembered their beauty four years later when he selected his battleground and his foes: he would build his new 3 Guys headquarters and 300,000-square-foot warehouse in Salisbury, North Carolina, and branch out from nearby Charlotte's ever-growing population. He would go head to head with Ralph Ketner's Food Town.

Gubay wanted all the world to know his intentions, even the loyal residents in enemy territory.

"Food Town is the best managed and most efficient supermarket in the United States, no doubt about it," Gubay told the Milford Hills Lions Club in Salisbury in 1980. "But Mr. Ketner and I are in two different businesses. Mr. Ketner runs a supermarket, and I run a discounter."

Gubay planned to drive a wedge between Food Town and its customers by offering lower prices. He didn't intend this newest price war to be subtle: His first store in Charlotte carried a 30-foot banner across its outside wall: "Opening Soon with Lower Prices than L.F.P.I.N.C." Gubay had only opened one store (in Charlotte) when he sued Food Town for $30,000 over its claim to have the Lowest Food Prices in North Carolina. "We've got the whole trade on the run," he boasted.

In many ways Gubay was like Ketner. He had $160 in his pocket after getting out of his country's navy and began selling groceries from the back of a truck. He worked hard but had little to show for it after opening stores and trying to compete with major grocery chains in his homeland. Then, like Ketner, he made a fateful trip to Dayton, Ohio.

While Ketner had traveled to Dayton to learn the workings of a low-price concept from Robert Stragand, Gubay went to Dayton for his sister's wedding. There, he saw American grocery stores for the first time and learned of yet another theory about cutting prices. He was told that customers only know the price of 28 particular items. If a store cuts prices on those 28 items – included were tea, sugar, coffee and other staples – then customers assume everything else is cheaper, too. Gubay returned to the U.K. and cut prices on the magical 28. Nothing happened. He still saw friends walking into his competitors' stores.

"With 28 specials, you can fool some of the people some of the time, but not all of the people all the time," he said once. "I believe that if you con people, eventually you'll be found out. When they see that 29th item, they'll know."

Gubay reduced all of his prices and cut his overhead. "Have you ever tried to eat overhead?" he would ask. "Tastes awful." His new formula worked. His theory for his American invasion was simple: "Give value for money. The tighter inflation goes, the more shoppers are going to have to eat with me."

The Welshman came on strong, appearing in his own television commercials and setting fire to $10 bills to illustrate the point that American customers must have money to burn because they pay so much for groceries. Gubay said his no-frills stores would sell at 15 to 20 percent below prices being charged. How? 3 Guys offered virtually no customer service. Groceries sat in their cartons on crude wooden shelves. His stores *were* warehouses: no ceilings, no floor tile, no chrome. Customers had to bag their own groceries in bags they brought from home, or 3 Guys would sell them bags at 3 cents apiece. Stores accepted only cash and food stamps.

3 Guys Limited also held true to the last part of its name by carrying only a limited variety of goods, about 700 items at first; later, about 2,000. Gubay acknowledged he could sell a customer only 80 percent of his or her needs. "We don't carry pickling spice," he said. "You'll have to go somewhere else for pickling spice." 3 Guys concentrated on fast-moving staples, canned goods and frozen foods, and allowed independent contractors to sell meat, produce and bakery goods in its stores.

Gubay even scored points with some Bible Belt customers by not carrying beer and wine, though it's most likely he couldn't buy it or sell it any cheaper than competitors because of legal restrictions. 3 Guys announced plans for 40 or 50 stores in the Carolinas with the Salisbury warehouse at the center of the wheel.

Publicly, Ketner and Food Town paid little attention, as if 3 Guys were an annoyance at best: "He knows he's not going to be able to sell groceries below cost," Ketner said. "He's just getting some publicity while he can. There's no law against telling a lie."

When WSOC, a Charlotte radio station, contacted Ketner to be part of a panel discussion about food prices, he agreed to participate after his secretary told him the "Reaction" talk show would include three regional competitors and Albert Gubay.

"I go down there, and who's there? Albert Gubay. Just the two of us," said Ketner. "And he's got two attorneys with him. So I asked the reporter before we went on the air, 'What's going on here?' He said, 'It's you and Mr. Gubay.' I said, 'Where's Winn-Dixie, Harris Teeter and A&P?' The reporter said, 'They were never supposed to be here.' "

Ketner hardly liked the arrangement. He and Gubay sat down at the microphones to the host's first question: "Do you two people dislike each other?"

"Well, I don't know," Ketner said. "I just met him. How do I know whether I like him or dislike him?" It wouldn't be long before Ketner had made up his mind. Gubay asked him whether Food Town would take down its LFPINC signs if 3 Guys opened its stores with lower prices. Ketner, covering up like a boxer stunned by an opponent's punch, said he didn't know. He resorted to the answer he had first given the Belgians: "It all depends," though he was scrambling to think what it depended on. Then it hit him.

"You've been quoted in the newspapers that you have so much money that your biggest problem is spending the interest on the interest," Ketner told Gubay. "Now I don't have that problem. We have to work for everything we make, so if you have that much money and can deliberately lose money to put us out of business, no, I won't give you brownie points for that. You might can do that, but it's just for selfish reasons. So you can jack your prices up the minute you get us out of business."

Ketner and Gubay continued for an hour, trading verbal blows. "The phone's been ringing like you're going out of style," the host told the two of them. Gubay accused Ketner of raising the price of coffee because Gubay had bought it cheaper than the shelf price at Food Town. "You bought yours for your warehouse a month or two ago," Ketner said. "We've had to re-buy at a higher price. We don't sell old coffee."

At one point, the men agreed to allow the host to buy groceries from each store to determine who really had the lowest prices. Gubay tried to turn Food Town's later decision to withdraw to his advantage. He issued a press release:

"Because Mr. Ketner withdrew from our contest," he said. "I am forced to draw one conclusion from Mr. Ketner's action: He feels that he cannot compete with 3 Guys consistently and maintain his claim of having the lowest food prices in North Carolina. For Mr. Ketner to continue to make those claims seems to me to be a blatant case of false advertising. I think it only fair that the public be told I was in for the full ride and eager to learn the outcome of our price contest. I pride my company on its willingness to have its feet put to the fire. I would still be willing to resume the experiment because I believe that the heart of what makes the American system of free enterprise so valuable to us is the atmosphere of free competition."

People asked Ketner later how he thought he'd done on the radio show against Gubay. On a scale of 100, Ketner said he could only claim a 49 and Gubay had probably gotten 51. "But he'd spent weeks," Ketner recalled years later. "Boy, he was pulling out figures quoting that we had so and so in our store and did this and that. But it was a lot better than if it had been just him."

Within five months of his first store opening and that January 25, 1980, radio broadcast, Gubay was overhauling his operation, saying he had made some "horrible mistakes." He began accepting checks and reduced the size of his stores from 42,000 square feet to a more Food Town-like 25,000. Customers complained that 3 Guys shopping trolleys were too big and unwieldy. Gubay replaced them with more conventional carts. In interviews, Gubay admitted that Food Town probably would be the last chain to feel the effects of 3 Guys' presence in the marketplace. He was just singling out Food Town because the chain was perceived as the low-price leader.

As documents were filed relating to Gubay's suit against Food Town on the lowest-price claim, it came to light that a 3 Guys executive, vice president Robert Hartley, went through a Food Town management training program between October 30, 1978, and February 24, 1979. Hartley had previously worked for Gubay in New Zealand and Ireland. Ketner accused Gubay of spying.

For the Food Town investors getting edgy about the 3 Guys challenge, Ketner had these words: "I tell my people to ignore 'em and keep chopping wood. Competitors are all the same; they're all trying to take my business and I'm trying to take theirs."

Housewives had problems with 3 Guys. They liked conveniences such as someone bagging their groceries and putting them into their cars. They liked clean stores, but the boxes and crates on 3 Guys' shelves contributed to dirt and a cluttered appearance. And why shop somewhere that only offered 80 percent of the things on their grocery list?

By spring of 1982, Gubay returned to the United Kingdom, leaving his operations in the hands of chief executive officer Trevor Wilson. Nothing ever came of his showy lawsuit against the LFPINC claim. By October 1982, both parties agreed to its dismissal without prejudice. On leaving, Gubay denied that he was skipping town.

Within four months, Wilson hired additional construction teams to reach the company's goal of having 20 stores by the end of 1982. After Bruno's, an Alabama-based grocery operation, backed away from its plan to buy 3 Guys, the employees and management bought all the company's stock from Gubay in 1983.

Gubay hadn't skipped town. He had abandoned a sinking ship.

Within two years of Gubay's sale of the American 3 Guys operation, it all began to unravel. Customers never accepted the stores' lack of service and variety in the warehouse atmosphere. A 3 Guys advertising campaign in 1984 used the slogan, "Our stores may be ugly, but our prices are beautiful." Sales actually became the ugly part. By 1985, the company was in bankruptcy. Six South Carolina stores were closed in what had grown to be a 29-store operation. A last-ditch attempt by senior management to join a grocery cooperative and salvage the 10 remaining stores fell through in early 1986 when they were outbid for the locations by Consolidated Stores, an Ohio-based chain that sells closeout merchandise under the name Big Lots.

The warehouse, ironically, would fall into the hands of Ralph Ketner and his Salisbury-based grocery chain. By 1986, Food Lion signed a lease arrangement with property managers in New York for the 288,000-square-foot distribution center Gubay had built for about $3 million in 1979. Food Lion had grown from 85 stores at the end of 1979, when Gubay came on the scene, to 388 stores by the time 3 Guys went belly up, putting CEO Trevor Wilson and about 300 other 3 Guys employees out of work.

J.T. Kluttz, a salesman for JFG Coffee, had gotten to know Wilson through calling on the company and offered to drop by his suburban Salisbury home one Saturday to help him with a lawn mower. The two ended up spending the afternoon tinkering with an old sports car instead. Toward the end of the day, Wilson surprised Kluttz by offering to sell him his house. He had already made plans to return to the United Kingdom.

Wilson proposed what Kluttz considered a bargain for the handsome home, but the price remained just out of Kluttz's reach. They talked more, and Wilson learned that his American friend owned some Food Lion stock that he could include as part of a deal. That was all he needed to hear.

"I've always wanted to own stock in Food Lion," Wilson said.

14. Big-game hunter

Tom Smith sat in his car waiting for the manager to arrive and open the Ketner Center Food Town. It was 7:30 a.m. The manager usually arrived closer to 8, but Smith liked to be early. Jeff Ketner was the same way. He thought he could score brownie points with the manager by showing up early, ready for work. When he arrived in the parking lot that morning, Jeff didn't like seeing that Tom had beaten him there.

The boys were friends, attending China Grove High School together. In the fall of 1958, Jeff had told Tom, a junior, about Food Town's plans to open a second store in Salisbury. The company would need more baggers, and Smith wanted a more dependable income than he was making on his family's farm. So about six weeks before the December opening of the No. 2 Food Town, Tom started as a bagger at the original store. He stayed with the work, which led to full-time summer employment – and the morning waits in the parking lot.

Jeff vowed to himself that he would arrive at the store before Tom the next morning, and he did, by driving into the parking lot at 7 a.m., a full hour before they were supposed to be at work. Tom arrived at his usual time, only to find Jeff sitting there waiting for the manager. Each morning the boys waited together in one or the other's car. They never mentioned the early hour or acknowledged they were trying to be first at work. The next morning, Jeff again pulled into the parking lot at 7 a.m. Tom already sat waiting.

Jeff beat him the next morning by arriving at 6:45. But the next day, Tom had arrived by 6:45. Meanwhile, the store manager never knew of the quiet battle going on between his eager young workers. He only knew that when he opened the store in the morning they were on time for work.

The boys finally figured out they were playing their game to an empty house, so they agreed on a reasonable time to arrive.

Many years later, when Tom Smith was president and chief executive officer of the grocery chain that became Food Lion, he continued to be the first to arrive at work in the morning. He would steer his conservatively styled Cadillac into the parking lot in the pre-dawn darkness, pull into a spot farthest from the headquarters building and walk across the expanse of asphalt that within two hours would be teeming with hundreds of cars. By 6 a.m., he was behind his desk, inaugurating another 17-hour work day.

Since boyhood, Smith has assumed he could accomplish a job by overwhelming it. He believes his sheer, determined effort at every task can bring success. As a boy, he delighted in picking the same amount of cotton as the adults working beside him. His greatest joy as an adult has become seeing others achieve, and experience the thrill of accomplishment through hard work.

"I would like to be remembered as having helped a lot of people achieve things," he said once.

Smith never allows himself to be satisfied. His drive comes from the thrill of accomplishing something new. His confidence springs from having asked himself time after time whether something can work, then figuring out a way that it can. He has Ralph Ketner's work ethic but handles problems differently.

"Daddy was the entrepreneur, the one with a creative idea, the one who put the system in place," says Ralph's daughter, Linda. "And then it got so big that it needed a good manager and developer of people, and Tom was that. But again, the thing that held it together, I think, made it so strong, was that they were both working from the same ethic. They had the same idea, the same culture for the organization. And then the evolution of the organization required two different kinds of gifts. Each one of them was there with the right gift at the right time."

Lion's Share

Ralph Ketner had a good idea. Tom Smith has been good at executing it.

"Tom Smith's better than I am," Ketner says. "He knows a hell of a lot of things. Now, he wouldn't have been able to have the ability to change the company, the concept, I don't believe. Because for one thing, he's probably not the type who would bet the company. Now I wouldn't want him there if he bet the company, but when you bet the company and it's not much of a damn company, it's a different ballgame. I would still have been working 100 hours a week if it hadn't been for Tom Smith, because until you get the right man, you don't delegate. They say 'delegate,' but hell, you've got to delegate to the right man. It's suicide to delegate to the wrong person."

Ketner said the magic words to Smith when he asked him to rejoin Food Town as a buyer. If he did the job, Ketner told Smith that morning, he could become president. He could have considerable wealth. He would have survived where others before him had failed and failed miserably.

That's all Smith needed to hear. Over the next decade, more often than not, when someone entered Ketner's office, he saw Tom Smith sitting there, writing down everything the president said. Smith became the student; Ketner, the great master. Just as Smith dedicated his career to becoming president, Ketner set out to prove himself right in choosing Smith.

"I think Ralph realized Tom had talent and Ralph made up his mind that Tom was going to work," said a former Food Lion executive. "Maybe the six before Tom would have worked, too. He (Ketner) just had this mental image that, 'OK, this one is going to work.' I think Tom came along at the perfect time. I knew or had heard about some of the other people who had been in and out of there. Some of them had some pretty good talent."

The lanky, boyish Smith stands more than 6 feet tall. He has a cleft chin and blue eyes. His hands feel a bit rough from the weekend work on his own farm. His brown hair remains thick, though at 50, touches of silver have invaded his temples. He wears

166

wire-rimmed glasses while doing paperwork, but during conversations he often takes them off, while constantly gesturing with his hands. Employees say he's a good listener, patient and demanding. He has a low-key management style that constantly emphasizes teamwork and working toward a common goal. Smith views himself as the hub on a wheel, the coordinator making sure things are done.

Though chief executive of a major corporation, Smith is easily accessible to employees and the public. He'll often walk out to the lobby to meet visitors who have appointments with him. Smith has never really become accustomed to employees standing to attention when he walks into a store. He still remembers (and likes to demonstrate) the two-handed method of packing groceries.

Smith reads all the mail addressed to him and takes extra steps to personally call a letter writer making a complaint. Or he'll follow up with a personal letter or one that can be handled with a standard form letter that he originally composed. His frequent television commercials for Food Lion – critics describe him as stiff, but earnest – have made him a celebrity of sorts, often disrupting his meals at restaurants. Because of his high public profile, people feel as if they know him and often address their letters, "Dear Tom."

Folks in the media have found Smith cooperative, if he views their intentions as honorable – that is, he doesn't like surprises and appreciates knowing beforehand where an interview and story are headed.

Like Ketner before him, Smith jealously guards the company and the people who work for it. He immediately responds to any perceived attack, no matter the source. Perturbed, he called editor Stephen Bouser of *The Salisbury Post* on December 31, 1990, to complain about the newspaper's frequent criticism of an experiment at Store No. 10 in Salisbury. Food Lion was in the midst of trying a new checkout procedure, using a system of ropes to line up customers and their shopping carts so that they were funneled to the next available cashier. Similar systems are used in banks and at airline counters. "The thing that's most disappointing," Smith told Bouser, "is that we have tried so hard to have the latest things for our customers, to have our stores very nice, and to have the things that we think will be in the stores of the future. And then to have it killed by negative publicity."

Smith blamed *The Post* for prompting the removal of the experiment in two Rowan County stores. While he had Bouser on the telephone, Smith also complained about the newspaper's publishing of a letter expressing disapproval of the checkout system, the use of plastic grocery bags and the dropping of several of the letter writer's favorite items. "It's just unbelievable that a letter like that would be printed, saying that customer service had gone down," Smith said. "Actually, we have never in our lives stressed customer service more than this year." He noted for Bouser that the Food Lion stores offer a customer a choice of paper or plastic bags.

When Tom Smith talks, the local paper usually pays attention. Bouser fashioned Smith's comments into a front-page story.

Born May 2, 1941, Tom E. Smith was the first child of Ralph and Cora Belle Smith. His sister, Brenda, was born four years later. The family lived outside China Grove on a farm that Ralph Smith had inherited. Rather than farm full-time, the father opted for a regular paycheck at Cannon Mills, where he worked in the construction department. Still, the farm provided many staples from its garden, and the family raised and tended a small collection of livestock. As a child, Tom relied on the hand-me-down clothes of a cousin about four years his senior.

Friends say Smith was born ambitious. As a six-year-old, he picked cotton on a neighbor's farm. Even as a child, he set an adult's 100 pounds of cotton a day as a picking standard and eventually reached it. Some of the first money he earned picking cotton went toward a new jacket, one that wouldn't be a hand-me-down. As an adolescent, he planted his own cotton patch and set out a large vegetable garden. He sold his cotton for savings bonds and bought the family its first freezer. He kept meticulous records of the sales out of his garden: lima beans by the quart, corn by the dozen. Ralph Smith would take his son's vegetables to Cannon Mills and sell them to plant workers who didn't have their own gardens. "At first, I started working for spending money," Tom Smith once said, "but then I found out I just enjoyed doing it."

Smith took school work seriously and graduated second in his class at China Grove High School, where classmates judged him "most studious." Growing up, he placed his ambitions squarely in business. He wanted to be an accountant – never even dreaming of occupations such as fireman or policeman. He knew he wanted to be in charge of a business some day.

Smith discovered with Food Town that he enjoyed the grocery business and considered it an important profession because people have to eat. He married former classmate Judie Bonds in 1960. They had a daughter, and Smith suddenly had a family he was trying to support while working and attending Catawba College full-time. He would prop his college textbooks on the steering wheel of his car and read his lessons as he traveled back and forth to work.

Even with these pressures, he excelled and was made store manager by the time he was 20. His marriage ended in divorce, however, and he delayed his college graduation by a year to work full-time at the C Street store in Kannapolis.

His whole life seemed to revolve around work schedules, even more so when he left Food Town and joined Del Monte. But his persistence paid off with his promotions at Del Monte. And he received the highest score in his unit on the proficiency test at the end of basic training in the Army Reserves, the military option he decided on while others were heading to Vietnam.

While Smith brought different talents to Food Town than Ketner, his workaholic attitude fit like a glove.

"The ethic that Dad started the company with was either adopted or completely in sync with the ethic that Tom had," says Linda Ketner, who worked for both her father and Smith. "I don't know whether Tom got it from Dad, or Tom felt the same way."

Lion's Share

Smith sets his daily alarm at 4:30 a.m., and pulls himself out of bed about 5. After getting his head start on others at the office, he leaves headquarters to have breakfast with friends. His lunches are much less involved, sometimes just a sandwich at his desk. When he's not on a business trip, his day at the office lasts until 6:30 or 7 p.m. He takes paperwork home, eats a late dinner and works until about 11. He works Saturdays and Sundays, although the schedule is less demanding. Smith believes the extra hours are necessary for the company to remain strong and continue to grow.

The desk in his modest-sized, functional office often has stacks of letters, memos and computer printouts for him to read. He might have a couple of new products on a nearby table that he wants to taste-test or examine for himself.

Smith takes pride in the management team of 13 vice presidents he has assembled and looks forward to the day that his own successor emerges from the development program Food Lion has in place. He wholeheartedly believes that the next president and CEO – he plans to retire at 65 – must have his or her roots with the company and know what every job entails: from bagger to meat cutter, supervisor to vice president.

Collectively, the company's vice presidents' traits closely reflect those of Smith. In 1990, the composite vice president was a white male, 47 years old, having worked 14 years with Food Lion and having more than 22 years experience in the grocery business. More than half of the VPs were from North Carolina. They tended to like hunting and fishing. They earned considerable salaries and owned healthy chunks of Food Lion stock. Their work schedules also mimic Smith's, as do their goals for having the company maintain its considerable success.

Some would say Smith's workaholic style has played havoc with his family life. He has divorced twice and was married for a third time in 1988 to the former Martha Robertson Hatley, a Food Lion employee herself. In interviews, Smith has acknowledged that he has always had to compress the time he gives to his family, though he disagrees that he has sacrificed his family life. With his two daughters, he characteristically tried to play hard and pack into an hour activities that other families may spread over four or five hours.

Smith has become wealthy from his hard work, but simple things on occasion give him the most pleasure. "Lots of times, if I work late on Friday night," he told an interviewer once, "I'll run by the store and get a steak, take it home and cook it, then take an hour or so to eat it. A real relaxed meal. I'm a big steak-eater. I guess I could eat steak every night.

"I guess a lot of people I know, they think I don't live an exciting life. But a lot of people, I think, look for excitement outside their work, and I get plenty inside my work."

Smith guards what private moments he does have on his 52-acre spread in southwestern Rowan County. An eight-foot-high wire fence surrounds the property. The gate has an electronic entrance, and guard dogs provide extra security. The stone and wood home lies off the road, hidden from view. Smith gave one instruction to the architects when they designed his home: make it comfortable.

Smith often trades his business suits for work shirts and jeans on the weekend and likes to drive a pickup over his farm or take a walk in the woods to unwind. His few extravagances include cars, a 1960 Corvette among them. And one room in his house is set aside for the animals Smith has killed on various hunting expeditions around the world.

Interviewers always seem to drag Smith into a discussion about his big-game hunting. They usually use the hobby to illustrate Smith's determination and persistence. He stalks his beasts the way he stalks the country for Food Lion, the reasoning goes. And through the years, most of Smith's interviews have been at company headquarters, where reporters have found it difficult to overlook various trophies stuffed and sitting on the floor or hanging from the walls. It could be a deer with a full rack of antlers, a wild turkey, a cougar, a mounted warthog or a red hartebeest.

171

Lion's Share

Prone to neglect vacations before 1980, Smith rejected the frustrations of golf and chose big-game hunting as his one diversion. His first trip to British Columbia was, typically, a freebie, but he soon became hooked. "I can go out hunting," he said in a 1982 company publication, "and it seems, for that short period of time, I completely forget about Food Town." But Smith's typical trips to places such as Zimbabwe, Alaska, Canada and New Zealand could hardly be called relaxing. Smith expends considerable physical effort stalking his prey. He also works, requiring his secretary to send him folders or shoeboxes full of mail and inner-office memos. He has gone hunting without firing a shot but still relishes the time away in different parts of the world.

Smith once hired a sea plane to take him and three other men to an Alaskan island, where they were to hunt for bear. The plane dropped them off, to return in a week. Though it was the start of bear season, the weather stayed so cold and snowy that the bears never emerged from their dens. Smith and his group spent the whole week climbing mountains and observing other wildlife. On another trip, he tracked a cougar through the mountains of British Columbia in five feet of snow.

The thing he likes best about displaying his animals at home or in the office is that each time he sees one, he recalls the story of the hunt and the landscape where the story was played out. But Smith has become reluctant to be photographed with his trophies after getting angry letters from animal rights activists.

One of his favorite hunts, interestingly enough, was for a lion. Smith tracked a certain lion for nine days and nights. One night, while napping in a tree, Smith woke to the roar of the lion. It had stopped under his tree, as if to mock him. On the ninth night of hunting, a rainy night, Smith perched in a tree waiting for the lion to make a mistake. His opportunity came the morning of the tenth day as the lion darted across a field in the pre-dawn darkness. Smith fired one shot and killed him.

The lion had underestimated his opponent. He had never heard the story about the two teenagers trying to beat each other to work.

15. A company culture

Wilson Smith caught a heavy case thrown from the pallet and, in one motion, set it down and ripped open the top with a razor. He then fielded another and another, repeating the routine, all the while telling his fresh-faced crew where to go with stock. "Send all of that canned stuff to Aisle 2," he barked. "Those belong next to produce on the far end." Smith never stopped moving. At age 56, he was working circles around the young boys, who would have watched in awe had Smith allowed them the time.

Dewey Preslar was dragging, but as a new clerk in a new store in Albemarle, North Carolina, he wanted to impress one of the company's founders. He and the others tried to keep up, stamping prices and throwing cans on the shelves at a feverish pace. Still, Smith always seemed to be a row ahead of them.

"Boys, let's take a break," Smith said finally.

He led them back to the break room, where they all got a Coke. The young men looked for a place to rest amid the clutter. Preslar kept his eye on Smith, who turned his Coke bottle up and downed the whole thing with one swallow. He slammed the bottle on the picnic table as he moved toward the door.

"All right, boys, let's get at it," Smith said.

That summer day in 1973 would live with Preslar. From then on, he knew the type of company he was working for and what would be expected of him. The day would help explain, whenever he questioned it himself, the long hours he put in as he advanced through the company ranks to become a risk and insurance supervisor.

Lion's Share

The men behind Food Lion learned the value of work early in childhood. Bob Ketner expected his boys to work on the farms and in his stores. Wilson Smith, forced to grow up fast, without a mother and an absentee father, started earning money with his wagon at age 8. Tommy Eller drew a regular wage as a 12-year-old at the A&P and had to compete at home with nine brothers and sisters. Jim Berrier was raised on the daily chores of his father's farm. Clifford Ray had carved his own place in the world by living off the land. They knew no other way to approach life and had proved to themselves time and again that anything was possible if they worked hard enough.

Hard work had kept Food Town from going under during those first 10 years of "research and development." Armed with a winning concept, the men who built it soon recognized that even harder work could allow them to grow beyond their wildest dreams.

In the beginning, these few men were the company. As Food Lion grew, their work ethic became the underpinning to the company's culture. Like Preslar, other employees – those who would stick with Food Lion – witnessed how hard their bosses worked. For some it became inspiration. For others, it meant resignation.

"Mr. Ketner, I want to quit," a young office employee told the president one day.

"You're doing a good job," Ketner said, "Why do you want to quit?"

"I come in in the mornings and you're here. It doesn't make any difference what time we come in, you're here. When I leave in the evenings, it doesn't make any difference what time I leave, you're here. I just don't want to work for anybody that works as hard as you do, because you expect it out of me."

"That's right, fella," Ketner said. "Let me tell you something. I probably make more money than you ever will. But I get happiness out of work. You haven't learned that yet, but I love to work. You need a job, 8 to 5. You'll be with your family, be with your kids and everything. Your route's different than mine. We both walk to a different beat of the drum."

The young man quit.

A definite Food Lion personality developed. Psychologists even test for it as part of the management recruitment and hiring process at the company. Tom Smith, the president and CEO, personifies the qualities. "An ambitious person," he says in describing the employee Food Lion looks for. "A person who would put forth whatever effort it took to make something work and wouldn't be the type of person who would reach a goal and feel relaxed. And the type of people that would really care about the people of the company because, again, in a growth company, you really have to tie the people and the company together to make it work. A person who is willing to change a lot, too."

From the beginning, Food Lion explains to a new employee that he has just set foot on a fast track.

Linda Ketner, Ralph's daughter, worked as a Food Town office receptionist when she was 14 and later headed the company's first training department in the mid-1970s. The successful Food Lion management employee, she says, had better be a workaholic, 8 a.m. to 8 p.m. weekdays and much of the day Saturday.

"You need to love to work," she says. "And you need to have a very understanding family. No hobbies. No other interests. You need to want to be the best. I don't think any of them, when I was working there, was working to get rich. Nobody had any idea it would be as successful as it is now. I know my dad never worked to get rich. I mean, when I was growing up, I never heard him talk about money, wanting things. Dad's the most unmaterialistic person I've ever been around. I don't think he ever made one cent that had anything to do with, 'Gee, I sure would like to make a lot of money,' or 'I'd like to have a boat' or 'I'd like to have a country house.' It wasn't his motivation. His motivation was he loved to work. He loved to achieve."

Food Town became Ralph Ketner's obsession, increasingly so with the success of his low-price concept. He expected the people who worked for him to feel the same way. The joke became that a good company could be made from the people Food Lion fired or forced to quit through the years, but a thread of truth runs through the statement. Not every person is Food Lion material.

"Ketner demanded a lot of himself," says onetime controller Harold "Hap" Roberts. "He demanded a lot out of all of us around him. He dedicated his life to it, I'll give him that, just as Tom Smith has dedicated his life to it. Ralph Ketner probably is the smartest man I have ever, ever been with in my life."

During his reign as president, Ketner dominated the Salisbury headquarters as he pored over every sales report, deliberated on every price, examined every lease, and doggedly got after his staff to answer his questions. He constantly searched for better ways to do things – especially methods to save money and time. He was never satisfied that the operation was working to its fullest potential or that every person was in the perfect job. That was all he needed to know to keep going. If Ketner had been asked to grade his company in the 1970s, when he was fully immersed in its operation, he probably would have answered "C+" even if he were sure Food Town was the best in the business. He would have given the competitors an even lower grade.

Ketner dictated memo after memo into a machine, and employees learned to dread directives with his familiar "R" signed at the bottom. He could cut an employee to the quick, and he could bring faithful employees to the brink of quitting.

"If you go to bed at night and you don't dream about Food Town, you are not doing your job," Ketner told Hap Roberts.

One day, soon after Roberts joined the company, Ketner rode with him from headquarters to audit a store. Roberts, a 22-year-old not far removed from college, was playing the radio in his Datsun 240-Z.

"Cut the radio off," Ketner ordered. "Get a memo pad out. If we think of anything we need to do we'll write it down as we go."

And whenever someone went into Ketner's office, he had better have a notebook and pen with him. Ketner would be sure to ask for something. Years later, long after he had left Food Lion, Hap Roberts would have a wreck one day trying to write something on the memo pad in his car.

But the people who understood the hard-edged Ketner and shared his desire to see the company be successful learned to deal with him and separated the brusque, professional Ketner from the likable, personal Ketner. They realized, too, how important Ketner's drive was in forging Food Lion's future. No one dealt with the numbers better. No one was a better buyer or tougher negotiator. No one could read a lease as well as Ketner. He knew warehousing, and he committed to memory the price of every item in the store.

The balding and wiry Wilson Smith provided the perfect counterbalance. Employees considered him a "people person" first, less intimidating, more like one of the guys. Smith was constantly in the field, setting up new stores, giving employees the chance to see headquarters people as flesh and blood. Smith never forgot Glenn Ketner's instruction to make customers and employees his top concern.

"He was quite a worker," Tom Smith says. "He was a hustler and real enthusiastic. I guess the thing I always remember about Wilson Smith was that he established in this company a care for employees. He just wanted to make sure that in everything that was done, the employees were kept in mind. He really put a spirit in the company that we've worked very hard to maintain. He was the pacesetter for that."

Without fail, every Christmas Eve, Wilson Smith paid a personal visit to the Food Town stores in his area, just to shake hands with the employees, wish them a Merry Christmas and thank them for the job they were doing. He continued the practice even after retirement. Stores he couldn't get to personally he telephoned.

Jim Berrier dealt with numbers and people. He put up daily with the rantings of Ketner and the directives spewing from his dictaphone, but he considered Ketner a friend outside the office, even vacationed with him. Berrier looked on Wilson Smith and Tommy Eller as brothers more than co-workers.

"Ralph was tough," Berrier says. "You had better get your work done. But I'm not talking in a negative way. When I would leave to go home in the evenings, Ralph expected me to bring some of my work home with me and do it at home. Glenn Ketner was entirely different. We'd get it while we were there, or we'd let it go."

Berrier took pills for his nervous stomach for 20 years while he worked at Food Town, and sometimes he felt like quitting. "But, you know, I understood. If I had not understood, I would have been gone. I'm glad I stuck it out, but it was rough."

Ketner blew his top one day when he learned that one of his managers was heading up a division of the local United Way. It led to a memo:

"It has been the unwritten policy for years that no director, or in fact no supervisor or store manager be encouraged to accept offices of president of any club because of the time it could take to properly fill that position. This also has included, and still includes the accepting of any position as a head of a drive, such as United Way, and by the head of the drive, I mean head of any particular division of a drive, because this entails a tremendous responsibility to carry out the obligation accepted.

"There are a tremendous amount of people who delight in getting these appointments and have the time to carry them out. Food Town people positively do not because of our expansion plans, etc. Every person in the executive capacity or management capacity is needed to perform their duties for Food Town, thus leaving no time to carry through with outside obligations, especially when these outside obligations conflict with Food Town hours.

"What I am saying in a nice way is, don't get involved if it means sacrificing hours that should be devoted to improving your performance with Food Town."

Ketner left the office early one afternoon. A buyer, seeing his boss exit, put his feet on the desk and leaned back to relax. But soon Ketner returned. Berrier remembers that the president really let his buyer have it. "It's just little things like that," Berrier says. "I had a little fellow working for me one time – he was a nice fellow – and he'd be sitting at his desk and sit sort of sideways and work. Well, that didn't suit Ralph at all, just seeing him doing that. You had to sit at your desk properly."

Berrier felt Ketner's wrath himself at times. When Food Town was buying the four mountain stores from the Giezentanner brothers in Asheville, Berrier and Ketner were among the crew taking inventory of the Black Mountain store. The Giezentanner men were there to make a count, too. Both sides worked at determining the inventory, before deciding on a figure that Food Town should pay for the store. Berrier counted all of the small merchandise near the front end checkouts: razor blades, candy, chewing gum, cigarettes, etc. Finished, he gave his figures to Ketner, who promptly grumbled, "Hell, no." He thought Berrier had overstated the inventory, but Berrier was confident in his figures. Ketner asked another man to recount Berrier's work, while the Giezentanner crew took in the whole scene. The recount came within a few dollars of Berrier's total.

"You owe that fellow an apology," a man from Giezentanner told Ketner. The apology never came.

"But that was my job and that was his job, and I can understand it," Berrier said many years later. "I told him I was glad he did it. He's sure of the total, plus I knew unless there was something unusual that slipped in that I was right."

One day Ketner came into the office area where Berrier and five women looked after the bookkeeping and announced that they should all memorize the multiplication tables – the 12th table up to 50. If an employee was verifying an invoice and had 12 items at 47 cents each, the employee would know the extension was $5.64 without wasting time by punching it into an adding machine or calculator. All the bookkeepers, including Clifford Ray's wife, Jean, followed through on Ketner's order and became proficient.

Ketner periodically tested them with flashcards. The student who hesitated on an answer was wrong.

"If I had to do it over," Berrier says of his Food Town years, "I probably would have gone through the same things. It was enjoyable, even though it was hell sometimes, too."

One of Ketner's famous feats with arithmetic dealt with counting train cars. One day he and an unsuspecting Hap Roberts were waiting in their car for a freight train to pass a crossing.

"Let's count the cars," Ketner told Roberts.

By then, Roberts knew he had to establish the exact ground rules. Do they count the locomotives, or start with the first freight car?

"Start at the freight cars," Ketner answered.

"Does the caboose count?" Roberts asked next.

"The caboose counts."

Roberts counted 96. Ketner came up with a number in the millions.

"How did you come up with that?" Roberts wanted to know.

"How the hell did you come up with 96?" Ketner shot back.

"There are 96 cars."

"I was adding the numbers on the side of the cars," Ketner said with a grin.

One day a warehouse manager in Salisbury called Ketner to task on his celebrated math trick. He challenged Ketner to take on the secretary fastest with an adding machine when the next train went through. A train finally came and Ketner stood stoically, adding the numbers on the sides of the cars as they passed, while the secretary's fingers flew over her machine. After the train passed, Ketner said his total aloud, and the group waited for the secretary to read her bottom line.

"They weren't exactly the same, but they were very, very close," Roberts recalls. Still, Berrier had to chuckle as they all left the warehouse that day. "Well, I guess we got one over on Ketner," he said.

Ketner heard him.

"You better double-check her work from now on," he said.

Ketner's office extension on the telephone system used to be "21." Clifford Ray always had a standard joke whenever he saw Berrier and Roberts coming through the door at the perishables warehouse on Julian Road. He would pick up his telephone and dial "21" on his rotary dial.

"I'm calling the man to see what the hell you all are over here for," Ray would say. But he would only let it ring once or twice and hang up. Once Ray went through his routine and on the first ring he heard Ketner's familiar "All right" on the other end of the line. Ray hung up the telephone quickly and said, "Hell, he answered it."

Linda Ketner remembers her father going to work at 8 a.m. and coming home at 6 p.m. He would eat and play with her and brother Robert for about an hour before spreading his work out on the dining room table for the rest of the night. The routine held true for weekends, too. But he was always accessible if the children had a problem. "He wasn't, 'Oh, don't bother me,'" his daughter says. "He was always available. He was trying to meet everybody's needs: Food Town's and ours. The man worked like nobody I've ever known before. And loved it. And that's the other thing I remember. He really left me with the sense that you really need to love your work. Because he was having a good time."

In her brief two years with the company, Linda Ketner thrived on the environment: "I remember literally staying up all night, working as a team, again, not because it was our department but because we all loved it. There were a lot of fights back then between Kroger and us and whomever. So a bunch of us would stay there all night, working on a layout and idea to respond. We just did it because we really felt like a team, and somebody had messed with us. We were willing to stay up all night and mess with them back, which was kind of neat. Never had that experience again."

No one ever said it out loud, but Food Lion executives were and are expected to work Saturdays. "Everybody just did it,"

Linda Ketner says. "We wouldn't have thought of not doing it. It's the most incredible work ethic I've ever seen. That work ethic and the efficiency of it were started by Dad and continued by Tom. You get a company culture and a company ethic. And if somebody didn't do it, they wouldn't be on your team. They'd look weird. It would be like somebody came in with three heads."

Linda Ketner fondly remembers her time with the company as "the best job I ever had."

"I'm not sorry I left," she adds, "because there's more to life than work. I reported to him (her father) and Tom at different points, and I loved reporting to them because they were fair and expected a tremendous amount. I loved achieving more than they expected. But there was more to life. I was single and living in Salisbury – Smallsbury."

Hap Roberts, a homegrown product, learned about the fast track early. He stayed with the company from 1972 to 1982, joining as a 21-year-old and retiring for health reasons at 31. As assistant controller and, later, controller, Roberts' duties at such a young age were considerable: He handled banking relationships and cash management, compliance with the Securities and Exchange Commission, investment policies, four-week income statements, shareholder relations, internal audits, acquisition and conversion of stores from competitors, inventory control, the company policy manual, weekly financial data transmittal, risk management, cash-flow projections, modified accounting systems and more.

"I just didn't want to maintain the pace that I had maintained," Roberts says. "At Food Lion, you go up or you go out. That's as simple as it is. I would have lost my family, I'm sure, if I would have stayed. I mean there were some times we would work 40 and 50 days straight when we were buying stores from competitors. My normal work week was 60 hours, and I would be there at quarter till eight and leave there at quarter of seven Monday through Friday, and Saturday I would work from nine to about one-thirty, quarter of two."

Roberts knew within a couple of weeks of joining Food Lion, then Food Town, that the environment wasn't his cup of tea, but he was hard-headed and young enough to want to prove himself. The stock options he took also were golden handcuffs. As a child, Roberts had ulcerated colitis and the residuals from that – complicated by job pressures – put him to the hospital three times during his last year with Food Town. He eventually had surgery that left him weak and susceptible to illness. He stayed rundown. When he became ill, he risked dehydration. He would go to the hospital for intravenous fluids. "I knew I couldn't keep on going like that and keep my family, my health and sanity," he says.

When he left Food Town, Roberts felt like he had lost a spouse. He loved and respected the men who had built the company: Ketner, Smith, Tommy Eller, Jim Berrier and Clifford Ray. "Mavericks built Food Lion," he says. "I don't know who's maintaining it now, but it was built by mavericks. I was spoiled by them. I loved them. I guess you get spoiled once you've been exposed and get a taste of that side of the organization."

Wilson Smith wore many hats through the years: advertising man, head of merchandising, store manager, operations head, store supervisor. His hours were like all the rest. When he was supervising the Asheville stores, he woke at 5 a.m., drove the two hours, supervised five stores, drove the two hours back and got up the next morning at 6 or 7 and headed out the other way. Smith gradually moved into store planning and development. When a location was found, Smith had the new store built, stocked it and turned it over to the area's supervisor, who did the hiring. At age 62, Smith was driving 1,500 miles a week.

"I wanted to stop," he says. "You see, the sad thing about it is, she (wife Evelyeen) raised both of our boys. I would leave in the mornings and they were either getting up and going to school or hadn't gotten up yet, and when I came home at night, they had already gone to bed. So the only time I saw them was on Sunday, and many Sundays we were out taking inventory, so I was just working all the time."

183

Lion's Share

Wilson Smith retired in 1979. By the end of that year, Food Town had grown to 85 stores in three states. Within a couple of years, Jim Berrier, Tommy Eller and Clifford Ray also called it quits. Ketner let up somewhat, handing over the presidency and day-to-day operations to Tom Smith, but he stayed chairman of the board until May 1991. The men's legacy had long been established: Hard work pays off. It filtered through the ranks so that store managers assumed the company persona and expected it of their cashiers, stock clerks and baggers.

Identicial twins Ronnie and Donnie Marsh spent their careers managing stores and watching their profit-sharing grow. The Marsh brothers confused a lot of people in Salisbury over the years. Not only were they a match physically, but their livelihoods also were eerily intertwined. From age 16, they worked at Food Lion stores in Salisbury. Tommy Eller first hired Ronnie, then, a few months later, Donnie. Ronnie spent 10 years in produce before becoming Eller's assistant store manager at the No. 1 store. About a year later, the store manager's job became his. Donnie labored 12 years in produce, served as his brother's assistant manager briefly, then became a store manager elsewhere in Salisbury. The brothers never wanted a promotion. That would have meant transferring, traveling and separating.

The brothers were so close that Ronnie repeated the sixth grade so he could stay with Donnie, who had fallen behind a year after a near-fatal fall from a tree. As adults, the twins eventually worked up to four weeks vacation a year. Each man spent a week with his family. The other three weeks they spent with each other hunting and fishing. On the job, they averaged 50-hour weeks, though remodelings or transitions often increased the average. Ronnie worked for 26 of his 27 years with Food Lion at store No. 1. Donnie worked 22 of his 27 years at store No. 10. Still, people couldn't keep them straight. Often someone asked one what he was doing in the wrong store or, "Which one of y'all is *my* manager?"

Tired of the job and wanting to spend time with their families, the twins retired together in the fall of 1990. Their profit sharing amounted to several hundred thousand dollars each.

With Tom Smith at the helm, Food Lion has not lost its reputation as a demanding place to work. In fact, Food Lion was a key focus in an October 22, 1990, article by *Fortune* magazine titled, "Do You Push Your People Too Hard?" Here's the beginning to that story: "Listen to a former store manager at Food Lion, the supermarket chain: 'I put in more and more and more time – a hundred hours a week – but no matter how many hours I worked or what I did, I could never satisfy the supervisors. I lived, ate, breathed, slept Food Lion. The hardest thing for me to be was to be a bitch. And I was a bitch. I had to be. They wanted 100 percent conditions, seven days a week, 24 hours a day. And there's no damn way you could do it.' "

The article angered Tom Smith. Rumors were he took that issue of *Fortune* out of any Food Lion where it was on the racks. Smith dashed off a letter to *Fortune* complaining that the magazine had left readers with a mistaken impression that Food Lion drives its people beyond their limits.

"The retail grocery business is a demanding profession that requires hard work and dedication," Smith's letter said. "However, Food Lion has in place an outstanding support system of training, education and supervision."

Food Lion officials cooperated on the story because the subject, they said, was supposed to be about productivity and how companies have found ways to be efficient. They were suspicious of the finished story because former employees quoted were unnamed and, apparently, the United Food and Commercial Workers union played a role in connecting the reporter with those workers. A union attorney also was quoted. "Food Lion treats people worse than anyone I've seen," he said.

Without a doubt, the six-floor headquarters building in Salisbury with its maze of offices – pedestrian, sterile and no-nonsense – rocks to a much faster beat than the slow-moving Southern community around it. Employees throughout the sys-

185

tem do the work expected of two or three in other companies. So say insiders and outsiders. "The number of employees per store is 50," said *Corporate Jobs Outlook!* of Boerne, Texas, in a December 1990 report, "whereas competitors' giant supermarkets may run 120 or more.

"While the huge supermarkets of competitors may have as many as 12 to 18 supervisors/managers, Food Lion stores operate with about seven. The firm has a high level of sales per employee: $117,226, compared to competitor Winn-Dixie's $97,351. Also sales per square foot of store space are 15 percent higher than Winn-Dixie's."

Brian Woolf, former vice president of finance for Food Lion, once said that when Food Lion took over other small chains, two-thirds of the employees left within six months. They were asked to work too hard.

But the company makes no apology for hard work, and loyalty to Food Lion among past and present employees runs deep, mainly because of that investment in the company culture.

Back in the late 1950s, Jeff Ketner took the Food Town work ethic to an extreme. The No. 2 store in Salisbury had little business one day. There were no groceries to bag. All the shelves were filled.

"Casey, what do you want me to do?" Jeff asked the store manager.

O.L. Casey learned his trade under Glenn Ketner, and he could always find ways to keep an employee busy. He told Jeff to clean the employee restrooms. So the teenager spent the next half-hour washing commodes and cleaning sinks.

"What next?" he asked, when he had finished.

"Well, let's go check those restrooms," Casey said.

Casey pointed out several things that could be cleaner. Jeff took care of them and returned to announce the job done.

"Let's look at them again," Casey said. Again, he nit-picked. Jeff knew this could go on all day. He decided to teach Casey a lesson. He got a disinfectant, flushed the water out of one toilet and thoroughly sanitized it. He put clean water into the bowl and locked the bathroom before going to retrieve Casey.

"Casey, I got those restrooms ready for you," Jeff said.

As Casey inspected the sanitized bowl, Jeff proclaimed it so clean a person could drink out of it. He promptly snatched a paper cup, dipped it into the bowl and threw back a big swallow of water. Casey's face turned red.

"My God, you must have them clean," Casey cried. "You can stop cleaning the restrooms now."

16. 1,000 things 1% better

Darrell E. Myers, a perishable foods manager at a Food Lion store in Danville, Virginia, looked at the soft drink machine in the employee break room and thought, "What a waste."

The machine was popular, for sure. All the employees knew where it was and how much the colas and orange sodas cost. They assumed the drink machine was working unless a hand-scrawled "out of order" sign told them otherwise. But the whole plastic front of the machine was lit up like a Christmas tree to tell people it was there, even though it already had a captive audience. Wasn't the store just burning good electricity for nothing? Wasn't *every* employee break room in the then 668-store chain?

Myers recommended turning off the drink machine lights as part of his entry in Food Lion's "Let's Eliminate Waste" contest for employees. Food Lion's management hardly viewed Myers' idea as trivial. Rather, they quickly learned from vendors that turning off those tubes that light up the drink machines is a fairly simple process. Do it in all the stores and maybe the company would save a couple hundred or a couple thousand dollars a year. Myers won a watch and a dinner with President Tom Smith.

Meet the penny-pinchers. While the low-price concept and work ethic are the bedrock of Food Lion's philosophy, the cornerstone is efficiency. Aggressive pricing will seldom survive long without a lean operation. And Food Lion is lean. A company credo, often repeated, is that Food Lion does "a thousand things one per cent better." Typically, in an industry where the cost of doing business averages 21 cents on the dollar, Food Lion averages 14 to 15 cents on the dollar. The money saved in operational costs helps Food Lion on price.

"With other companies I work with across the United States," says Linda Ketner, who became head of her own consulting firm, "they don't have the desire to be efficient. It's kind of like it doesn't occur to them, and it occurred at Food Lion every single minute. Not every day, every minute of your job, it was, 'How do we do this more efficiently? How do we save money?' "

The grocery industry's expense rate has been climbing steadily in recent years. "Supermarkets' critical competition is in expense rate control more than retail pricing," wrote William Walsh in *The Rise and Decline of the Great Atlantic & Pacific Tea Company*. "It is relatively easy to offer lower retail pricing when your cost of doing business is lower than the competition's. Historically, the financial community has attributed A&P's decline to prolonged sales deterioration stemming from the failure of management to follow population movements out of the big cities and into the suburbs and Sun Belt areas of America. In truth, A&P's deterioration can also be traced to management's failure to maintain effective cost controls."

Supermarkets have always taken pride in their low net profit margins. The industry average has been about 1 percent of sales for many years. The 1 percent is achieved by assuring that gross margins exceed expense rates by 1 percent of total revenues. "Long-term profitability and growth favor the operator who can scrape that 1 percent net profit out of a reduced expense rate," Walsh said, "as opposed to the operator who must add 1 percent extra to an otherwise competitive price structure to achieve profitability."

Despite its reputation for low prices, Food Lion has continually dazzled the industry with consistent net income margins that are more than double the average. In 1989 and 1990, the margins were 2.96 and 3.09 percent, respectively. Efficiency is a major reason.

The war on waste goes back farther than the day that Jim

Lion's Share

Berrier turned off lights in the ladies' restroom to save money with Ketner's Inc. Charles Allmon, the seasoned editor of Growth Stock Outlook in Chevy Chase, Maryland, likes to call Food Lion the best-managed supermarket chain in America. "I'll buy that," Ralph Ketner agrees. "I mean, when I ran it, it was. And now with Tom running it, it's even better.

"We always had the efficiency. When you start with as little money as we did, you start lean and mean. Nobody flies first class. Nobody does this. Nobody does that. You work 70, 80 hours a week. In fact, we would have been bankrupt, out of business the first 10 years, had it not been that we were so efficient. Now that didn't show up in the net results. In other words, the percentage. It maybe cost us 18 per cent to operate then. Eighteen per cent was probably the bare operating cost you could have because your rent was so high and you didn't do any volume. So as our sales started going up, the volume was the answer to our problem. Our problem was not inefficiencies, or anything else other than the fact of lack of volume, and once I cured that, then we were off and running."

Smith likes to say that Food Lion does a thousand things one per cent better because of the few things one can do in the grocery business that are totally new and different. So the tiny things, taken collectively, add up.

The company saves everything it can use again. Food Lion recycles banana crates as bins for the health and beauty aids it ships from warehouses. Used envelopes are saved for inner office mail. When a new trailer is purchased for distribution, the company takes off its new tires, puts recaps on the trailers and uses the new tires as replacements for the large fleet of tractors. The meat departments sell ground-up bones and fat for fertilizer, bringing in a million or so dollars a year. In newspaper advertising, the company goes for three-quarter-page ads rather that full pages. For television commercials, the company saves money through in-house production utilizing its own star, Tom Smith.

Typically, stores blow heat from the motors on refrigeration and freezer units out of the store. Food Lion recycles that heat to

190

warm stores in the winter. Some of the cold air escaping from the units also is captured by the stores in the summer to aid in air-conditioning. Sensors in offices and bathrooms turn off lights automatically when the rooms are not in use. A computer at Salisbury headquarters douses the lights in stores throughout the system after their 11 p.m. closing times.

The energy conservation measures in the late 1980s were said to save each store $1,000 a month. With 800 stores, the chain saves $9.6 million annually through energy conservation.

A warehouse employee reasoned once that lighter cartons should be stacked under the heavy ones because it takes less effort – and possibly less time – to pick up a light carton near the floor than it does a heavy one. Makes sense, management said.

After moving to its Harrison Road warehouse in Salisbury, the company looked closely at how it was unloading rail cars. The practice had been to park the rail car and unload it case by case using several employees. Food Town talked manufacturers into slip-sheeting. Loads of merchandise were placed on pallet-sized pieces of cardboard, so a forklift could grab the cardboard and carry it and its merchandise to a pallet. No employees were needed to lift the cases. The practice became the industry norm.

When trucks head back to the warehouses from stores, they "back haul" milk crates, bread trays, cardboard or merchandise they can pick up from a nearby manufacturer.

Not until the late 1980s, would Food Lion allow itself the luxury of a full-time attorney on the payroll. Of course, one of the great examples of the company's efforts to cut down costs was the 1983 name change: realizing that going to "Food Lion" would require only the purchase of two new letters for signs, thus saving $500,000 over the possible purchase of four new letters.

Through the years, Food Lion has scraped for every nickel – to the point of being maniacal. Inner office memos from the 1970s reflect that frenzy, revealing that company officials routinely went on paper chases. They were after employees spending too much for lunch, charging personal miles on the company car,

191

using the store telephone for long-distance calls, buying unnecessary magazine subscriptions, sleeping single (not double) in motel rooms, paying too much for car washes, purchasing unneeded office supplies and more. Every day seemed to prompt new memos aimed at determining how each penny was spent, finding ways of getting money back or suggesting how to change procedures to save money.

Controller Hap Roberts sent out a memo February 8, 1978, to a supervisor who had gone just 39 cents over the lunch limit for 10 people attending a grocery managers meeting. "John," Roberts wrote in the memo, "please keep in mind that our lunch limit for meetings and everything else is $3.50. In the future, please try to stay within this limit, if at all possible."

Jim Berrier once noted for operations manager Lawson Saul that a pair of Food Town employees had taken separate rooms at the Matador Motor Inn in Columbia, S.C., the night of May 18, 1978. "Lawson," Berrier wrote, "please follow through to see that all personnel, excluding directors and above, stay double occupancy in motel rooms whenever possible."

Roberts dashed off a letter in 1976 to the *Harvard Business Review*. In it, he noted that Food Town had paid $18 on a one-year subscription for an employee who had left the company. The employee was receiving the magazine at his home. Roberts asked that the subscription be canceled and a check be sent to Food Town for the issues not used. "If credit cannot be issued in this way," Roberts wrote, "please send the remaining copies to Food Town Stores."

Ralph Ketner wrote a memo to Roberts and Tom Smith in August 1979 wanting them to make sure employees flying on departures from Greensboro were not overlooking cheaper rates from Charlotte to the same destination. And vice versa. Vince Watkins, director of organizational development and later a vice president, gave Food Town employees training sessions on how to keep telephone calls short. The company made sure employees paid for gasoline at self-service pumps. Ketner demanded that weekly logs be kept for supervisors and directors being paid mileage and that the logs be cross-referenced with what the company had determined was the actual distance between locations.

Berrier sent out directives in 1979 that no store manager was to buy his own office supplies. It had come to Berrier's attention that one store paid several dollars more for pens than headquarters would have paid.

In 1980, auditor Mike Foley, while looking at individual store telephone bills, noticed a number of long-distance calls at a Columbia, S.C., store going to an unfamiliar number. Some sleuthing determined that the number belonged to a girlfriend of an employee who used the company telephone to ring up $83.90 worth of calls over a three-month period. The employee repaid the money, and Hap Roberts calculated the wage expense that should be deducted from the employee's paycheck for the company time he used to call his girlfriend. The memo, directed to loss prevention officer George Seger, happened to cross the desk of Tom Smith, who scribbled across the top a note to Lawson Saul: "L.S., In my opinion, this person should be fired. He was stealing from us." A series of follow-up memos reveals that the employee was fired, relating to another discovered theft.

An employee could expect a memo if he or she did not turn in a receipt, no matter how little the expense. Likewise, an employee had better have a good explanation for any request for money or equipment. Tom Krieger requested a new calculator for each of his supervisors in 1977. He received a note back from Roberts: "I will need to know what the supervisors will be using the machines for and approximately how much time each week they would be using these calculators." Krieger wrote a response on the bottom of the same memo – personnel were instructed not to waste paper – that said the calculators would be used to figure budgets, sales and sales per employee hour. He estimated usage at three to four hours a week. "Used calculators would be fine," he wrote.

Food Lion people on the road often spent time explaining why they had stayed a night, say, at a Hilton rather than Howard

Johnson's motel or why they stayed overnight when they could have commuted to a meeting early in the morning. Company policy used to allow $1 per night for personal long-distance calls from a motel room. The finance department always required an employee to pay any additional charges.

Ralph Ketner even wanted memos to be efficient. On May 19, 1978, he sent a memo to all his vice presidents, directors and supervisors: "I receive letters and notes which require much concentration to read because of the fact that the person writing same apparently was in a hurry. I realize that some of my notes are illegible, also. Please, in the future, let's do attempt to write in such a way that the person receiving the note will know what has been sent. I, too, will try to improve my hand-written notes."

Interestingly, it was the constant memos and paperwork that Tommy Eller judged a big enough inefficiency to force his retirement. Someone at headquarters had a love of paper that Eller, a supervisor, found exasperating. The home office required the supervisors to fill out check sheets on each visit, and Eller had to fill out one on Monday, two on Tuesday, Wednesday and Thursday and three on Friday and Saturday – a total of 13 forms.

Eller would try to trace his paperwork sometimes, only to find all the reports tied up in bundles on a secretary's desk.

"What do you do with those?" Eller asked the secretary once.

"I just save them," she said.

"What are you going to do when your room is full?"

"I'm going to throw them away," the secretary said.

At every meeting Eller would fuss about the paperwork. "You would get a letter from one guy giving information – a new product or new policy or new procedure," Eller says, "and the first thing you know you would get two letters from somebody else to tell you to be sure to read the letter from this other guy." Eller finally kept count one week of all the forms and correspondence he handled, in addition to working the stores and driving 600 miles. The number came to 1,162. He complained, but it didn't let up. He decided to teach someone a lesson.

On all the letters and memos he received for information, Eller would write "OK," sign it, fold it up and direct it back to the original sender. The guy at headquarters who Eller says loved all this paperwork finally sent Eller a letter saying, "Tommy, it's not necessary to answer all this correspondence. I'm just sending it to you for your information." Eller took the letter, wrote "OK" on it and sent it back. His mail started to slow down.

"Some of the guys didn't have enough confidence in doing what they would like," Eller says. "They were afraid they would do something and get their butts chewed out about it, so they would write a letter about it so they could say, 'I told him.' "

Fed up after five years of what he thought was too much paperwork, Eller retired in January 1982 at the age of 54.

In recent years, Tom Smith's management team has tried harder to avoid the writing of memos when a telephone call or poking one's head in the door for a brief conversation would suffice. The company officials also shun the formation of any long-standing committees, whose meetings might lead to an inefficient use of time. Task forces may be set up to address issues as they arise, but they are dissolved once the matters are settled.

Management successfully fosters attention to detail through the whole organization with contests to eliminate waste. It has shed light on a whole new level of nit-pickers. Jimmie Harvey, a driver in Clinton, Tennessee, suggested that Food Lion install wind deflectors on its tractor-trailers to make them more aerodynamic and lead to better gas mileage. The deflectors have become standard equipment on all new Food Lion tractors. Dewey Brisson, a driver from Dunn, North Carolina, told the company that each Food Lion store did not need two aluminum dock boards. Although each store was routinely provided a pair, only one seemed to ever be in use at one time, Brisson observed. Why not take the extra boards from each store and use them to outfit new stores? The company was intrigued that it might not have to buy dock boards for its next 600-plus stores.

Faye Smithson, a store manager in Lawrenceville, Virginia,

recommended that hangers brought to stores by linen services be bundled and sold to customers. Linda Angell, customer service manager for a Food Lion in Lexington, North Carolina, said stores should ask its bank to return paper clips and rubber bands used in making regular deposits. Store manager Ray Pledger in Norfolk, Virginia, puts a roll of tape at the end of each aisle in his store so stock boys can use it to fasten loose labels on jars and cans. It saves steps and time. Cherrie Ault, a customer service manager for a Food Lion store in Knoxville, Tennessee, said the stores that sell greeting cards should use any leftover envelopes for store business.

Food Lion has used its cost-saving ways as material for television commercials explaining how operating efficiently allows the company to lower more prices. Ralph Ketner sees a downside to that practice. "Every time we explain to our customers how we save you money," he says, "we're telling our competition how to get competitive. So there's a fine line there as to which one costs you the most and which benefits you the most."

A reporter once asked Ketner what steps Food Lion was taking to deal with a pending recession. "None," he answered. "If I told you some way I could improve, I'd be telling you about something I got careless on."

In 1990, Ketner decided to throw a dinner for the salesmen who used to call on him when he was buyer for the old Excel Grocery Co. He invited 53 of the salesmen to a dinner at Slug's restaurant in Charlotte.

"In case you're wondering," Ketner told the group, "It's pretty obvious Food Lion didn't pay for this. Ralph Ketner paid for it, because there would have been no shrimp cocktail – there would have been no dinner. If I turned in this expense account to Food Lion, Tom would have to approve it, and he wouldn't write 'No' on the front of it, he would write, 'Hell, no.' If I trained him properly that's what he would do."

"You trained him properly," a salesman in the audience said.

17. Grow or die

"I don't know any grocer or anybody else who wants to stay small. They all dream about building something bigger. The whole country's growing, our cities, schools, labor unions, everything. I don't see how any businessman can limit his growth and stay healthy."

When John Hartford, the "Merchant Prince" of the Great Atlantic and Pacific Tea Co., said those words to a *Time* magazine reporter in 1950, his A&P grocery chain was the world's largest. Maybe it was a blessing that Hartford died without ever having to witness the decline of his company.

Hartford never saw A&P abandon its growth, turn its back on efficiency, betray employees or throw on a trash heap what it had always done best – sell groceries for less, depend on high volume and satisfy the customer. Many Americans filed away for future reference A&P's fall from giant to also-ran.

So it's not surprising that at every turn in its dramatic growth, Food Lion has heard from a barnyard full of Chicken Littles. When it first sold groceries in only small-sized North Carolina towns and cities such as Rockwell, Lexington, Mount Airy and High Point, people asked whether the Salisbury-based company could ever handle more stores and put them in larger cities. Food Town answered that question with its first store in North Carolina's biggest city, Charlotte. Food Lion gradually became the top grocery store in the Charlotte and Greensboro/Winston-Salem markets, and today is the state's largest publicly held retailer.

Lion's Share

Then came the question: Could Food Lion manage its growth when it challenged entrenched competitors in other states? The answer, again, was yes. Now the doubters want evidence of Food Lion's ability to grow and compete in one of the bigger U.S. metropolitan markets. The company set out to prove that point in 1991. But it has been the sheer total of stores – and the scores of stores opening each year – that has scared even the loyal investors back home and raised the eyebrows of stock analysts and industry executives nationwide.

Food Lion went from 15 stores in 1971 to 30 by the end of 1975 – a 100 percent increase, even though it was only 15 additional stores. From 1983 to 1987, Food Lion increased its number of stores from 226 to 475 – more than a 100 percent increase, again, but this time the jump represented 249 new stores in a year's less time. By the end of the decade, Food Lion showed a net gain in a single year of 115 new stores, or the opening of one store every three days.

How can the grocery chain contend with such growth without a wheel coming loose, as it had for A&P? Low prices on dog food and the recycling of banana crates can't be the whole answer. Food Lion has always run into the assumption from doomsday outsiders that a company that starts out small and grows so fast has to hit a serious roadblock ahead. But the company's insiders have dispelled doubts of their own by recognizing that their system works. This system's main components include buying, merchandising, store location, distribution, training and incentives. Taken as a whole, it's a simple approach: Buy more for less and buy it all out of one location. Make stores convenient to the customer and in close proximity to warehouses. Teach an employee fast, so he can hit the ground running. Give management a reason to work hard. The basic structure was in place when Food Town had 50 stores, and it remains intact with Food Lion's 800 stores. Customers, employees and shareholders must know what to expect, so Food Lion keeps applying its successful formula day after day.

Jerry Helms, retired senior vice president and chief operating officer, recalled once how people asked, "How will you ever run 700 stores?"

"It's easy," he replied, "I don't know. We've never run 700." But it isn't something Food Lion's management frets about, because the company officers are never fearful of confronting a new company philosophy

. Their jobs stay well-defined.

"Owner-operated stores are successful, in part, because everyone understands how the boss wants things done, and complies," wrote William I. Walsh in his book, *The Rise and Decline of the Great Atlantic & Pacific Tea Company*. "Similarly, chains can be most successful when everybody understands the company policy and complies, when policy is respected as the corporate flag, when it reflects bedrock principles and not just this week's changes in management attitudes."

This employee confidence in the company's basics spills over into the stores. Customers will find that a Food Lion store in Winston-Salem, North Carolina, will look the same as one in Charleston, South Carolina, or Knoxville, Tennessee. And shoppers find reassurance in knowing grocery prices will be the same in every Food Lion they visit. The company does not adhere to "zone price" strategies. A shareholder finds comfort in knowing that Food Lion won't deviate from its all-out growth, thanks to the system it has in place.

"I think in the '70s we were looked on a little bit as a renegade because we were odd and different," Tom Smith says. "People still didn't think we'd make it. They thought it was a situation where maybe luck was carrying us, that we had overextended ourselves. In the '70s you'd always hear, 'Well, you've got 50 stores now, and that's good, but can you do this when you get 70 stores?' And then it would be, 'Can you do this when you get 100 stores?' There are certain things in which we proved ourselves, I believe."

Lion's Share

One of those things is buying. Suppliers, brokers and analysts consider Food Lion the best in the business. The two key ingredients are "forward buying" and "centralized buying," concepts Ralph Ketner practiced for Glenn Ketner's Excel Grocery Co. more than 35 years ago. Indeed, some people give Ketner credit for raising the concepts in the grocery industry to an art form.

Food Lion will buy bottles of ketchup by the train carload – months worth of ketchup for all of its stores – if it can strike a deal and take advantage of cash discounts. Once the product is bought at a deal price through this forward buying, the company will not have to buy it at the normal bracket price as long as it has a supply in its warehouses. The savings show up in prices on the shelves.

"Our forward buying has always been for the benefit of the consumer, never to make money." Ralph Ketner says. "But you make money by having the lower price and increasing sales. So my philosophy is to do things conducive to low prices and the sales increase will take care of the profit."

Food Lion takes advantage of the many, many trade promotions in the industry by allocating large working capital and lots of warehouse space to buying. It buys any item it finds a deal on, not just a selected few, and not just things that sell exceptionally fast. It thereby takes full advantage of the inefficiencies of the trade promotion system. Brokers and suppliers find it to their advantage because Food Lion buys in quantities never contemplated by other chains.

The company also seeks out deals on products it knows its customers want, rather than waiting for the manufacturer to make the first move. Again, manufacturers listen because of the volume Food Lion buys and sells. Individual buyers at Food Lion have tremendous leeway to sign for the big orders without consulting buying committees. The company may even drop a national brand item if it isn't on deal, and wait for the next deal. On the deals, Food Lion couldn't care less for the gifts that come with promotions – microwave ovens, televisions, trips. They tell salesmen they'd rather have a bigger cash break, although the vice presidents have been known to take a group vacation overseas at the expense of manufacturers.

The emphasis on "forward buying" is reflected in Food Lion's balance sheet. More than 85 percent of the current assets at the end of 1989 were taken up in inventories. The typical supermarket chains practice "turn buying" – buying enough to keep the shelves stocked. If competitors do practice "forward buying," they confine it only to the fastest-moving items.

Salesmen have mixed emotions about dealing with Food Lion. The strain of haggling with a Food Lion buyer is evident on their faces as they wait in the reception area at Food Lion headquarters. Sometimes it's a tortuously long wait for a few minutes with a buyer. The salesmen know they have to catch the buyers' attention. It's difficult to get a product into Food Lion, partly because the company carries limited lines. A Food Lion store may have one or two sizes on a product, not four or five.

Brokers and suppliers respect the company, however, because Food Lion stores move their products, give them good display and price and never ask for special favors – that is, nothing illegal. But the buyers are tough.

"The word 'tough' sounds mean," Tom Smith says. "I prefer to say they're good buyers and that they buy right for Food Lion. It doesn't mean that we take manufacturers, or that we're doing anything wrong. In fact, we work very closely with the manufacturers, but it takes a lot of work on the buyers' part. It isn't a matter of saying, 'We need some corn today, let's just buy it.' It's a matter of studying corn and seeing when is the right time to buy. Is this a good deal or should we wait or should we buy a lot? So it's a very intense job. And they're tough in that we expect a lot from manufacturers but, in turn, any manufacturer will tell you, 'Food Lion has tough buyers but we like to deal with them because they're fair and they move our product and when they say they'll do something, it happens.' So I hear 'tough buyers' more times used as a compliment than I do as a negative."

Ralph Ketner ran roughshod over brokers. To Ketner, the

secret in buying was selling. When he was still working for brother Glenn's Excel Grocery warehouse, Ketner struck a deal one day on strawberry preserves offered for $4.74 a case: 39-and-a-half cents a jar. Sitting in on the bargaining discussion was a broker and the president of the packing company.

"Jerry," Ketner said to the broker, "I'll take 1,000 cases and ship them all out to the stores. We'll sell them for 39 cents, won't make a penny, but I'll distribute them for you, if you'll sell them to me for $4.68."

"No, Mr. Ketner," the president said, "I won't take your deal."

Ketner moved toward the broker and said, "Jerry, would you mind introducing this gentleman. I got confused when you introduced me."

The broker told him the president's name.

"I got his name all right. His title got me messed up."

"I'm president," the man said.

Still looking at the broker, Ketner said, "Jerry, I'll take 1,000 cases for $4.68 a case."

"No, Mr. Ketner," the president said again.

"Jerry, you didn't tell me he married the boss's daughter. I'll take 1,000 cases for $4.68."

"No, Mr. Ketner."

"Well, Jerry, you didn't tell me that he inherited the company and that's how he got to be president."

"No, I didn't inherit the company," said the president, becoming even hotter under the collar as Ketner again said he'd take 1,000 cases at $4.68 a case. "Mr. Ketner, I don't know what's wrong with you, but you just can't understand I'm not taking it."

"I have to admit I'm kind of confused," Ketner said. "We established you're the president. We established you didn't marry the boss's daughter. We established you didn't inherit the company. With those three known factors, I've got a right, I think, to assume I'm talking to an intelligent person."

"Well, I'd like to hope you are," the president said.

"Well, I would, too. But you tell me what intelligent person turns down a thousand-case order. We're only six cents a case apart, at $60. With Uncle Sam's 50 percent tax bracket, that's $30 they want to pay. That leaves you $30. Now the State of Virginia says let me pay 7 percent. That's $2.10, so we're $27.90 apart on 1,000 cases, packed 12 to a case. I'm going to move 12,000 units for you for $27.90. Now you tell me what intelligent person would turn down your order?"

"Write up the damn order," said the exasperated president.

Centralized buying goes hand in hand with "forward buying." Food Lion buys groceries for all of its stores from its Salisbury headquarters, accounting for the tremendous volumes the chain can sometimes order for its nine distribution centers.

"When I used to work for my brother Glenn," Ralph Ketner says, "I used to think how stupid A&P, Winn-Dixie, Colonial and everybody was to have a buying office in every division in every community where they had a warehouse. My God, the figures – and this was before computers – the figures would tell you what the movement was. You don't need a buyer in South Carolina. Now I read the other day that Winn-Dixie is thinking about doing this (centralized buying). A&P is thinking about doing this. Thirty-five years ago – hell, any fool knows you ought to do it."

Again, it's a matter of efficiency, flying in the face of a longtime industry practice of decentralization. The brain trust in Salisbury makes all the major decisions on buying, pricing and merchandising. Store managers in 800 different stores aren't deciding how to merchandise product. The home office decides, freeing the managers to focus on staff and service. The same goes for price. The mix of groceries in stores is adjusted somewhat for regional preferences, but the allocation of space for vendors depends on a product's performance. On beer sales, for example, if the Budweiser distributor sells 50 percent of a store's beer he gets 50 percent of the shelf space.

When Food Lion built its warehouse in Petersburg, Virginia, it made little sense to Smith to have buyers in Salisbury and Petersburg. Consider the time one buyer spends studying one company's deals, advertising and future goals before he places his order for Food Lion. Why not have one person spend two hours doing the research rather than two people spending four hours?

A&P learned with its decentralization and the creation of up to 33 divisions that malaise set in. Restriction on the authority of executives out in the divisions led to new ways to pass the buck and blame others for failures. Turned loose from central control, weaker units failed. The company culture that used to be so well-defined for A&P became more like a confederation of tribes all marching to their own drum beats.

"A national chain, be it corporate like Sears or franchised like McDonald's, must retain central core policy control or risk losing the identity which brings it success," William Walsh wrote in analyzing A&P. "Policy is the heart without which a multi-linked corporate being cannot sustain life."

Smith gives an example of how the customer benefits from good buying and how the company widens the price difference between itself and competitors: "You add on to your spread by buying right. If we pay 90 cents for something, mark it up 10 percent, then we're at 99 cents. If somebody else pays a dollar for it, marks it up 10 percent, they're at $1.10. There's a 10 percent spread there, even though we got the same markup on it. You take your six or seven percent that our efficiency also saves and add on to it to get additional spread."

· · ·

In placing its stores, Food Lion took to heart the real estate adage of "location, location, location."

The modern Food Lion store typically covers 29,000 square feet, possibly up to 33,000 with a deli/bakery. This size of a store is big enough for one-store rural towns and small enough to saturate big cities in a way superstores cannot. While the trend has been toward large combination stores that cover an acre or more and rely on attracting customers from many miles away, Food

Lion sticks with its compact, mid-sized stores. Thus, Food Lions become neighborhood stores serving retail trade areas of fewer than 7,000 people, but they can afford smaller per-week volumes than larger stores. In 1990, Food Lion stores averaged $138,000 in sales per week. The philosophy: Three smaller stores conveniently located are better than one superstore that may be difficult to reach for a large segment of a city's population.

The smaller stores are cheaper for developers to build, and their size makes them easier fits into good locations that big stores have to decline because of the lack of space. Food Lion's "inkblot" formula for expansion during the 1970s and 1980s aimed at putting every store within a 200-mile radius of a distribution center. This saves money by reducing drive time. The inkblot strategy, until recently, had the growth rolling out from the edges while also filling in or "intensifying" the inkblot inside those boundaries. An example of what some competitors consider Food Lion's overkill: Salisbury, a city of only 24,000 people, has five Food Lions within its corporate limits. But placing new stores in the saturated areas allows them to come under the umbrella of print and television advertising already in place. Regional supervisors also can cover more ground without much more drive time of their own.

The stores have the same basic layout throughout the chain. Customers can expect to find the produce, meats, frozen foods, dairy products and groceries in about the same locations in each Food Lion. The merchandising sticks with groceries and stays away from luxuries such as lobster tanks, boutiques, hardware, pharmacies, clothing, fishing rods, videotapes, fancy imports or gourmet foods. Store decor is simple. Don't expect departments to be identified by expensive neon signs unless vendors paid for them.

Food Lion signs 20-year leases, and almost all of the new stores are placed in strip shopping centers, often with a drugstore as one of the tenants.

"The thing I think we do different from other grocery chains"

Tom Smith says, "is that we have been fortunate enough – guilty, or whatever word you use – in not jumping into a trend."

Food Lion stayed away from generic brands because they were poor quality products, or at least viewed that way by consumers. Only recently has Food Lion gone more into its own private label on products judged to be of high quality. The company also avoided going to scanners at the checkout stands in the beginning because management determined it would not pay for itself. "So we stayed off of it," Smith says, "whereas a lot of companies jumped on it and really ran their expenses up. Now we're getting into scanning because the savings are there."

When Food Lion was first attempting the warehousing and distribution of health and beauty aids, Smith traveled as far away as California to examine ways of handling the items at the distribution centers. The trend at the time was toward semi-automated and fully automated selection, but Smith noted that the highest number of items being pulled in an hour was 125. He knew that couldn't be efficient, so the Food Lion warehouse went with a strictly conventional setup in which employees managed to pull 325 pieces an hour. They later voted to increase that standard.

"Sometimes the economical way is to sort of go backwards based on technology and do it another way," Smith said. "When we were putting this warehouse up, there were completely auto-mated warehouses – warehouses that worked like a big vending machine. And I don't think any of them operate any more. It would have been very easy to say that's got to be the wave of the future, but I remember studying them. It would have cost us twice as much to operate."

Food Lion has not been conservative when it determines that an innovation can save time and money. It was one of the first grocery chains to be completely computerized. The grocery chain also has been innovative in its approach to labor. In the warehouse, Food Lion pays the employees who fill store orders based on productivity with no limit to their pay. The more items they pull, the more money they make. The chain demands certain minimum levels of productivity in the warehouses, stores and Salisbury headquarters. Baggers learn the two-hand method of packing. Stock boys must reload shelves at a rate of 50 cases an hour.

When Linda Ketner joined the company in the mid-1970s, her training department helped start a move toward labor scheduling. It determined for each store how many people were working at any particular hour of the day, then tried to schedule workers according to the hours they were needed. The scheduling has been modified through the years, but old-timers in the stores resented the interference with their work schedules.

"Where they might have 60 people at work on Fridays between 2 and 4, now it said they only needed 40," Ms. Ketner says. "So they started going, 'No, it's impossible. We can't do it.' Labor scheduling is used by supermarkets all across the United States now. Food Lion was one of the first. They schedule the labor according to the sales. Now a computer does it. We used to do it by hand."

Cashiers would be timed with a stopwatch to determine how fast they could average sending someone through the checkout line. "Then we started hiring cashiers based on how fast they could work," Ms. Ketner says. "Again, that's standard operating procedure for supermarkets, and we were one of the first to do it."

Ms. Ketner, who holds a degree in sociology of organization, talked her father into hiring her and establishing the company's training department.

In the earlier days of Food Town and even into the LFPINC era, a typical Food Town store manager joined the company as a bagger after dropping out of school. Through the years, he was promoted to stock boy, assistant produce manager, produce manager and assistant store manager. Within about 15 years, he became a store manager. He never really gained any experience in the meat department – few store managers came from that end of the business. He knew nothing about the warehouse. All of a sudden, the sleepy chain he works for takes off.

"So he winds up managing a business that may do $10 million

a year with a high school diploma, at most," Ralph Ketner says. "And so you were limited on what you had to work with. Nowadays we get these alert, sharp kids out of college, put them on a training program, and we don't care whether they've ever been in a grocery store."

As fast as Food Town was growing, the chain needed more people in management positions to be store managers or supervisors. With A&P's growth during its own heyday, a critical problem had been how to produce store managers on demand to run the thousands of "Economy Stores" spread out in 29 states. A&P's John Hartford devised a manual small enough to fit in a shirt pocket that explained rules for cleanliness, ordering, receiving, inventory control, pricing and how to control costs. The book also taught salesmanship, courtesy and a strict adherence to the company motto. For the time, it was the only means available to A&P to get its procedures across to new managers.

Ms. Ketner's department of three – herself, Jerry Franklin and Richard Torrence – began recruiting people removed from the grocery tradition. They enticed business majors from colleges and placed them into an accelerated program. "We wanted to be able to train someone to be a store manager within a year," Ms. Ketner says. "And that required partially an ability to learn quickly in an academic way instead of a hands-on way."

A trainee still received on-the-job training in each department but he also was poring over written material and videotapes in his free time. "We wrote it, and we worked with all the vice presidents and got all the things they wanted in it and made sure everything was framed as it should have been," Ms. Ketner recalls. "It was an industry that just hadn't been in touch with human resources, even though it's very human resource dependent. And it does have a tradition of using people and spitting them out. This was really a progressive step that Food Lion was taking to say, 'Hey, our labor cost is our highest cost of doing business. We should try to train, nurture and develop these people.' Food Lion, I think, was one of the earliest to recognize the importance of managing the human resource more effectively."

Tom Smith gained some valuable insights during his days with Del Monte, a company he considered at the forefront in training. "At the time," he says, "I saw a vast amount of the retailers that were not well-trained, a very poorly trained industry, the retail grocery industry. So one of my big goals when I came to Food Lion was, 'Let's get us a good training department together. We can set ourselves out separate from the others.' We started on that and we've just worked and worked and worked to get to the point that we offer to train anybody in our company. That's been one of the backbones that has carried us."

Early on, the program also allowed Food Town to train existing managers who were, in a way, victims of the old system. They often were afraid to challenge the way things were done in the meat department because they knew nothing about it. The meat manager used that to his advantage. By putting the store managers through the training program, it standardized operations and gave them hands-on experience in every facet of the operation, including meats. No longer could the meat manager pull the wool over the store manager's eyes.

The program is modular, designed for each section of a store. A trainee has to pass a test for each module. "If operations hadn't gone along with some of this stuff, we would have been in deep trouble," Ms. Ketner says. "Some of the ideas were quantum leaps for Food Lion."

The company started a library for continuing education. It has an extensive lending collection of audio training tapes and books that employees sign out on their free time. Completion of a certain number of training units (credits) becomes important information in employee evaluations and decisions on advancement.

"If you're growing at 110 stores a year, then the chance for advancement is great," Ralph Ketner says. "For every 10 stores, basically, we have a grocery supervisor, a meat supervisor and a perishable. So that's the equivalent of one for every three and a third stores. So you have about 35 new supervisors every new year. Well, Winn-Dixie may not have 35 supervisor positions open in five years. So your chance for advancement in our company is so great that people want to come work with us."

By 1991, Food Lion had 12,000 in its training program, and Linda Ketner's small training department had evolved into "organization development," complete with its own vice president, Vince Watkins. Director Mitch Yatsko considers the company's Management Succession Planning (MSP) program the cutting edge for the grocery industry. Rapid growth forces Food Lion to identify the right people with the right skills at the right time to step into management jobs. Smith, for one, still believes a Food Lion bagger can become president of the company some day. But if that happens, he will have traveled a somewhat different road than Smith took.

Store managers usually single out employees with potential and recommend them for manager positions. The MSP program then kicks in. The employee begins receiving management and technical training as he or she scales the ladder to store manager, supervisor, director, regional supervisor and beyond. Yatsko says the company has seen part-time baggers go through the company ranks to become regional supervisors responsible for 65 to 70 stores.

"I'm very anxious," Smith said in a 1990 interview with *The Salisbury Post,* "for the next president – I don't know whether it will be a bagger, it could be a cashier, it could be a stocker, it could be a meat cutter – to come from that type of background. My whole desire is that every vice president and every president of this company comes out of this company. And the reason I want that so much and would like for that person to have been exposed to all the jobs in the company is that they'll know Food Lion.

"I think it's so important – a company like this that is so efficient and so precise – that we know what it feels like to be that bagger and know what the difficulties are. So when you're here making decisions that affect that bagger, you've got a feel for baggers and whatever other jobs in the company."

The company depends heavily on psychological evaluations that measure the Food Lion personality. But other tools used for evaluations are career plans, computer tracking and efforts employees make at continuing education. The real opportunities in management come in operations, because of the number of stores being added each year. The ranks of store managers and store supervisors are growing rapidly. At headquarters, Food Lion usually has openings for computer specialists, buyers and people interested in real estate and construction management.

Even with the company's desire to promote from within, it has been forced to hire outside the company because of a five-year plan, launched in 1990, to grow by 20 percent a year. In recent times, up to 50 percent of new store management was coming from outside the company ranks.

Incentives for working Food Lion's long hours include some of the industry's best health insurance benefits, plus stock options and profit-sharing. These benefits allowed longtime Salisbury store managers Ronnie and Donnie Marsh to retire at age 44. The company's profit-sharing plan sets aside up to 15 percent of what an employee working 1,000 hours or more annually earns per year. The full amount has been placed in the plan since 1970. A cashier who makes about $16,000 a year could expect to have built up $236,000 in 20 years. A store supervisor making $41,000 a year could build up to $604,000 in profit-sharing after 20 years. A meat manager earning $37,000 a year could retire with a lump sum of $400,000; a store manager's total could reach as high as $700,000, depending on when he joined the company.

The plan has done well because 25 percent of it is invested in Food Lion stock.

The stock purchase and option plans serve as additional incentives throughout the ranks. On becoming a store manager, an employee is given the chance to buy 100 shares of the company stock over a five-year period. A supervisor is given the chance to buy 1,000 shares over five years. During a recent 10-year stretch, a store manager's original 100 shares grew to be worth $104,000; a supervisor's 1,000 shares ballooned to $1 million.

The stock option plans have made millionaires out of many of the vice presidents. Their salaries rank well with other executives in North Carolina. Jerry Helms had risen from a produce clerk in 1958 to a senior vice presidency and a salary well over $300,000 a year before retiring in 1991.

In retrospect, Tom Smith's breakfast meeting with Ralph Ketner those 20 years ago proved quite lucrative. Ketner followed through on the incentives he had offered. Smith, the first person to be given a stock option with the company, owned more than 2.6 million shares of Food Lion stock by the end of 1989. His annual salary had become more than a half-million dollars, buttressing John Hartford's long-ago observation that a businessman must grow to stay healthy.

18. Roll 'em

When the television camera's red light came on, an over-whelming feeling of deja vu swept over Ralph Ketner. He was suddenly a frozen, frightened student again, taking his public-speaking class for the fifth time back at Tri-State College in Indiana. That red light came on and Ketner forgot that he was president of a fast-growing grocery chain recording his first television commercial in an Atlanta studio.

Ketner knew what he wanted to say but stumbled over the sentences. If he could tell every person face to face why Food Town would save them money on groceries, he'd be great. But the nameless, faceless audience behind that camera was unforgiving. Every second seemed an eternity.

Ketner had been selling the LFPINC concept for 10 years before he walked in front of that television camera. One evening years earlier while playing bridge with regular partners John Hartlege, Jim Summers and Eddie Post, Ketner noticed that Hartlege was serving instant coffee from a competitor's store.

"John, I didn't know you were a wealthy person," Ketner said.

"I'm not," Hartlege answered.

Ketner had hooked him and their audience of two.

"Well, you can afford not to trade at Food Town," Ketner continued. "It's obvious you must be wealthy, if you can afford that luxury."

"How do you know I don't trade at Food Town?" Hartlege wanted to know.

"You paid 60 cents more for this instant coffee than we sell it for. I don't know where you bought it, but I know where you didn't buy it."

At the bridge club, Ketner could have passed for a preacher giving a Sunday morning sermon to a packed house. He spoke to his bridge partners like a wheeling, dealing car salesman. But Ketner couldn't bring that ease of delivery to the television camera. Stiff – that's what he was. Stiff as a board. He spent nearly four hours on his first commercial and all of the takes were lousy. Ketner had had enough with himself and the television camera.

"When I left the office this morning," he told the crew around him, "I was president. Unless somebody fired me, I am still president, and nobody can fire me. So hell, I'm president, and I'm telling you now that I'm not doing any more commercials. Either take one of the ones I've done, or forget it."

Shortly after that first commercial appeared on television with its high-pitched, nasal introduction of "Hi, I'm Ralph Ketner," a woman spotted the company president in one of his grocery stores.

"You're Ralph Ketner, aren't you?" she asked. "I want to tell you how much I appreciate your coming across so truthfully on TV."

Ketner began to think maybe he hadn't been so lousy after all.

"Anybody who looks as bad on TV as you do wouldn't be on there if he weren't telling the truth," the woman added.

Ketner smiled, but inside his ego was crumbling. "Lady," he said, "you know how to take away a compliment before it settles in."

Only prodding from daughter Linda had provoked Ketner to try television in the first place.

"I hated them with a passion," Ketner says about the commercial taping sessions. "God, I hated them. I'd rather work a week than do one. That camera, if you say 'uh' or take one second too long, you have to do it over again."

Food Lion hired Tom Crabtree in 1980 as vice president of advertising, and he inherited his reluctant actor. Crabtree tried not to offend his boss by telling him he was lousy. "Mr. Ketner, that was good but ..." he would say, adding some advice about how to improve the next take. Ketner, growing more exasperated with every minute, didn't want it sugarcoated. "Tom, if you tell me ever again that was good, but ... damn, if I'm not going to fire you. You get my hopes up and then you put them down. Start off with, 'Mr. Ketner, that was another lousy one. We'll do another one.' Then I'll understand."

Ketner had always enjoyed tweaking the competition's nose in his newspaper advertisements. He was especially good at taking a competitor's claim and twisting it inside out, much the way he had given his own interpretation to his father's "I don't care what you do" statement when he was a kid wanting to walk a cow to the Rimertown farm.

There was a time when most of his competitors were sponsoring games to attract customers. Ketner ran a newspaper advertisement telling shoppers that if they wanted to play games, they had a better chance at winning in Las Vegas. At Winn-Dixie, for example, he figured out that the chances for winning a $2,000 cash prize were one in every 255,111 visits to the store. Shoppers could count on winning that $2,000 once every 4,905 years of weekly shopping. "If you were shopping 3,000 years before Christ," his advertisement said, "it was your turn to win."

A&P claimed it had the 'lowest overall prices." Ketner responded by running an ad with a large picture of a pair of overalls next to the words, "A&P claims they have the lowest overall prices. Food Town doesn't sell overalls, so we don't know if their claim is true. But we do know that Food Town has the lowest FOOD prices. If you need overalls, go to A&P. If you need food, come to Food Town."

Another competitor, Lowe's, liked to boast that it had the "Lowest Prices Anywhere." Food Town answered with an ad showing a map of the Earth and asking the consumer to find Anywhere. The ad ended, "For the lowest prices in North Carolina, South Carolina, Virginia, or Georgia, come to Food Town."

In the early 1960s, Food Town bought five train carloads of

dry dog food. Though it paid the same price as other stores – $2.07 per 25-pound bag – Food Town sold the dog food for $1.99 a bag, taking an eight-cent loss on every sale. The competition sold the same bag for $3.99. Food Town suggested customers take the $2 savings on dog food and put it toward a T-bone steak for the dog's owner. More than a few customers did exactly that.

Not every advertising tactic worked. In August 1981 Food Town dropped a two-day-old campaign offering cash to customers who could find lower grocery prices elsewhere. The company canceled newspaper advertisements saying, "Food Town wants to bet you 5 to 1 that you cannot buy groceries for less anywhere." A similar ad was broadcast on radio, promising to pay five times the difference between the price of 20 items bought at Food Town and the same items bought elsewhere. A woman from Charlotte received a check for $89.55 from Food Town after paying $115.78 for groceries she could have purchased at 3 Guys Ltd. for $17.91 less. Her neighbor claimed a check for $54 before the campaign was scrubbed.

Food Lion steadily moved away from specifics in its ads to the broad strokes of selling its concept. And in the move, it has filtered more and more money toward television.

Ketner eventually took to his television role and came up with his own ideas. He decided to offer his personal check for $3 to anybody who shopped at Food Lion, spent at least $15 and felt he didn't save money.

He opened a checking account and had a form letter saying "Enclosed is my $3 ..." and the letters started coming in. "Then I realized," Ketner says, "that just because these people are wrong, you don't want to give them $3. And so I changed the letter. I started off, 'You're entitled to my check for $3. Now, I want to tell you some of the comments from our customers.' " His letter included testimonials about Food Town having the lowest prices and the results of a survey from the North Carolina Food Dealers revealing that Food Town was lower on 97 percent of a 300-item list that had been surveyed.

Rather than sending the people $3 cash, Ketner sent them a $4 gift certificate. "If you still want your $3 back," he wrote, "send me the $4 gift certificate back. But you owe it to yourself to try us."

It was a lesson that Ketner had learned from brother Glenn. "If you're going to make something good, start off with it and then ask the questions," Ketner says. "It would have been easier for me to start off trying to explain and not give them the money. You don't want to try and fool people. Hell, tell them the truth. People will beat us on some features, but we're looking at your total bill."

Food Town once hired actor Mason Adams as its pitchman. Adams was the solid-citizen managing editor from the popular early-'80s "Lou Grant" television series. He told a *Salisbury Evening Post* reporter he liked the Food Town commercials because they were straightforward, without gimmicks.

But Food Town management didn't like one aspect of the plugs by Adams. "I was shocked at that time what it cost us," says Tom Smith, who had just become president of the chain. The Food Town brain trust was worried, too, about having a professional actor sell its groceries. Why should anybody believe Mason Adams? He was just being paid to say some lines on television.

Management decided no more actors would be telling the public about Food Town. It should be an officer of the company speaking for the company. It suggested commitment and sincerity, even if he wasn't professional. By early 1984, Smith inherited the job, and began looking for new ways to sell the concept.

"The thing we wanted to do when we got into low pricing was to tell people, 'Look, we've got low prices all throughout the store,' and you really can't do that much by putting a couple of prices down," said Smith. "Everybody says they're the lowest, everyday supermarket. So we felt that we had to give people reasons to see that we were lower."

Tom Crabtree, who had his own ad agency in St. Louis before joining Food Town, also gave birth to other commercials – sans Ketner or Smith – that always seemed to have an amusing touch, while pushing Food Town's low prices.

Lion's Share

Winner of several industry awards, Crabtree wrote commercials about an animated clay Food Lion super hero who came to the rescue of a woman customer held prisoner in a high-priced supermarket. Crabtree starred in one advertisement himself in which he told the audience that "saving money on groceries is serious business" – all the while someone is drawing over his face on the television screen with a black grease pencil. Benny the Butcher told viewers about a Food Lion pamphlet on nutritional meats and recipes in the 1950s style of the "Dragnet" police series.

By not spending his whole career in the grocery business, Crabtree brought a different perspective to his job. "It's not hard to do TV," Crabtree said once. "Any 10-year-old can write a TV commercial. They know how to do the expected. We try to do the unexpected. Try to show the marketable difference in an unexpected way. Kroger has 'Cost Cutter;' Winn-Dixie has '10,000 low prices.' Nobody believes you have the lowest prices unless you tell them why."

Sticking to its cost-conscious philosophy, Food Lion determined that its own in-house production of television commercials would cost less. The company recoups the 15 percent commission it might pay on contract with an outside agency. Traditionally, Food Lion has spent a third to a half of one percent of sales on advertising – about a fourth of the industry average. A typical television spot for the company in 1987 cost $6,000.

Some Food Lion ads are common-sense, straightforward descriptions about how recycling cardboard and having computers turn off lights in empty rooms save the company millions of dollars a year. Others feature lighter, humorous touches with the increasingly more polished Smith as the star.

One ad featured Smith explaining how Food Lion saved money by doing its own commercials. As he talked, the commercial purposely exaggerated the homemade aspect of production. A clock fell off the wall. The camera swiveled wildly as Smith attempted to turn with it. Finally, the film broke and flapped to the end.

Smith has been featured as everything from a tap dancer to a basketball player competing against the amateurish efforts of the competition's weekend specials and come-ons. A 1991 script for a Food Lion television advertisement often seen during ACC basketball games or during the local evening news is typical:

The scene: *Outside a Food Lion store. At the front door, employees on a ladder are struggling to put up an anniversary sign with the dates, 1957-1991.*

Tom Smith *(speaking from the parking lot of the store)*: "Don't make plans to attend Food Lion's 34th anniversary sale. We're not having one. We're not having a Fourth of July sale. Or a Labor Day sale, either. Matter of fact, at Food Lion, we never have a sale. That's because these customers *(by now, a swarm of customers are heading for the front door of the Food Lion)* don't like saving a few cents on a few items a few days out of the year. They want extra low prices on all their groceries every day of the year. *(The crowd has continued to get larger. Smith has been picked up by two burly guys moving toward the store with their backs toward the camera.)* That's why almost seven million *(he's shouting now)*, I said, seven million customers shop at Food Lion each week. They don't like sales, either!" *(He has been carried away into the store. The Food Lion logo then appears on the scene with the words, "Extra Low Prices, Everyday!")*

The hardest thing to do is relax, says Smith, who fought early on to control his eyebrows. "They used to travel about five inches up and down his face," a crew member once said, "and now they're only a few inches."

Trying to look easy and natural in a commercial is what makes it so difficult. "It really works on people," Smith says, "and I know you think, 'Thirty seconds, that's not much.' But the thing that people don't realize who have never done a commercial is when you've got to say it in 30 seconds, every word has to get in there, and every word pretty well has a meaning, and it's got to fit. A lot of times, it doesn't flow like regular conversation. You've got to be ready for somebody to say, 'Now, we want you to speed up a little bit, slow down over here, want you to smile there, want you to hesitate here, want you to look at this person over here. And besides that we want you to be walking sideways because that looks right on camera.' "

Smith has even included his mother in one television spot about Food Lion's adding a motorized shopping cart in each store for people who have difficulty walking. Mrs. Smith hot rods around the store like a race car driver before crashing into a display, as the company president stands helplessly in front of the camera.

The tap-dancing commercial proved to have a longer life than most. A piano plays "Yankee Doodle Dandy" as the camera shows a woman's feet in red and white tap shoes with the Bi-Lo logo prominently on the sides. She and other dancers wearing shoes from A&P, Winn-Dixie, Piggly-Wiggly, Harris Teeter and Kroger appear in succession, all plodding along out of step.

A voice off camera says, "A lot of supermarkets go through a song and dance each week to get customers. But some of their routines just don't work. They get out of line with high food prices. Try to cover up with a few fancy weekly specials. Or get out of step with gimmicks like games or double coupons."

(Now, on stage, come the shoes of a good tap dancer, a man, whose blue and yellow shoes display the Food Lion logo. The voice continues:)

"But there's one supermarket whose extra low prices have been getting rave reviews from critics for years now. Food Lion. Catch our act."

(The camera cuts to a shadow of a dancer with top hat, cane and tails. It's Tom Smith, who finishes his dance with a showman's bow.)

At Christmas, Smith is seated in a den beside a Christmas tree when a Food Lion animated clay character developed by John

Lemmon of Charlotte comes down the chimney as Santa Claus. Smith tries to give a serious Christmas wish to all of Food Lion's customers as the lion gets a claw caught in Smith's sweater and begins pulling a thread. Soon one of his sweater's arms is gone. Smith ends the commercial with a Christmas wish and a warning to watch out for "Santa's claws."

An example of a Food Lion educational commercial is made at a Food Lion warehouse on the subject of recycling cardboard. "Who says money doesn't grow on trees?" Smith asks. "It does at Food Lion, beginning at the cardboard baler in every Food Lion store. It takes a lot of timber to make a bale like this, so we send it back here to the warehouse. Last year, we sold almost 100,000 tons of cardboard and paper from our office and stores for recycling. That amounted to almost $5 million. A big savings on your grocery bill and a big savings on our forest lands. Because at Food Lion, when we save, you save. And so does our environment."

Of course, the competition doesn't allow Food Lion's commercial claims to go unchallenged. Harris Teeter disputed the recycling commercial with a radio spot that claimed Food Lion's big savings are as big a myth as Paul Bunyan dragging his pick ax to form the Grand Canyon. "Tom Smith," the commercial voice says, "wants you to believe that recycling cardboard will save the environment and lower the national debt and save you money on your grocery bill. Everybody recycles cardboard, Tom."

Because Food Lion commercials are seen during Atlantic Coast Conference basketball games, Smith has become easily recognized throughout the region. His resemblance to former University of Virginia basketball coach Terry Holland also helped people associate Smith and Food Lion with the popular sport. The exposure has caused Smith to be stopped on the streets of San Francisco and in the hills of Scotland by customers who happened to be visiting those places when Smith was there.

Then again, there are places where Smith is a stranger. Food Lion went into Kentucky and saw that its prices were considerably lower overall than the competition, but sales didn't reach expectations. "I was really surprised," says Smith, "Gosh, the price spreads were so far apart. So we had to get started, and one of the ways we do use print is with price comparisons. Here's what they've got; here's what we've got. People in Kentucky were looking at the lowest price on big items, and that's how they chose their supermarkets. So we've got to break that habit. When we got there, the competition went boom, boom, boom with low prices on a few items, so it made the educational process a little tougher, because you had to say, 'Forget about what you've been used to and look at this concept.' "

The problems in Kentucky were minor compared to the reception Food Lion received in Tennessee. The grocery chain was regarded as an outsider and rumors spread that Food Lion was owned by communists and that the tail of the lion in the store's logo had something to do with Satanism. A gas station attendant spotted the Food Lion logo on the front of a company supervisor's car and refused to pump any gas for him. Something had to be done before the damage was irreversible. In this isolated case, Food Lion deserted its anti-celebrity philosophy and went looking for a face familiar to all Tennesseans.

Crabtree courted Minnie Pearl of the Grand Ole Opry and hired her for $15,000 to do a dozen commercials for Food Lion in Tennessee. Everybody knew and felt at home with Minnie Pearl's traditional "Howdy!" salutation. The fear of Satanism dissipated. Food Lion could go on with the business of selling groceries.

19. Breaking new ground

It was hot, even by Florida standards, on August 16, 1987, when Food Lion's first three stores in Jacksonville opened their doors. With the thermometer pushing 100 degrees and humidity making it feel even hotter, shoppers lined up outside the new stores to see for themselves what all the hullabaloo was about.

The most popular guys in town this day were the Pepsi representatives giving away free samples to those waiting outside. Security officers kept people in line, allowing a batch to enter as others left.

"There could be little doubt that something unusual was happening here when the Food Lion stores opened," *Supermarket News* reported. "Although they offered nothing unusual in size at 25-29,000 square feet – and nothing in service departments apart from a deli in two of the stores – shoppers by the hundreds besieged the stores on opening day and for several days thereafter."

Food Lion's founders had looked forward to this day. They were opening stores in Winn-Dixie's backyard, challenging the big chain that they believed had once tried to run them into bankruptcy. They have maintained that the move into Florida was nothing personal against Winn-Dixie. The cold-blooded Food Lion chain intended to slice itself as big a piece of the Florida pie as it could, grabbing business from anybody.

Florida was the new frontier in the '80s. It had already been discovered by Safeway Stores, Kroger, Lucky and Pueblo International. Eight hundred people a day were moving to Florida, making it the third fastest-growing state in the Union behind New Hampshire and Arizona. The state's population was expected to climb from 12.5 million to 15 million by the end of the century. "Any operator who builds a store can be sure there'll be a residential area nearby soon," said William Weaver, president of the Florida Retail Grocers Association. No longer a haven for retirees, Florida claimed three million people in the 25-44 age range, the money-spending baby boomers.

For Food Lion, Jacksonville was just part of its inkblot strategy down the Southeast's coast. Food Lion had grown to a 500-store chain by oozing stores across the landscape, much the way spilled ink moves across paper. Food Lion's Vince Watkins, vice president for special projects and development, said the company liked Jacksonville because of its strong economy and the presence of the military. The hub of the north Florida operation was already under construction – a million square foot distribution center in Green Cove Springs, just outside Jacksonville.

Winn-Dixie was getting nervous about Food Lion's entry into Florida . The market-share leader with 25 percent of the region's sales, it had the most to lose. Winn-Dixie had just acquired 30 stores from Super Valu in Jacksonville in a deal that included a 400,000-square-foot warehouse.

Food Lion had figures that showed Jacksonville's grocery prices to be the seventh-highest in the state, and the chain launched a nine-month barrage of television commercials announcing that its arrival would cause competitors to lower prices. Winn-Dixie countered with an ad depicting garbage men tossing the nameplates of failed competitors on a scrap heap. The ad ended with Winn-Dixie proclaiming itself "unbeatable."

With Ralph Ketner setting the precedent, Food Lion has never been reluctant to single out the competition in advertisements. When the company was expanding into Florida, it went on television with a buggy of groceries. "You can buy these groceries at Winn-Dixie for $114 in the Carolinas," the ad said. "Here they cost $158."

It's a theme Food Lion uses to its advantage: Grocery prices are lower in stores in every town that has a Food Lion. Tom Smith often ends similar ads with: "We just wanted you to know who lowered your grocery bill."

Winn-Dixie took the bait and lowered all its prices in Jacksonville just before Food Lion opened. And there was Smith, taking the credit on TV commercials while noting that Winn-Dixie was still charging the same old, higher prices in Atlanta where it had no competition from Food Lion. Winn-Dixie insisted it lowered prices in response to all its competition – not Food Lion. But the damage was done.

"Winn-Dixie's claim of low prices in Jacksonville is nothing new," Smith said in one commercial. "They've been making the same claim where they compete with Food Lion for years now. A Winn-Dixie shopper here in Jacksonville who usually spends $100 each week for groceries has been paying $14 more each week than a Winn-Dixie shopper in North and South Carolina. Fourteen dollars more each week! Aren't you glad Food Lion's coming to town?"

Within nine months an industry study found an overall grocery price decline of up to 6 per cent in Jacksonville, according to *Food People*, a grocery industry publication. Food Lion captured 2.4 per cent of the market share in its first year with Winn-Dixie leading the area with 36 per cent.

"Winn-Dixie is currently a vulnerable company," Ken Gassman Jr. of Wheat, First Securities in Richmond, Virginia, told *The Greensboro News & Record* in 1987. "The market has become far more segmented. Winn-Dixie is still trying to be everything to everybody. You have to pick and choose your niche. That's what Food Lion has done a really great job of."

By mid-1991, Food Lion had 37 stores in Jacksonville and had advanced to third in the market with a 14 percent share of the business.

Food Lion, meanwhile, continued to push into Florida. It bought five Florida Choice Food and Drug stores around Daytona

Beach in February 1988 from Kroger and converted them to its cookie-cutter format by removing the pharmacies and other expensive service departments. As Florida's population continued its shift from the heavily Hispanic southern areas to the central cities of Tampa and Orlando, Food Lion planned a new warehouse in Plant City, Fla., and announced plans to have 1,000 supermarkets across the Southeast.

As Food Lion moved into Tampa Bay, its biggest competition was Kash 'n' Karry, a company that had staked out the low-price image and top sales figures. Food Lion concentrated on getting convenient locations for its neighborhood stores, serving a retail trade area of fewer than 7,000 people.

But while the competition couldn't slow Food Lion's growth, the State of Florida put on the brakes. Tough laws regarding construction and public services were passed by the Florida legislature. The state was growing too fast. The laws meant that it would take Food Lion 18 months to get a new store site approved, as opposed to about 12 months elsewhere. Industry analysts speculated that Food Lion would have to change its format to keep growing.

Tim Simmons of *Supermarket News* wrote in 1989 that Food Lion would have to come up with stores offering more "services and higher margins for value-added products." In other words: raise prices. "Since Food Lion's hunger for growth is unlikely to be sated, it seems inevitable that the company will venture into new territories and new formats."

Simmons proved half right. Food Lion wouldn't change the format of low-price appeal developed for rural Southern towns. It would find new territory. Though it already had plans for a new distribution center in Greencastle, Pennsylvania, to open territories in central Pennsylvania and western Maryland, it was time to take Horace Greeley's advice: Go west.

In the company's boldest expansion move ever, Smith announced April 10, 1990, that Food Lion would move into the Dallas-Fort Worth area with 40 stores and a warehouse by the fall

226

of 1991. It seemed like the right move. A growing company needs room to grow, and Food Lion needed a new challenge.

The north Texas region around Dallas already had 874 super-markets for its seven million people. Don Smith, executive director of the Austin-based Texas Food Industry Association, said he was "appalled and surprised" by Food Lion's decision to enter Texas.

There were factors in Food Lion's favor. The Texas economy had just suffered through an extended recession, but analysts believed that it was ready to rebound. The real estate market was attractive. Food Lion representatives caught a lot of Texans off guard when they began asking about potential store sites in an area littered with abandoned, bankrupt strip shopping centers.

Food Lion's plans for Dallas-Fort Worth didn't include the frontal assault that it used against Winn-Dixie in Jacksonville, Florida. Texans didn't know Tom Smith, and the company didn't want to come on too strong with its low-price pitch, fearing that people would equate low prices with warehouse grocery operations.

The Texas advantage that Food Lion saw for itself was that its stores could be placed near residential communities. Many of the big stores in Dallas are located at main artery locations as much as seven miles from customers. The leading competitors include three chains with leveraged-buyout debt: Tom Thumb, Skaggs/ Alpha Beta and Kroger. Grocery prices in the Dallas-Fort Worth market were as much as 20 percent higher than those Food Lion charges, and it would be difficult for the stores with big debt to cut prices.

"Food Lion's presence in this market will save every man, woman and child in the Metroplex more than $100 per year on their grocery bill," Smith said in a story in the *Texas Food Merchant,* a publication of the Texas Food Industry Association.

The only nagging concern for Food Lion about its entry into Texas was gaining acceptance. Industry analysts claim that Food Lion's style has its limits. Will people in a metropolitan area be satisfied with lower prices? Texans are less willing than Northeasterners to sacrifice variety and service for price, one analyst said. Food Lion plans to make the convenience of its stores in and around Dallas as big a selling point as low prices. 7-Eleven, the convenience store chain, had an 11 percent share of the Dallas-Fort Worth grocery market before Food Lion arrived.

Robert Dietz, columnist for the *Dallas Times Herald*, said that Cullum Company's Tom Thumb-Page food and drug chain would be Food Lion's principal target in Dallas, but the local stores have worked hard on serving individual neighborhoods. "It's no accident that in the Love Field area Cullum operates a high-end Simon David store stocked with gourmet foods demanded by an affluent Park Cities population, while less than two miles away is a Tom Thumb store offering fajita-cut meats and low-priced rice and beans that are the staples of the heavily Hispanic adjacent neighborhoods. And only a couple miles from that store is an Oak Lawn unit that sells a large variety of health foods demanded by aging Turtle Creek yuppies seeking to stay fit if not young." Dietz says that it won't be easy for Food Lion to learn the eccentricities of the Dallas neighborhoods. Food Lion officials say they won't have to. All their stores are the same.

PaineWebber retail supermarket analyst Gary Gilben of Houston says, "Cullum is pretty well established as a hometown chain – and that's going to be hard for Food Lion to overcome." Still, Cullum is carrying $424 million in long-term debt from management's buyout of the business in late 1988.

Food Lion projected 80 stores for Dallas-Fort Worth, and began plotting which way to expand: north to Oklahoma, south to Houston, or east toward Shreveport, La.

"With their operating strategy," said analyst Ed Comeau of Oppenheimer and Co. in New York, "they can open stores wherever they want and still make money."

20. Thorns in the Lion's paw

"When we started in this industry," says Dewey Hill, chairman of Hill Food Stores, a 31-store chain in Whiteville, North Carolina, "there was a Food Lion. But it was called A&P."

A&P's tumble from the top of the industry heap has been blamed on a variety of problems. But they all go back to one: A&P got too big to be concerned about details. It was expanding so fast that existing stores were allowed to fall into disrepair. Wages to unionized workers ran costs up and to save money the workforce was cut. Shoppers were left waiting in the checkout line while a couple of harried bag boys tried to assist half a dozen cashiers. The careful attention to low prices – the bedrock of the A&P philosophy – softened.

Could the same things happen to Food Lion, despite its attention to the crucial elements of pricing, "forward buying," centralized control, distribution, training, incentives and efficiency?

Some obstacles loom like possible thorns in the Lion's paw. They include aging stores, customer expectations, expanding product lines and labor demands.

Every Food Lion store is modernized after 10 years. Food Lion uses a new technique to put new shelving on top of old shelves to make the process faster and less expensive. The company's standard lease is for 20 years, and once a lease expires a store is usually remodeled or moved to a better location.

Tom Smith says convenience has become a customer's chief concern after price. "And we offer convenience in quite a number of ways," he says. "One way is that we locate frequently. We work on convenience by sticking strictly to groceries so people don't have to shop through a bunch of other stuff to get to groceries. We think having a good-sized store, but not a monster where people have to walk so long, is convenient."

Convenience takes the form of two express lanes for customers. Plenty of cashiers man the checkout lanes, and bag boys continue to load groceries into customers' cars. Computers fill slots at the front of stores for cashiers to quickly check the prices of unmarked merchandise. Scanners in new stores have speeded up the checkout process.

Food Lion's competition in Dallas is claiming that the invader will suffer if its stores won't carry certain regional favorites. But, as tastes have changed and new products have flooded the market, Food Lion has expanded its line of groceries to as many as 16,000 items. (Competitors' bigger stores have 20,000 or more.) Smaller stores in the Food Lion network have had to stretch their aisles, deepen their shelves and triple-deck their meat cases. Upright door cases for frozen foods have replaced the open, coffin-like frozen food cases. Customers have been offered more oat bran cereals, specialty breads, bottled water, low-calorie frozen foods and microwave products.

Demand for more convenience foods, as well as more fresh produce, puts additional pressure on Food Lion's low-price philosophy, competitors say. "I think Food Lion is beginning to change its policy because it is finding that the competition is beating it by offering variety," the president of a Southern grocery chain told *Supermarket News*. The weekly publication, based in New York, ran a front-page story in 1989 titled, "Food Lion's Changing Course," in which it suggested that the company "may be moving upscale in a way that would be counter to its ultrasimple philosophy of operating small conventional stores in small towns – stores that offer the lowest prices in a relatively narrow product range."

As evidence, the publication said the chain was moving

toward bigger stores, more groceries, more private label, more scanners, more deli-bakeries, more frozen foods and expanded produce. Tom Smith didn't appreciate the implications that Food Lion was deserting its basic philosophy.

"I was quite shocked when I read your article," Smith wrote the editor. "If the article had not mentioned Food Lion, I would never have recognized that the article applied to Food Lion." He continued that the story was misleading, inaccurate and a disservice to the company.

Kay Norwood, an oft-quoted securities analyst with Interstate/Johnson Lane of Charlotte, said Food Lion is obliged to move not only toward more products but toward higher priced products as well: "Food Lion's reasoning is that since people are working more and buying more frozens, and especially convenience foods, Food Lion must offer more to maintain market lead. It's simply offering what the customers want."

Lee Wilder, analyst at Robinson-Humphrey Co., Atlanta, contends that Food Lion will have to offer more costly perishables to stay competitive. "I see Food Lion expanding produce, seafood and poultry," he said. "A few years ago poultry only meant dead birds, but today there's a whole range of products. New products are always coming out, and there are categories today that did not exist five years ago."

Another analyst who follows Food Lion suggests that the cookie-cutter stores won't work in areas as diverse as Pennsylvania and Texas. "Food Lion may run into its problems as it enters a more heterogeneous environment" analyst Gary Giblen said. "Diversity in stores means extra costs. Although I expect the firm to perform well, I see its prospects being less exciting than before, and the future won't be quite as rosy."

Tom Smith tells his people "You're either getting better or falling behind." He drives himself relentlessly and expects the same from others as he looks for ways to continue to grow and stay profitable. Speaking at a business symposium at Catawba College in 1990, Smith said Food Lion's success hinges on six ingredients:

training, incentives, finance, distribution, management and phi-losophy. If it can do those six things right, sales will hit $14 billion by 1995, he said.

"These boys from North Carolina are hard-driving operators," said *Growth Stock Outlook* in 1989. "We compare them to Wal-Mart. In the years ahead, we suspect that Food Lion might well become the biggest supermarket chain in the U.S."

That hard-driving style doesn't suit everyone. Labor organi-zations have jumped at the opportunity to criticize Food Lion in hopes of sparking enough internal debate to lead to a union vote some day. But the union denies it's in an organizing posture when it comes to Food Lion.

Food Lion wants to keep labor unions at bay. Before its expansion into Dallas-Fort Worth, the company had avoided metropolitan areas and their union pressures. Ketner's philoso-phy: Union wage scales increase the price of groceries. Food Lion's own insatiable need for qualified employees drives its pay scale and, the company believes, makes its wages competitive.

The United Food and Commerical Workers distributed leaf-lets when Food Lion opened some stores in Virginia, contending the Salisbury, North Carolina firm pays 15 to 40 percent less for labor than competitors. Mike Earman, then special assistant to the president and director of membership administration and training for UFCW Local 400, said the company's profits stem in part from a high turnover rate, which keeps the employees from obtaining benefits. This claim later manifested itself in a union-supported suit against Food Lion that could have significant implications.

The union filed the suit on behalf of Rickey Bryant, who was fired from his job as assistant manager at a Food Lion store in West Columbia, South Carolina. It charges the company with an illegal scheme to deny employees profit-sharing and health benefits. Bryant, a nine-year employee, was fired in March 1988 for "gross misconduct" after receiving three unsatisfactory performance reports within a few months. Employees fired for gross miscon-duct are not allowed extended health benefits. Bryant, who would have been fully vested in the profit-sharing program and eligible to receive $67,000 by the end of 1988, was able to collect only $30,150 under the terms of the plan. The remaining $36,850 was reallocated to the accounts of the remaining plan participants. Food Lion called the suit "just one more attempt by the United Food and Commercial Workers Union to harass and pressure Food Lion into recognizing the union without regard to employee sentiments in the matter."

Diana Henriques wrote in *The New York Times* April 22, 1990, that Wall Street had virtually ignored the unflattering and troublesome union lawsuit against Food Lion. "Litigation, of course, is long and Wall Street's attention span is notoriously short," The Times said. "Still it's hard to understand why the Food Lion case has gotten so little notice on the Street."

David H. Grigereit, an attorney with the Arnold & Anderson law firm in Atlanta, says Wall Street simply recognizes the case has no merit. The Atlanta attorneys work for Food Lion.

"The UFCW claim that Food Lion had a scheme to fire its employees to deny them profit-sharing money is absurd on its face," Grigereit says. "If Food Lion management didn't want employees to get profit-sharing money, they wouldn't have to have a profit-sharing plan. In fact, during the year that Rickey Bryant was discharged less than 50 employees were fired who would otherwise have vested 100 per cent in the profit-sharing plan at the end of that year. What the union ignores, however, is that at the end of that year, several thousand employees remained employed with Food Lion and did vest 100 percent in the plan."

The attorney for Food Lion says the union claim that the profit-sharing plan is designed to benefit top executives is equally absurd. More than 75 percent of the Food Lion employees 100 percent vested in the plan are hourly employees. In 1990, the company had 21,945 employees participating, and the plan paid out more than $25 million to qualified employees and their dependents.

The union filed a grievance in 1986 with the U.S. State

Department, charging that Delhaize, the Belgian company that owns a majority of Food Lion's voting stock, had violated standards of the Organization of Economic Cooperation and Development. Started principally as a vehicle for international economic development, the OECD subjects member nations to fair business practice laws. The grievance said that Delhaize has violated those standards because Food Lion uses its advantages in labor costs to drive competitors out of markets it enters. The union's goal was to apply pressure to Delhaize in Belgium, forcing it to apply pressure to Food Lion in the United States.

The general secretary for the International Federation of Commercial, Clerical, Professional and Technical Employees acted on behalf of the UFCW in a June 20, 1989, letter to Guy Beckers, then chief executive officer of Delhaize: "It is clear to us," the letter said on behalf of it UFCW affiliate, "that the best overall strategy for Food Lion would be to negotiate the recognition of the United Food and Commercial Workers International Union."

"Any such 'negotiated' recognition without regard to employees sentiments," Grigereit says, "would be unfair labor practice under U.S. law and would flagrantly violate Food Lion employees' freedom of choice."

The UFCW also has participated with a Belgian union official in strikes against Delhaize in Belgium. Grigereit says the UFCW acknowledged its own coercion against Food Lion in the May/June 1989 issue of the *Union Leader*: "Two Belgian unions are pressuring Delhaize to recognize Local 400 (UFCW) and negotiate a fair contract for their exploited American workers."

Grigereit contends that all of the UFCW activity against Food Lion has to be viewed within the context of the union's "corporate campaign" strategy. The union has employed this strategy for six years, Grigereit says, to coerce recognition of the UFCW "without regard to the desires of Food Lion employees."

The UFCW attempted to force a labor vote among Food Lion workers in 1980 with a traditional card-signing campaign, requiring a "show of interest" from 30 percent of the employees in a unit.

Grigereit says the union failed miserably at this effort, leading to the corporate campaign's "pressure tactics."

The union has promoted consumer boycotts against Food Lion. Company officials also accuse the UFCW with pressuring employees to sign union authorization cards, trespassing into stores, planting smear stories in newspapers and harassing customers.

"Food Lion points to the fact that employees have not requested an election for union representation as 'evidence' their employees do not want union representation," Earman, the UFCW official, said in August 1989 correspondence to *The Salisbury Post*. "If you follow that logic," he said, "I guess the citizens of the Soviet Union do not want freedom and democracy either.

"Local 400 would readily accept the decision of Food Lion workers about union representation if Food Lion would allow the issues to be discussed and then let the employees make their decision without threats, harassment and interference by the company. Food Lion has captive-audience meetings with their employees in Virginia stores to brow-beat the employees about the 'evils of unionization.' They do not allow employees to hear the other side of the story and then let them make their own decision."

Company executives have said they will do everything legally possible to keep unions out of Food Lion stores, claiming that the company's wages are comparable to those of other supermarkets in Food Lion's market area. In the past, Tom Smith has cited a Cornell University study that found Food Lion's turnover to be less than the industry average. The Almanac of American Employers rated Food Lion 73rd out of 500 U.S. companies in a study based on wages, benefits, stability and advancement opportunity. Food Lion was the top-rated grocery chain. Kroger ranked 360th; Safeway, 460th; and A&P didn't make the list.

"They are a very turned-on bunch of people," says one observer about Food Lion employees. "And why not? They've all made money on the Food Lion stock."

Lion's Share

"We are convinced that one of the foundation stones of our success has been our non-union status," said Tom Smith in part of a statement circulated to stores. "We are convinced that unions have a tendency to create an antagonistic relationship between employees and management. Once you have employees and management fighting each other, cooperation and teamwork simply cannot exist. It is through cooperation and teamwork, with management and employees working together for the common good, that Food Lion has been a success. That is why we're opposed to unions at Food Lion and will continue to be so.

"No employee is ever going to need a union to keep their job or to receive fair treatment with good wages and good benefits at Food Lion. We are convinced our employees do not need a union."

Because of the company's expansion, one competitor says he has been predicting for five years that Food Lion would have trouble getting qualified employees. Smith acknowledged in 1991 at least some concern about predicted labor shortages. "It's always a priority," Smith said in addressing a Carolina Business Summit. "We added 8,000 jobs last year. It's more of a challenge as the labor pool gets thinner." But Smith believes Food Lion will be an employer of choice so that even with a labor shortage there will be enough people to fill Food Lion openings.

"It takes proper pay to attract the people you want," he said. "We maintain competitive pay scales so we're selecting from what's available, not what's left over."

Smith noted that 150 initial job openings at the Texas distribution center attracted 3,000 applicants. Meanwhile, published reports said Food Lion was offering people incentives to sign up for a training program in Dallas.

"All is not rosy on the labor front," wrote Steve Weinstein in *Progressive Grocer* in September 1990. "While the Food Lion system may encourage loyalty, some say it discourages initiative. An official of one chain that employs quite a few former Food Lion people, says they left 'because they felt the company was cold and impersonal, and they had no real feeling of security there.

236

Also, under the rigid Food Lion system, there is virtually no decision making at the store level and it is difficult for managers to become really involved in their communities.' "

Even if some employees (or former employees) are disgruntled, *Progressive Grocer* said, there's no doubt that Food Lion's financial incentives will continue to provide enough personnel to staff its many new stores.

Another troublesome area in the past has been Food Lion's confrontations with the National Association for the Advancement of Colored People. The company was one of 22 targeted by the NAACP in 1984 to sign a "Fair Share Agreement." The companies were asked to formally agree to increase minority representation in management and to do more business with black-owned companies.

"Food Lion was the only supermarket chain that wouldn't even meet with us until we staged a two-month boycott," said Fred Rasheed, who negotiated the agreement for the NAACP. "They started out saying that we should be happy to shop at the stores and get their low prices. Even today the relationship isn't very warm. It's a tough, no-nonsense type of company."

Dr. Benjamin Hooks, executive director of the NAACP, threw down the gauntlet to Food Lion in demanding increased black employment, more management positions for blacks, black representation on the company board of directors, more business directed toward minority companies and more contributions toward non-profit black organizations.

Hooks called Food Lion's claims that it was saving the black community $6 million a year through lower food prices "hogwash." He said that blacks were entitled to better jobs at Food Lion "even if we didn't buy a single loaf of bread there."

When Food Lion wouldn't sign the NAACP's Fair Share Agreement, picketing of stores in Salisbury began in July 1984. Salisbury's black community didn't wholeheartedly endorse the boycott. The Rev. Reid White, pastor of White Rock AME Zion Church in nearby Granite Quarry, said that he didn't feel the

Lion's Share

NAACP had done everything it could to avoid the boycott. "I'm not convinced that I can go and tell a grandmother making $217 a month to boycott when we have seen a 50 per cent increase in employment of blacks in the past four years." The audience at the Salisbury-Rowan NAACP chapter meeting jeered White as he read from his prepared statement. One man asked if he were on the Food Lion payroll.

Sensing the potential damage, Food Lion hired a New York public relations firm, Hill & Knowlton, and began its own campaign to blunt the criticism. The company said it had started placing grocery stores in minority neighborhoods that other chains would not enter. Total black employment at Food Lion was 12.6 percent, up in four years from 8.4 percent. Food Lion said it had 86 blacks in management, representing 5.4 percent of 1,596 officials and managers. The NAACP listed among its demands in July that within two years the company have: 27 blacks in executive management, 25 black store managers, 30 black assistant store managers, 20 black management trainees and 100 black department managers.

By September the boycott was history. News that Food Lion had signed an agreement with the NAACP was announced at halftime of predominantly-black Livingstone College's football game in Salisbury. In reality, the agreement was watered down to the point that Food Lion said that it merely reflected company policy. Hooks said it called for Food Lion to hire a consultant to deal with minority entrepreneurship, increase its business with minority-owned banks, advertisers and insurance agencies, increase overall black employment and set up a consumer advisory council to monitor its compliance with the agreement. Food Lion later claimed an entirely different agreement had been reached.

The Salisbury Post said in an editorial that Hooks needed a show of strength to ward off challenges to his leadership within the NAACP. Even after the smoke had cleared, it was unclear who had won. At Food Lion's insistence, the contract was not called "Operation Fair Share." The company called it a "Statement of

Principles" and the contents were kept largely secret. One specific was made public: "Food Lion confirms its present manager training program should increase black representation from 79 to 158 by 1987."

"Use of the word 'confirm' is interesting," *The Post* editorial said. "It seems to back up Food Lion Vice President Eugene McKinley's assertion that the agreement merely takes note of minority-advancement plans that the company already planned to put into effect anyway."

McKinley wrote The Post a lengthy letter, claiming that the newspaper's stories had been misleading or incorrect. Food Lion was not required to hire a consultant to deal with minority entrepreneurship. It had agreed to explore the use of a consultant with respect to a minority purchasing program. The company didn't agree to increase the amount of business it does with minority-owned banks, advertisers and insurance agencies, but it would entertain bids from any sources. The agreement did not set up a consumer advisory council to monitor Food Lion's compliance with the agreement. Food Lion would simply set up a consumer advisory board to explore ways to continue "high quality service and otherwise enhancing relations with its consumer market."

Food Lion hadn't given away much, but it had patched up relations with the black community by being willing to negotiate. Several years later, McKinley was presented the local black community's highest award for humanitarian service, the Martin Luther King Award.

21. The Carolina hot rod

Members of Salem Lutheran, a modest country church just west of Salisbury, had about $20,000 in 1988, but wanted to build a new educational building that would cost more than $90,000. Somebody suggested that the congregation invest in Food Lion stock. By the time the church was ready to begin construction, the reasoning went, the stock probably would have increased significantly in value.

Food Lion already had made 87 Rowan County investors millionaires by 1988. An original $1,000 investment was worth about $14 million and would grow to more than $20 million by 1991.

The church council took the matter to the congregation and the members voted to invest their building fund money with the hometown grocery chain. Unfortunately, after six months the stock had dropped a point and didn't appear to be heading toward any dramatic upswings.

Some members of the congregation accused the church council of "gambling" their money in the stock market, so when the church's Food Lion stock finally showed a small profit, it was sold. There had been no six-month miracle, just a 10 per cent gain.

Co-founder Ralph Ketner, whose personal fortune is now worth more than $100 million, never promises that people will get rich quick on Food Lion stock. He always says that if investors are patient, Food Lion will pay off.

But patience is a virtue that is lacking even in church congregations. Expectations of Food Lion's growth and profitability are such that anything short of spectacular sends the 10,612 investors living in Salisbury and Rowan County into a tizzy. From 1976 to 1990, Food Lion sales and earnings grew at a compound rate of 29 to 30 per cent, and return on equity never dipped below 20 percent – it averaged 32 percent from 1986 to 1990. In 1990 the company earned $172.6 million – a net margin of 3 percent in an industry that, again, averages around 1 percent.

Ralph Ketner characterized Food Lion's dramatic growth with the illustration that if the company's sales were a one-inch block in 1968, when LFPINC took hold, they reached as tall as a nine-story building by 1990.

Stockbroker Sted Morris calls Food Lion "the Carolina hot rod." But brokers unfamiliar with Food Lion look at a portfolio heavy with the grocery stock selling at 30 to 40 times earnings and gag. By all conventional yardsticks, the stock is overpriced. Similar national chains, Winn-Dixie, A&P and Giant Foods, are selling for around 16 times earnings.

"I think their biggest challenge is that everybody is expecting such phenomenal increases from them," says John A. Howard, analyst at Carolina Securities Corp. in Raleigh, North Carolina. "At some point, as they get bigger and bigger, they just can't maintain that kind of growth."

But the memory of a 5-for-1 split in 1970 and that September day in 1971 when the stock went from $19 to $31 as a result of a recommendation by *Growth Stock Outlook* won't die. The first question on stockholders' minds at the company's annual meeting each May is, when will the stock split again?

The stock split has been the engine that has driven the Food Lion investment machine. A share bought in 1957 for $10 has multiplied into 12,960 shares. The original $1,000 investment was worth $23 million in mid-1991. The splits began in 1963 (4 for 1) and continued with regularity: 1970 (5 for 1); 1972 (2 for 1); 1976 (3 for 1); 1979 (3 for 1); 1982 (3 for 1); 1983 (2 for 1, A and B shares); 1986 (3 for 1, A and B shares); 1987 (2 for 1, A and B shares).

Lion's Share

The original investors may think themselves lucky that Ralph and Brown Ketner and Wilson Smith called in 1957, but there have been other fortunes made since the company went public. A $1,000 investment in November 1970 bought 83.333 shares at $12 each. Through splits (not counting the five-for-one split in February 1970), each of those shares was 54,000 shares by 1991.

Of the scores of millionaires in Rowan County, North Carolina, alone, many of them still work for Food Lion. The company has shared its phenomenal stock growth with its employees to the point that a dollar up or down on Wall Street means big money to everyone in the company. The bottom line has become: Work hard so the stock will go up.

"Basically, if you look at each of our vice presidents, you look at me, you look at Mr. Ketner, we never had anything personally," Tom Smith, chief executive officer, told *The Salisbury Post* in 1990. "Over the years, we've been able to build something personally by the way of stock and by the way of profit-sharing, but we always realized that the only way we built that was because of Food Lion. So you just naturally put Food Lion first – now I'm not talking about obnoxiously first – but that's what has made everything we do possible. We do work mighty hard."

Smith owns 1,098,690 shares of Food Lion Class A stock and 1,555,948 shares of Class B, about $35 million worth in 1991. If the stock goes up a point, that means $2.6 million to him. Food Lion's leaders don't intend to let the fickle forces of Wall Street damage the stock's value. Company directors obtained authority from shareholders in 1989 to purchase up to 16.2 million shares of outstanding Class A voting stock, and up to 15.9 million shares of Class B non-voting stock. "The board of directors may consider repurchasing shares of common stock if, in the future, the volatility of the market causes the price of the company's common stock to fall to a level which leads the board of directors to determine that repurchases would be in the best interest of the company and its shareholders," a proxy statement sent to Food Lion shareholders in 1989 said.

The company has yet to exercise its authority to buy up its own stock, but it would certainly buy shares to support the price of the stock should it fall to "a ridiculously low level," company spokesman Mike Mozingo said.

Confidence in Food Lion stock is such that investors themselves go into a feeding frenzy should the price fall to attractive levels. When the Belgians put 3 million shares of non-voting stock on the market in October 1983 at $10 per share, they were all sold by 2 p.m. on the first day. Voting stock was selling for around $13 a share that day, but the two stocks – voting and non-voting – have stayed close in price. "Voting doesn't mean anything anyway," said Marvin Edens, broker for Interstate/Johnson, Lane in Salisbury. "Most people don't vote and if they do the Belgians have control of it."

Edens saw the confidence in Food Lion for himself in October 19, 1987, "Black Monday" on Wall Street, when the market took one of its most historic nose dives: 508 points. In the midst of all the turmoil, an investor walked into his office and wanted to buy 10,000 shares of Food Lion because it was down from 22 to 14. By the next day, the stock had recovered to near its starting point, and the investor sold, adding another chapter to the Food Lion legend.

"I've been buying Food Lion for 20 years," Edens says, "and I feel like I owe a lot of my success to it." Back before his brokerage had a minimum commission, Edens sold investors five and 10 shares of Food Lion at a time. "A lot of those people are rich today," he says, "and Food Lion is sending a lot of kids to college."

The company's success has become a part of Salisbury folklore. One man sent his portfolio to be managed by a Boston company, and the broker called wanting to know if he had any emotional attachment to Food Lion stock. It was not a stock that the brokerage regularly watched, and he wanted to sell it. The investor said he had no emotional attachment to the stock – but it was the only thing he had ever made money on. The Boston broker sold the stock for $12 a share, and within nine months it had climbed to $18.

Ned Cline, the onetime *Salisbury Post* reporter who wrote the paid advertisement for Food Lion's "Big Change" in 1968, went on to become managing editor at the *Greensboro News & Record.* He regrets the day he took $300 in cash instead of $300 worth of stock. "I have calculated since, of course," Cline said in January 1991, "that if I had taken his offer of stock and just left it alone to grow, my $300 would be worth somewhere in the range of $500,000 today. So much for my business expertise."

Even worse news for Cline: His calculations were a bit off. If $300 would have purchased 50 shares in 1968 – the going price then was $6 a share – his number of shares would have grown to 162,000, thanks to the many splits. That number of shares valued at the average price in early 1991 of approximately $15 a share would have had a value of $2.43 million.

Twenty men started the Buy-Rite Investment Club in Salisbury in 1958 and each invested $10 a month. The club bought Food Town in its early years and continued to invest in it. In 1986 the club had almost three-quarters of a million dollars, mainly due to Food Lion. "Our gain was 1,876 percent at an average cost of 40 cents a share," one of the original members, W.M. "Bill" Younts Jr. said once. Later the club decided to spin off 5,200 shares to each of its remaining nine members.

Fred Stanback, a businessman who was in an investment club with Ralph Ketner in the early '60s, bought some Food Town stock and later sold it. But Stanback had second thoughts and repurchased stock. One of the company's biggest individual investors by 1991, he owns nearly 1 percent of the company.

Archie Rufty, the largest individual stockholder with roughly 10 million shares, didn't buy in the beginning. "I've never forgiven Wilson Smith for not calling me," said Rufty, who went to church with Smith. Many of the original stockholders went to either Smith's church, St. John's Lutheran; Ralph Ketner's, First

Presbyterian; or Brown Ketner's, China Grove Baptist. "I was driving a '51 Nash," Rufty said, "so I guess he thought I was too poor."

"Not at all," said Smith. "We thought you were too tight."

Rufty eventually moved from Salisbury to Las Vegas, Nevada, where there is no intangibles tax – as there is in North Carolina.

While Food Lion may have been a gamble in 1957, it has become well known among growth stock gurus today. It is considered the 70th favorite stock in the nation among investment clubs. Gene Walden's book *The 100 Best Stocks to Own in America* listed Food Lion 42nd. He gave the company five stars, his highest rating, for earnings, stock and dividend growth. Walden's top 100 outperformed the stock market year after year by "possessing that winning combination of superior product development and innovation, management savvy, marketing genius and exceptional service to shareholders."

Scott and Stringfellow Investment Corp. chose Food Lion as one of 11 stocks that investors with long-term objectives should consider in 1991.

Changing Times magazine in 1991 listed Food Lion among 66 companies whose earnings per share rose in each of the previous 10 years. Two other grocery chains made the *Changing Times* list: Albertson's and Weis Markets. "Folks need to eat in good times and bad," the magazine said.

U.S. News and World Report listed Food Lion as one of the 100 best stocks to weather a recession and bear market on Wall Street. Giving heavy weight to earnings per share, the *U.S. News & World Report* ranked Food Lion 25th on its Top 100.

Forbes magazine ranked 1,078 stocks in January 1991 in terms of growth, the stock market and profitability. Food Lion was 133rd in growth with average sales increases of 26 percent over the past five years. The survey placed Food Lion 28th on its stock market performance list with its price up 269 percent over the past five years and a price earnings ratio of 26.2. *Forbes* ranked Food

245

Lion's Share

Lion 73rd in profitability with its five-year average return on equity of 32 percent. Among supermarkets and convenience stores, Food Lion was second only to the Arden Group. It was ranked ahead of Albertson's, Weis Markets, Giant Foods, Bruno's, Winn-Dixie, A&P and 20 others in the magazine's comparison.

More than one stock analyst has referred to Food Lion as the Wal-Mart of grocery chains: an appropriate label considering how similar the two companies are. Both are hometown firms with hometown approaches and hometown problems. And both have been amazingly successful.

In his book, *Sam Walton, the Inside Story of America's Richest Man*, Vance H. Trimble refers to Walton as "an old-fashioned promoter in the P.T. Barnum style." Another description of Walton: "Overlaying everything is a lot of the old yard rooster who is tough, loves a good fight and protects his territory."

No truer words could be said of Ralph Ketner, a feisty man whose blood pressure stays incredibly low, even into his 70's, because he loves to compete. He never shied away from a calculated risk. The traits served both Ketner and Walton well, even though they fired blanks sometimes. Walton had his share of brainstorms that didn't work. Ketner came up with a few himself, such as the discount on sales tax, though that gimmick's failure may have worked had the government not stepped in.

But the similarities go way beyond the leaders of the companies. Wal-Mart, like Food Lion, decided to conduct its business well off the beaten paths of most large corporations by setting up shop in the small city of Bentonville, Arkansas. "The best thing we ever did," Walton told *Forbes* once, "was to hide back there in the hills and eventually build a company that makes folks want to find us. They get there sometimes with a lot of trepidation and problems, but we like where we are. It's because of the work ethic, because of the chemistry of the people up there and the support we get. We're much better off than if we'd gone to Chicago."

Wal-Mart headquarters in Bentonville is a bit austere. The corporate offices are tied into the company's first big warehouse, as is the case with Food Lion. The typical office at both companies is tiny, overcrowded and part of an elaborate maze, often confusing to the infrequent visitor. The lobbies are filled with sales representatives who work at makeshift desks fashioned out of briefcases on their knees. Hundreds of hometown residents flock to the annual meetings held in their small towns, and letters pour into headquarters by the thousands each month with praise, criticism and suggestions. All of the mail is answered.

Wal-Mart and Food Lion each built their success with conveniently placed stores in small Southern towns. And while their demeanor is often "down home," the sales people calling on both firms soon realize that the buyers demand price concessions and deals on large quantities of goods that promise high-volume sales at "everyday low prices."

Buyers for the grocery chain and the discount department stores are considered the toughest in their respective industries. Both Walton and Ketner preach centralized buying and, some would say, often went at distribution backwards by building numerous large warehouses first then spotting stores within convenient (and efficient) driving distances around them. With this arrangement, Food Lion and Wal-Mart trucks can deliver merchandise to stores within a matter of hours.

Both companies are fanatical about efficiency. Edwin L. Underwood, a stock analyst with Scott & Stringfellow in Richmond, Virginia, once noted that the North Carolina-based Rose's, a discount department store chain, faced considerable pressure from Wal-Mart because of the Arkansas chain's low operating expenses. "Wal-Mart is doing 100 things 1 percent better," Underwood told a *Winston-Salem Journal* reporter once. The statement sounds strangely like Tom Smith's claim that Food Lion does 1,000 things 1 percent better. Each company solicits cost-saving ideas from its employees and passes out awards for those that are implemented. The companies harp on energy conservation, recycling and controlling administrative expenses.

The chains rely heavily on corporate planes to cover their vast territories. Routinely, Tom Smith and his vice presidents hop on planes to visit other regions, as do the executives of Wal-Mart. Both companies place great weight on the importance of visiting stores and seeing what effect decisions at headquarters have meant at the critical employee level.

Tommy Eller and others learned from Glenn Ketner that customer satisfaction came first: Again, "If you're going to make it good, don't make them mad," Glenn Ketner instructed. Listen to the words of a Wal-Mart store manager interviewed for Vance Trimble's book: "It will be silly for us not to give him (a disgruntled customer) a new item. If he goes away mad, maybe he'll knock off a dozen customers. He'll never tell you he was displeased. He goes and tells everyone else."

Retail giant Sears, which has lost the distinction of being the country's largest retailer to upstart Wal-Mart, probably paid Wal-Mart the highest compliment of all by going to an everyday low-price concept though it didn't seem to halt Sears' slowing growth in recent years. In the mid-1980s, Winn-Dixie reacted to Food Lion's stunning gains by resorting to its "10,000 low prices."

When it came to expansion, Wal-Mart and Food Lion took some gambles. Food Lion jumped the Mississippi River into Texas, took on Winn-Dixie in Florida and has taken a bold step into Pennsylvania. Wal-Mart's targets outside of its traditional Southern stronghold have been the Northeast and California.

Wal-Mart takes the Food Lion posture toward unions. Sam Walton has argued that his employees already have better wages, benefits and bonus incentives than a union can deliver. Both chains offer great opportunities for advancement – stories of stock boys moving up the ladder to earn six-figure incomes are retold in each. Sam Walton, not unlike Ralph Ketner when he was president, drives his people relentlessly and gets rid of employees not producing to his standards. And many Wal-Mart employees retire early, complaining of burnout, while taking with them healthy chunks of profit-sharing money.

The successes of Wal-Mart and Food Lion crept up on people.

In the '70s, investors often overlooked the companies as they plugged along from their obscure locations making faithful stockholders richer each year.

Heading into the 1990s, Wal-Mart boasted 250,000 employees, 1,500 stores in 22 states and $26 billion in annual sales. Food Lion cracked the Top 10 in size among grocery store chains with $5.584 billion in sales, 23,071 full-time workers, 24,205 part-time workers and 778 stores by the end of 1990.

Each firm rose from humble beginnings in the Eisenhower years. Each went public with its stock in 1970. Each saw its stock split eight times between 1970 and 1990. All of Wal-Mart's splits were two-for-one. A Wal-Mart investor with 400 shares in 1970 had 102,400 shares by 1990. The Food Lion investor with 400 shares going into 1970 (before that year's five-for-one split) would have 1,296,000 shares today.

It may be just as correct to call Wal-Mart the Food Lion of discount department stores.

22. Lifestyles of the rich and famous

It sounded like a good idea for a story: A small-town company turns 87 investors into millionaires. Producers of the television show *Lifestyles of the Rich and Famous* packed their people and equipment off to Salisbury in the summer of 1988, but there was one problem: Nobody would talk to them.

While the original Food Lion investors were certainly rich, they didn't consider themselves famous. Finally, Paul Ritchie agreed to go on camera and tell about Food Lion because he felt that the story ought to be told. It is one of those "only in America" stories about dedicated people who started with nothing and built something beyond their wildest expectations.

Ritchie is typical of the original investor: unchanged by the money. He still lives in the same modest house where he has lived for more than 40 years. He does admit to enjoying a "nice car," usually a Cadillac. He's given his wife and children a good share of his stock but feels a responsibility to do the right thing with his Food Lion money. He was meeting with representatives of Lenoir-Rhyne College, a private, Lutheran, liberal arts school in Hickory, North Carolina, on the day he was interviewed for this book.

Those original investors in 1957 didn't plan on becoming millionaires. They believed in Ralph and Brown Ketner and Wilson Smith. "I just trusted them, that's all," said G.K. Brown, a friend of Smith's and founder of Salisbury Engravers, who invested $100 in '57.

"I forgot about it," Brown says of his original 10-share investment. "I just let it out of my mind. I didn't worry about it. If I lost it, I lost it." Brown said he took notice again when the stock started "going to town" and even bought more. He retired in 1981, and he and wife Lucy, spend a lot of time at their second home at North Myrtle Beach, South Carolina.

Dr. Glenn Kiser, the pediatrician who retired at age 37 to care for a wife with a progressive illness, originally invested $300 in Food Town but spent the next eight years buying five shares here and 10 shares there.

In 1963 he heard about Food Town's convertible debentures. "I jumped at the chance," Kiser said once. "I bought the full $25,000 Food Town would allow any one family to buy. By buying these convertibles, which paid a good rate of interest, it would enable me, hopefully, to have a chance to obtain more Food Town stock. That was the good part, the convertibility. When these convertibles were called in a few years later, it meant that I had, for the first time, a sizable amount of Food Town stock. There were rumors of hard times at Food Town, but I was jubilant. I honestly never, ever had a bit of doubt that Ralph Ketner, et al, would come through. He did."

Kiser studied the stock market and made a good living by dealing in stocks. "I did not buy Food Town stock out of ignorance," he said. "I bought Food Town stock over an extended period of time because I knew and believed in Ralph Ketner."

Harold Melton, owner of Salisbury Cut-Rate Furniture across the street from Ketner's on East Innes Street who invested $200 in 1957, suffered a blood clot September 23, 1968, and his doctor told him to quit work. He liquidated his business and retired to his home in Granite Quarry. By the late 1980s, he had 134,000 shares of Food Lion. "I've been blessed, and I'm thankful," Melton says. "It's something I never expected."

Charlie Barger, the newspaper Linotype operator from *The Salisbury Post*, retired and spent his golden years playing golf and tending a garden off the first fairway at his son's course, Corbin

Hills. He gave stock to his children and grandchildren and when he died his estate was valued at $1.3 million.

Helen Goodnight sold her stock in the late '70s to buy a special birthday present for her husband, Cress. He bought her five shares of stock in 1957 as they struggled with their own clothing business on North Main Street. Helen and the children decided to give Cress a membership in the Salisbury Country Club and a golf cart for his 50th birthday. "There has never been a happier man," she said. "We are so thankful he had this pleasure for the years he had left." Goodnight died in 1984. Mrs. Goodnight's grandchildren count themselves as modern-day Food Lion investors.

VA chaplain George Hood, who bought 10 shares in his wife Rena's name in 1957, died 10 years later and never saw the company, or his investment, take off. Mrs. Hood sold some of her stock to help with the expenses of putting son Frank through graduate school.

Zula Marlin, Wilson Smith's sister-in-law who invested $100 in 1957 with husband Richard, says the dividends today are "real nice." Richard died of a heart attack in 1984, and Zula has moved to Spencer, adjacent to Salisbury. She sold some stock after her husband's death and has given some to her grandchildren. She said the stock was also good for her father, P.L. Wyatt, who originally invested $200. The dividends supplemented his railroad pension and paid for his care in a nursing home during his last years.

The three Hurley boys – Jim, Haden and Gordon – were given 100 shares each by their father in 1957, held on to most of their stock and are owners of the town's newspaper today.

Haden Hurley says he's lucky to still have some of his because first wife, Doris, wanted a house along the fifth fairway of the Salisbury Country Club. An appraiser told Hurley not to pay more than $30,000. The house was sold to another bidder for $32,000.

"Thirty thousand dollars was a lot for me then," he said, "and I'd listed everything I could to raise the money, including Food Town, which Mr. (Ernest) Hardin said might bring $4,000 if he could find anyone to take it. Well, I dodged a bullet by being $2,000 short on the bid.

"I sold a third to the Belgians in 1974, and it sure helped. Anyway the success of Food Lion has meant so much to so many. The original stockholders – with one exception – have been extremely generous in helping people and Salisbury in particular. I doubt there is a person in Rowan County that hasn't benefited from some donation of Food Lion stock either directly or indirectly." Haden Hurley is retired and lives in Florida.

Gordon Hurley also sold some of his stock to the Belgians. "People say today, 'I bet you wish you hadn't sold any of your Food Lion,' " he says. "Hardly. The money from Food Lion has enabled us to do things for ourselves and others that would have been impossible to do on our salaries and other side income." Gordon Hurley is president of Post Publishing Co., and he and wife, Carolyn, have two sons. "I told Carolyn I should put Ralph's picture over the fireplace in our condo in Blowing Rock."

Jim Hurley, publisher of *The Salisbury Post*, has used part of his Food Lion fortune for the benefit of his community. He led a $28 million fund-raising campaign for Catawba College, and he and his wife, Gerry, contributed $1 million to endow a school of humanities. He encouraged Archie Rufty to join him in putting up $200,000 each for the new Rufty-Holmes Senior Center, also built with donations from the county government and the public. Holmes was his mother's maiden name, and a garden financed by the family has been named in her honor along a portion of Salisbury's City Park. There are other beneficiaries: a college soccer team that needed uniforms, a school program that came up short of funds, deserving students who needed a boost.

Hurley says that if his brother, Haden, could have sold his stock for $4 a share in the early '60s he might have sold his, too. "As my wife, Gerry, and I began to buy stocks on a very limited basis, we'd send our 'portfolios' – you really couldn't call what we had a real portfolio – to companies for evaluation," he says.

Lion's Share

"Almost everyone advised the sale of Food Town because it was too large a percentage of our holdings. Julian Robertson, a good friend who was a broker with Kidder, Peabody and Co., told me not to sell regardless of what the 'experts' said, even those in his own brokerage firm."

Sage advice from a shrewd investor. By 1991, Salisbury native Robertson was considered the best money manager on Wall Street. It was his father, Julian Robertson Sr., who thought he was speaking to his banker friend Bill Smith when grocer Wilson Smith called him about investing in Food Town in 1957.

In 1971, Jim Hurley sold some stock to build a house in the North Carolina mountains near Boone. As editor of *The Salisbury Post*, his telephone rang with complaints from readers almost every night.

"One night I counted 22 people calling to disagree with an editorial, an article, mistakes in a wedding writeup or what not, and I told my wife, 'If we don't find a way to get out of town, I'm not going to live to be 40.' So we bought a house in the mountains for $37,500, built a retaining wall and furnished it nicely – altogether an investment of about $55,000.

"In our family, we were taught that you could borrow money for education, for equities or equipment for the business, but we weren't allowed to borrow for clothes, cars or carpets. And certainly not for a second home. So I sold enough Food Town to buy the house and furnish it. But, you know, I have never regretted that purchase. The fact is, it probably saved my life. Spending weekends away from the public, reading and relaxing was a great way to reduce tension and to reflect quietly on long-term goals for *The Post* and our family. And, so, even though we may have suffered a monetary loss from the stock sale, we gained much more in peace of mind than we lost in money.

"The wealth Food Lion has generated for me has enabled me to make a difference in many phases of life in this town. No matter how much you'd like to see some things done, you've got to have money to do them. My wife warns, 'Don't you dare misfigure when you're giving all this money away.' I tell her, 'I'm not giving money away. I'm investing in our community,' and I appreciate Ralph Ketner and Food Lion enabling me to do it."

Jim Woodson, the lawyer who used Food Town stock to make a quick profit in the 1970s, bought what surely has proven to be the world's most expensive lawn mower. Had he kept his stock, it would be worth more than $3 million today.

"I kid Jim Woodson that I lost more money on my house at Hound Ears than the $3 million he lost on his lawn mower," Jim Hurley says. "His reply: 'I'll swap my lawn mower for your house.' "

Helen Black's original 50 shares, bought for her by doctor husband Kyle, sparked a hidden interest in the stock market. "My 50 shares was the catalyst," she says. "The strategy of any investment is not to lose it. I always kept faith in it as it struggled to survive. I'd never known anything about stocks before, but I just got real interested and wanted to learn more." She bought some ITT, took courses, read financial magazines and got hooked.

"I've done all the investing for Kyle, and the office portfolio has done really well," she says. Mrs. Black took charge of a trust set up for her father-in-law and eventually became a director of First Charter Bank in Concord. "Without Food Town," she says, "I would never have known about stock. It opened up a whole new world to me and has brought me much joy and us financial success."

Frank Hinds, the former Ketner's store manager who ran the big Winn-Dixie in Salisbury – and matched all of Food Town's early specials – retired from Winn-Dixie in 1985 and went into the advertising specialities business with his wife, Jean.

Hinds turned down several offers to go to work for Ralph Ketner and Food Town. "I remember one time while I was eating Thanksgiving dinner, the phone rang and Ralph was on the phone," Hinds says. "Ralph said he would make available $10,000 worth of stock and arrange financing for it. Well, if anybody could be sick about what might have been, it would be me."

Jim Berrier retired as office manager for Food Lion January 1, 1982, at age 58. "I felt like I wanted to get out while I could enjoy a few things in life before I got too old," he says.

Berrier said he retired shortly after the company hired a psychologist to quiz company officials about their ambitions. "I told him I didn't want to be president, didn't want to move up, and he thought that was terrible," he says. "At my age, and at that time, I was happy where I was. If I was younger, I would have gone for it and if I had been offered some of these positions, I would have worked like hell. But after you get so old, I don't believe in trying to do too much additional drive, because you've done it all your life anyway. I was happy."

Berrier quit a millionaire, and he and wife, Uzeal, still live in the same house in which they have lived for years on U.S. 52 east of Salisbury. They also own a house at the coast.

Berrier says he's always amazed at Food Lion's growth. "I couldn't tell you where all the Food Lions are today because they move so fast and open up so many stores. I'll see a new store once in a while and say 'I didn't know that.' " Berrier believes Food Lion must keep growing: "If they're not, there's something wrong with our company. We have a lot of good men, and men who were willing to strive and go a little farther. I really had the idea that our company would one day be as big as Winn-Dixie. I always did."

Hap Roberts, controller, left the company about the same time as Berrier, who had recommended him for the job. Roberts had declined the position of vice president of finance in 1980 because of his health problems.

Roberts operates a small Salisbury accounting firm with his former Food Town associate, Gary Morgan, and is on the board of directors of Ryan's Steakhouse. "Everything that I am professionally," Roberts says, "I owe to Ralph Ketner and his men."

After retiring from Food Lion, Tommy Eller bought a small

256

chain of convenience stores called Spee Dee Mart. He applied the LFPINC principle to the store's beer, soft drink and cigarette sales, cutting prices and generating traffic. Eller says his stores sell beer cheaper than anybody – except Food Lion.

Eller and his wife, Jeanie, gave $150,000 in Food Lion stock in 1988 to the Baptist Children's Homes of North Carolina to build a dining hall at a boys camp in Cameron, North Carolina. Eller convinced another donor to give $100,000 and Food Lion, through two statewide Community Way projects, contributed $112,000. The Jeanie C. and Thomas O. Eller Chuckwagon was the first building erected in the camp's million-dollar expansion.

"We've been very, very fortunate," Mrs. Eller says. "We wanted to share with the less fortunate, to some good cause where we would enjoy seeing someone else enjoy the gift."

Eller was one of the driven men who established the Food Lion work ethic. He once worked four months of 18-hour days to get a store reorganized and back on track before his doctor made him take five days off. Despite the rewards it brought him later in life, Eller didn't do it for the money.

"Money doesn't make you happy," he says. "The lack of it can make you unhappy, but I don't think money makes you entirely happy. There's a lot of times when I say, 'Damn, I was crazy.' I'd sit back there in the produce department and I'd talk to myself. You know, you have good days and bad days. I'd say if this damn stock ever gets worth $100,000, they can take it someplace and shove it. But the funny thing is, when it got there and the ball started rolling, you just didn't want to turn it loose. You wanted to keep going with it. We had a lot of fun."

Clifford Ray, Eller's good friend and produce buyer encountered health problems. He had two heart surgeries in the '80s and fought cancer for several months before dying May 20, 1991. His horse, Charcoal's Delight, won the 1990 amateur world grand championship for Tennessee Walking Horses in Shelbyville, Tennessee, for the fourth time. Ray showed the horse 46 times during a three-year period, and Charcoal's Delight won 41 blue ribbons. A wall in his den had shelves filled with trophies, plaques, photos and ribbons.

Ray said once that he always knew Food Town would make it, despite hard times. He held on to his stock. "The main thing the money did for me," he wrote for one family history, "was to give me security. One of the times I was in the hospital and the doctor wouldn't release me, it felt good to know my medical bills could be covered regardless. But I tell you, when I was under the knife, I found out that no amount of money was gonna help me."

In his basement at home, Wilson Smith still practices his gift for making signs. Old grocery habits are hard to break. But instead of mixing drop chalk and water for a window paint solution, Smith has the more sophisticated colored markers. Friends routinely turn to him for a class reunion banner or signs for the Kiwanis Pancake Festival.

In rather quiet fashion, Smith and his sons set up the Smith Foundation to share their success. "God really has been good to us," he says. He and wife Evelyeen have paid the scholarships of five residents of the Baddour Memorial Center, a model home for mentally retarded adults in Senatobia, Mississippi. Many other contributions have been made anonymously.

Smith stayed on the Food Lion board of directors until 1984 when he was asked to step down to make way for more Belgian representation.

Establissements Delhaize Freres et Cie were represented by Jacques LeClercq, Gui de Vaucleroy, Raymond-Max Boon and Charles de Cooman d'Herlinckhove on the Food Lion board of directors entering the 1990s. Guy Beckers, one of the original board members representing Delhaize, has left the board. The Belgians have made more money than anybody on the growth of Food Lion. An incredible fortune has grown from their $8 million investment in 1974 and $11 million in 1976. The Belgians owned 44 per cent of the company in 1991: 62,195,642 shares of Class A and 80,295,642 shares of Class B. The value of their investment was roughly $3 billion by 1991.

Glenn Ketner never returned to the grocery business after leaving Winn-Dixie, despite being released from his non-competitive agreement in 1959. His brother, Ralph, called him "the smart Ketner" and "the only Ketner with any money," but Glenn's contributions to the Food Lion saga came in the ethics and ideas he planted in his employees. He was a perfectionist and a gentleman, and the founders of Food Lion wanted to run their stores the way he had run his.

Glenn Ketner still operates Rowan Investment Corp., the company that leased Store No. 1 to Food Town in 1957. Glenn and wife Addie established the Ketner Foundation to benefit their community.

Brown Ketner and son Jeff operate the Apple House Cafeteria chain. They both remain grateful for their years in the grocery business. "I learned what it is to struggle and survive," says Jeff, "what good things can happen to people who work."

The enmities from the lawsuit Brown filed against his brother, Ralph, and the other Food Town principals are gone. Brown became interested in nutrition and brings his father's principles of value to his cafeterias.

Linda Ketner, Ralph's daughter, lives in Charleston, South Carolina, and is vice president of KSI, a management consulting firm. Among her clients are General Foods, Rose's Department Stores, OMNI Magazine, the National Grocers Association and the American Speech, Hearing and Language Association.

As chairman of the Mayor's Council on Homelessness, she is working toward obtaining state funding for affordable housing in South Carolina. In 1988, her father gave $1 million to the Trident Community Foundation, the major source of funding for the homeless shelter in Charleston. "It's part of my inheritance," Linda says. "My father said, 'God, you're doing so many good things, Linda, and I want to support them. Why wait till I die?' "

Her mother, Ruth, lives with her husband, Stuart Hope, near Georgetown, South Carolina, and remembers her daughter as somebody who was always finding another child who needed a warm coat. Her parents quietly bought a lot of coats, Linda says.

She appreciates the brief time she spent with Food Lion and says it shaped her opinions about work and what it ought to be.

Linda remembers the day when she overheard her father deliver a tongue-lashing to an employee while she was helping the company develop its training program.

"You're going to have to stop doing that some day, Daddy," she said.

"I told her she was right – but not yet," he said.

That day has arrived for Ralph Ketner. He officially retired in May 1991 and, as chairman emeritus, has moved his office to Ralph W. Ketner Hall at Catawba College.

Ketner and wife Anne gave Catawba $3 million to establish the Ketner School of Business and build a three-story classroom building. The big gift was the cornerstone of the successful $28 million fund-raising drive headed by Jim Hurley. Gifts of Food Lion stock were said to make up $15 million of the total.

One can look out the window of Ketner Hall across Barger-Zartman Dorm – Zeda Barger of Faith gave $750,000 in Food Town stock to refurbish the women's dormitory – and across the campus to the Julian and Blanche Robertson Community Center. In the Ketner building is the Tom E. Smith Auditorium, the Rufty Forum (named for Archie and Frances Rufty), the Eller Administration Center (named for Jeanie and Tommy Eller), the Food Lion Executives Faculty Office and the Ralph W. Ketner Office, provided by son Robert Ketner.

Ketner, a trustee of the college, was walking across campus one afternoon when he spotted a license tag: "RWK SOB." He recognized his own initials and the epithet that followed. He began to ask some questions. He had a good laugh after finding that the license tag was on the car of business professor, Dr. Erik Oldenburg. He intended the tag's letters to stand for the "Ralph W. Ketner School of Business." Ketner keeps the license tag in his office.

The big gift to Catawba was the first of many by Ralph and

Anne Ketner. There is the Ralph W. Ketner Hall at the National 4-H Center in Chevy Chase, Maryland, so named after the Ketners donated $1 million toward the building. Then there's the $1 million gift to the homeless in Charleston. Ralph was so moved by Linda's work there that he and Anne helped build a new shelter and soup kitchen in Salisbury. Ralph gave a million dollars to Duke University, alma mater of son Robert. He and Anne bought Salisbury's Wallace Building, a brooding, turn-of-the-century hulk in the center of town, and turned it into a $3 million apartment, office and retail complex. "We want it to be a gift to the city we love," said Mrs. Ketner when the project started. In April 1991, that's just what they did – gave it to the city along with another $927,000 to finish the project.

Both the Ketners have been important benefactors of the Nazareth Children's Home near Salisbury. They funded the construction of a home for independent living for boys and the renovation of a similar home for girls, named in honor of his mother, Effie Yost Ketner. At Christmas, they hand out 500 gift certificates to the needy for $10 in groceries at Food Lion.

The Ketners' latest idea is to help working people own their own homes through a program that provides low-interest loans with modular houses and appliances at cost. The only requirement: $300 down and the ability to make mortgage payments, which usually run less than most people's rent.

"If you have money and don't use it," Ralph Ketner says, "it isn't worth anything. You don't ever miss it if you give it to people. I believe it's true that you make a living with what you get, but you make a life with what you give."

23. Epilogue

A reporter once asked Ralph Ketner when he would be satisfied with Food Lion's growth.

Never, Ketner said. He owed it to his customers to bring a store – and lower grocery prices – to everyone that he could. Ketner received letters from people, lots of them. Some begged him to open a store in their town. Others were angry about something and wished they could shop somewhere else that had prices as low – but they couldn't. When a tornado destroyed a Food Lion store in Bennettsville, South Carolina, Ketner opened mail from customers asking him to hurry and rebuild. Prices in the town's other grocery stores had gone back up.

The men who started Food Town didn't set out to get rich. In fact, they were foolhardy to quit their jobs with Winn-Dixie. They just wanted to get back to the friendly business of running a grocery store for people they knew and liked.

They didn't like the big chain's numbers game. To a man, they were renegades. If they failed, so be it.

There are so many ifs in their story:

• If Winn-Dixie had made good on its promise to build a big warehouse in Salisbury, Food Town might have never been started.

• If Food Town's founders had known about the Securities and Exchange Commission's laws, they might not have telephoned their friends and raised the money they needed to start the business.

• If Ralph Ketner hadn't read about Bob Stragand of Dayton,

Ohio, who had been experimenting with low prices to raise volume, LFPINC might not have been started and Food Town would still be a struggling little chain.

• If Tom Smith had stayed with Del Monte ... If the Belgians had never called ... If the company had been satisfied with having 100 stores, or 200....

None of those things happened, of course, and Food Town became Food Lion. The company has had a profound effect on the people of Salisbury. Everyone wishes he had invested way back when, but Food Town didn't look like much of an investment in 1957. It wasn't much in 1967 either.

Ralph Ketner could see some ominous handwriting on the wall that November day in 1967 when he holed up in a Charlotte motel room. He had nothing to lose, he figured. "It was time to bet the company," he said. Thus was born that odd expression: LFPINC.

The original investors showed faith in the men who started Food Town. They knew them personally, trusted them, admired them. They didn't plan on getting rich. Many had never invested in stock before. A lot of them didn't know what they had, even after Food Town began its spectacular growth. Ralph Ketner's sister, Dot, called him one day complaining about her teaching job. He asked her if she remembered the stock he had given her. She told him that she didn't see how 10 shares of stock would make much difference to her. She could hardly believe it when he told her what those 10 shares were worth. She didn't have to teach, if she didn't want to.

She called later and told him, "Ralph, I didn't hate going to teach today at all."

The favorite statistic about Food Lion around Salisbury is how much the original $1,000 investment has grown. By 1991, it was close to $23 million. But there's not a single one of the people who invested $1,000 in 1957 who still has all of his original stock. Bill Alsobrooks, the Southern Railway mechanic, may have been the last to break his up. He gave some to his sons.

Lion's Share

Most of those investors realize how lucky they are. Few let the money go to their heads. Many are thankful that they have been able to provide something better for their families, that they are financially secure, that they have been able to help others. People who shared their good fortune found that their stock grew back, leaving them with even more than before.

Ralph Ketner sees money as a way to keep track of success. But he also understands money. He knows that the less of it you have, the more important it becomes. He never forgot the lessons of his father, Bob Ketner, about charging only enough to make a living, not a killing.

Food Lion has been successful because Ketner hit a nerve with the American public. He promised to save his customers money. He didn't cheat on the concept once he saw that it worked. The more successful his idea grew, the more he cut prices. His fascination with it turned to obsession. His employees followed Ketner's example and themselves became impassioned with keeping costs – and prices – as low as possible.

Ketner has passed Food Lion's baton to Tom Smith. There will be no more "betting the company." Smith's job is to steer America's fastest-growing grocery chain in the right direction. It won't be easy. Recently, a man being detained as a shoplifting suspect for eating grapes in a store successfully sued Food Lion for $30,000 – $10,000 a grape. Big companies are big targets. There will be other obstacles ahead.

Analysts say that Food Lion can't maintain its pace of expansion. They say that it will have to change its strategy. They say its price-earnings ratio is out of whack, and the numbers indicate it's not a wise investment. It wasn't a wise investment in 1957 either.

From a single store at Ketner Center on West Innes Steet in Salisbury had sprung 800 stores by May of 1991. They were spread over 11 states. At the end of 1990, Food Lion had 312 stores in North Carolina, 86 in South Carolina, 173 in Virginia, 63 in Tennessee, 41 in Georgia, 83 in Florida, 6 in Maryland, 3 in

264

Delaware, 4 in Kentucky, 5 in West Virginia, and 2 in Pennsylvania.

By the end of 1991, the company planned to add 40 stores in Texas, and some officials dared to whisper a goal of 2,000 stores by the year 2000. But there's hardly time to look back and admire a job well done. Food Lion's leaders follow a simple notion: grow or die.

Food Lion did allow itself a brief pause in 1990 when it erected a marker outside its Store No. 1 that says: "Food Lion Inc. Founded here in 1957 by Brown Ketner, Ralph Ketner and Wilson Smith. Now a major U.S. supermarket chain." All three men attended the modest ceremony.

Eased by the years into a much slower pace, the founders looked up at the sign as if it were a mirror to another time. They were carried back to that freezing day in December 1957 and a store with a frozen gravel parking lot. They thought of a store trimmed out in yellow, blue and shrimp pink colors. They stepped again on the Magic Carpet automatic door. They saw 53 shopping carts lined up at the parcel pickup. They pictured a loyal employee with bloody feet. The day truly was one of the most exciting, and satisfying, of their lives.

No sooner had Food Lion erected its historic marker outside Store No. 1 than company officials announced it would be closed. An empty Kmart building about a block north offered more room inside for the ever-increasing number of products and more parking outside for the higher number of cars. The founders were among the first to understand the move. The customer comes first. Sentiment be damned.